PRECARIOUS LEASE

Jacqueline Feldman was the recipient of a Fulbright grant for her reporting in Paris, where she lived for many years. An Albertine Translation Laureate for her previous book, *On Your Feet: A Novel in Translations*, which features her translation of a story by Nathalie Quintane, and a graduate of the EHESS-Paris, she teaches expository writing at the University of Massachusetts Amherst. Her essays have appeared in *Triple Canopy*, *The White Review* and the *Paris Review*.

'Feldman's *Precarious Lease* is marked by erudition, astringence, biting wit, and the perspicacious awe of a seasoned examiner of our time, attributes bound to be hallmarks of her work for years to come. Diving under the rubble of social and class collapse, Feldman deftly manoeuvres between investigative reportage and essayist forays while weaving through this tapestry a tone so sharp yet compassionate, so personal, it feels like a friend delivering dire news from the front lines of the world.'
— Ocean Vuong, author of *On Earth We're Briefly Gorgeous*

'In *Precarious Lease* Jacqueline Feldman follows her curiosity about alternate forms of living into the heart of north-east Paris's squat scene, and takes the reader with her, asking fundamental questions about how we live together under late capitalism, and the relationship, in France, between freedom and bureaucracy, marginality and the state. It's completely fascinating, an American in Paris memoir like no other.'
— Lauren Elkin, author of *Scaffolding*

'Jacqueline Feldman's *Precarious Lease* offers an enthralling immersion into the confluence of 2010s-era social and political activism, Parisian and French real estate and the margins of the global artworld. Multimodal in its storytelling, encompassing critical journalism, social history, the precision of documentary writing, and more, *Precarious Lease* also holds up a mirror to our current capitalist moment and suggests other ways of imagining our world.'
— John Keene, author of *Counternarratives*

'Like the diary of Samuel Pepys, *Precarious Lease* is not so much reporting or even memoir as full-on history writing. Biased in the most important and necessary ways and at the same time telepathic, translucent, and hard-won, Feldman's attempt at an account will make you rethink citizenship and all the hideous fictions associated with contemporary real

estate. It will also remind you of the sacred and anarchic power of description.'
—— Lucy Ives, author of *Life is Everywhere*

'To trust a writer's insight, we must first trust their eyes, must be able to see what, how, and as they see. In *Precarious Lease*, Jacqueline Feldman trains her vision – indeed all her senses – on the striking, insistent particulars of the culture of squatters in Paris. Feldman assuredly, brilliantly, guides us through their unstable circumstances, through their fraught world. At every turn, the urgent, vivid, vitally empathic prose of *Precarious Lease* is grounded in a sense of our shared, our undeniable humanity. That is where revelation springs from. You heard me right: Jacqueline Feldman's *Precarious Lease* is a revelation. This is a masterful, elegant, powerful book.'
—— Richard Deming, author of *This Exquisite Loneliness*

'Destined to become a classic of literary reportage, *Precarious Lease: The Paris Document* honours the poetry of facts in its vivid, boldly intimate depiction of artists and artists manqué struggling and dreaming in the squat houses of Paris and its peripheries. In its narrative sweep, the photorealism of its details, its sure grasp of cultural and subcultural history, its confiding tone, and its indelible portraits of eccentrics, rebels, and visionaries, Jacqueline Feldman's deep-hearted and brilliant firsthand account offers us nothing less than utter enchantment.'
—— Garielle Lutz, author of *Worsted*

Fitzcarraldo Editions

PRECARIOUS LEASE

THE PARIS DOCUMENT

JACQUELINE FELDMAN

chercher et savoir reconnaître qui et quoi, au milieu de l'enfer, n'est pas l'enfer, et le faire durer, et lui faire de la place

There is a stretch of the Paris border where the city ends as if in a cliff. The natural slope of the land is visible in the hill of a park. Around it, accommodation for the rectilinear has been made, and buildings sit flat, the streets terraced. On the descent you pass the Métro Pré-Saint-Gervais, obscure stop of a circular. You cross the Boulevard Sérurier, one of twenty-two bending along the city's perimeter and named for Napoleonic marshals. There are tramlines, taut of wire, and the Périphérique highway, the city's ring road, which throws light. From there the suburbs fall away to the northeast, the land below them sinking. This view serves to dignify the area's desultory pizza parlors, its bar, and its other bar, the one for placing bets.

I went there one October afternoon to look at a construction site. I had moved back to Paris after three years away, and I still knew this address by heart. It was written as if unsettled, as a range: *58-62, rue de Mouzaïa*. A few more buildings and the road runs out, Sérurier taking the relay. I had come from that direction.

Because of the building's location, because of its many tall windows, it could reflect the weather over the suburbs. Within Paris it served those suburbs as an embassy, as one of the occupants, one of the squatters, had long ago told me. Police evicted those squatters in December 2013. Since then, for four years and ten months, the building had stood empty. It was empty as I took it in, in 2018. At a glance, I saw the windows had been replaced. A sign put up by the city indicated construction would run through 2020. But the glass was black and clean. The building's stories, eight in number, glittered. Below them lay four basements.

I wouldn't be able to see it in full. Sheet metal hid a man who was shouting, a worker, a temporary wall.

Concrete gapped to show its supports, twisting, rusted. Across the first story snaked words, engravings, a 1974 work by the French sculptor Catherine Val. Menacing nouns, they were nearly oracular: *Storm-Cold-Wind-Cold*. Shaped like a hinge, the building was wider than it was tall. Caught in the fold of its wings was a sizeable courtyard where the occupants had, I knew, cultivated bamboo and, in their idiosyncrasy, trussed up a disco ball. Far oversized, ten feet across, it cast a fractured light into every room.

Yards away, a man was watching me. He stood still, as I did, and on the same sidewalk. The messy hair and baggy clothes scanned, from where I stood, as homelessness—I looked away. The stare could not be returned politely. He has the right, I thought—a French expression. I am looking at the city, and this man is looking at me. Moving, I also felt, would have provoked him, a feeling I can't have been glad to register. Years ago we might have both gone on ahead into that building. I trained my attention on more signs hung by the municipal government, temporary, detailing the history of the place: something to read until 2020, consolation. Here, or around here, lay rebellious Belleville village, incorporated into Paris in 1860. Quarries came to my mind, as did defensive ramparts called the Thiers Fortifications. At their base extended a no-build zone on which drifters contrived shacks of salvage and scrap, building all the same. The Brutalist architectual movement had in the twentieth century bestowed on Paris this edifice for use by a regional Directorate for Health and Social Affairs. (The architecture was "inspired by 'bunkers,'" as one could read in the local paper, *Le Parisien*.) I used my phone to photograph the signs. One gave the squat's name, Le Bloc, an acronym of the squatters' devising for *bâtiment libre*, "free building," *occupé citoyennement*, "occupied by citizens" though with an adverb that is nonstandard, as "citizenly" would be in English. One look at it, and a homeless man comes and stares at you accusingly. The sign's summary made much of "art" produced within but did not say what kind of art it was. A professional managing the project had told *Le Parisien* of an intent for "certain works" to remain. Many were murals, immovable. "Because there's some very interesting stuff," the project manager continued. Their employer would be converting the building to housing for students and "young workers"—130 students, 65 workers, with 14 "artists" to be accommodated across the extent of its studio space. The state had transferred title for 6.7 million euros, which amounted to a 76 percent discount. That renovation would cost twenty-two million. As far as deals go the building's sale had been stagnant, hopeless.

I looked up, and the man was gone.

I started back the other way. The Rue de Mouzaïa holds, unusually in Paris, many country-style houses—brick walks and fitted shutters, brimming planters—along a wall of which I saw a window only painted on. It was a false signal. Curtains had been depicted, billowing.

That street empties out into the Rue du Général-Brunet, which quickly flows into the Rue Botzaris, one border of a crescent-shaped park, Buttes-Chaumont. On that street that day I recognized a boot-shaped sign, swaying above its clapboard storefront. In the months after Le Bloc's eviction, in that quiet season, I had brought the cobbler my own boots, which I conceded had to be resoled. I passed them over the counter. He looked back in horror. They were too far gone. Nothing to be done. I had worn down the heels to triangles. I looked at those heels with the man, as he did, almost ashamed.

I got home to find a letter from Le Général, which I recognized by my own handwriting. This was the envelope I had addressed, stamped.

¶ I could write about a man who considered his integrity to consist, if not principally then partially, in the repetition of stock phrases. Knowing they got old, Le Général slipped them in as subordinate clauses—*comme je vais toujours bien jamais mal*—as jokes, jokes for me. Alongside a recto and verso of schoolboy cursive he'd left himself no margin. For an instant it looked as if he'd written on the envelope itself, though he had not, and momentarily I regretted that I hadn't also sent paper.

Le 27 octobre 2018. Formally dated, with that period after, and located: *Rouen. Ma chère Jacqueline.*

> *What a magnificent moment, to receive your letter, thank you Jacqueline, for having taken a few moments to write me; it gives me pleasure to have some news of you and of the advancement of your book project; as for me I'm off on yet another adventure, that of prison and of the deprivation of liberty, but as I'm always good, never bad, and as normality of life for me is really different from that for the vast majority of French people, a typical day, understanding that I've since met half of those interned here, wake up in the mornings at 7 or 7:30, it's trash pick up and mail at first whether external or internal (cultural services, medical services, any request), one walk a day in the open air, for me the walk is from 12:45 to 1:15 (the only moment when I have access to one of three phone booths [send me a French number and I'll try to call you, the administration will without a doubt call you to confirm]); as I'm taking care of a sick detainee I leave my cell relatively regularly, I accompany him in all his moves; I'm already familiar with three-quarters of the surveillance and external personnel, a library (I go fairly regularly [three times a week]), a "philosophy coffee" activity, but that's already been postponed twice so what*

else to tell you, that normally I should receive a prize from the Malraux Foundation, new contacts at the Mayor of Paris, a project of creating a cryptocurrency...
With these few words I leave you in pen but not in heart, hoping to read of you soon: take care.

An elegant close, I thought. He prided himself on his French. He signed off, then, as "Le Général," with a big, sweeping X, having added a more modest X above his writing's every *i*.

I didn't know what he was in for. I had last seen him in Nîmes, a city on the Mediterranean, in 2016, August, breezy but hot.

I could write about him that day: two hours late, owing to a headache. He blamed it on the chlorine of a pool he had been using, which was, he said, beautiful. He was really unwell. He lay on a bench, and I sat at its head. The major sound was that of buses circumnavigating an esplanade now and again, like a weather event. From a distance I heard children laughing, echoes of a fountain: we might have been sunbathing at the end of the world.

Or so I noted down. Le Général was in camo gear, his usual. The soles of his sandals were peeling. His physical deterioration was subtle enough that I couldn't ask about it directly, or felt I could not. A few front teeth had been, as I remembered, missing. Now more were gone, leaving the constants: motile brown eyes, a round face, short salt-and-pepper hair. Olive-skinned, he was of Portuguese extraction, for people of his parents' generation in France a non-white racial category. My height, a little fat. Short of breath. In better health he'd sit flush with a chair's back to lean forward nimbly, claiming territory.

"Even as I speak with you, I see you this way," he said, making a gesture of parallax with both hands to show

how there were two of me. On a forearm were scratches, raw. He was speaking of a chicken farm in Haiti, an ambition. "The next step is to go there in person and be energetically, financially, digitally independent." He pulled a bankcard from a pocket, given to him "for business." He did not say by whom. Neither would he reveal the source of a second windfall, the use of a villa where he professed to be staying. He lay back and tugged off his cap, sunglasses. His eyes were squeezed shut, sockets pink with fatigue. He draped his arms over his face. Silence. A fly landed in an armpit and crawled a moment before moving along. I had offered to take an earlier train to Paris, where I was staying with friends. He had rejected the idea. I offered to take us to lunch, out of the heat. I was impatient. I'd come all this way, come from New York. It was as if my listening was something not quite freely given, irrecoverable even as I was the one who required of myself to find out what had happened to Le Général. I prompted him, starting the tape. I chose the humiliation of taking him seriously as he was wasting my time. He sat up, swigged from a water bottle that I had brought, and sighed. Behind him, a man coaxed a dog to its hind legs. It drank from a fountain. "Everything I can tell you about Le Bloc I've already told you," Le Général said. At Le Bloc he had been "in [his] element."

Born Antonio Joaquín Xavier in a Portuguese coastal village, a suburb of Porto, 1969, the baby was quickly relocated to a bad suburb of Rouen, France, where he attracted disaster. On an early birthday, bathwater scalded half of his body. As a man he'd boast about the accident, showing off scars lingering along one foot. A slippery toddler, a child who disappeared, he fell, sleeping soundly, between bed and wall. The search took his mother an hour. At twelve months he vanished among market stalls to reappear adopted, playing with a pack of dogs. His stepfather would mount alarms. The boy tampered with them, a burgeoning electrician, and escaped into the night. A prodigy, he ate two sandwiches daily so his mother would allow him out to buy bread. He read comic books before he could read, decrypting the pictures. When he couldn't buy a new release, he stole it. By five he had built up a skill set. He credited his criminal imagination to the luck by which he'd grown up in a shoddy residential tower, public housing called an HLM. The world was unfair to him, fair game. His stepfather didn't like to catch him wandering. "So I had to find a solution," the debutant realized, "and fast." He got to know the library. He crossed a forest and came upon another suburb. He went swimming in the water tower. In the first squat he opened, in Rouen proper, a hallway trailed from the front door to a desk, where the young man sat and watched pedestrians who never caught him looking. The feeling was one of achievement. He developed expertise as a locksmith, this by now proficient electrician, all of which he would draw on in opening additional buildings. He issued checks, he said, from a bank of his own invention, for which he would claim to have served only part of a sentence. "There was an error," he clarified. "So I was set free." All grown up, he turned his attention to auto theft. Every unsavory enterprise compelled him. An aging thief when I met him, he had failed as a murderer. "I had to understand why I lived in an HLM while others lived in little houses with gardens," he said. "I left like Tom Sawyer, to discover the world."

Throughout France he was called, in his travels, Mr. X, until while sleeping on the plaza at La Défense, the Paris-area business district where activists had taken up a protest against austerity, he met Stéphane Hessel, a figurehead of the French Left. Actually he met Hessel in Montreuil. Hessel dubbed him Le Général. Le Général would never know why—but, as he told me ingenuously, it stuck. It stuck in Paris. In Portugal, he went by Joaquín. In Monaco, he was known as Tony.

Call him what you like, I am writing of him as he spoke of himself. "I'm not an innocent man, Jacqueline," he'd say, only to explain it with another favorite: "I live inside the margin of the margin of society." He had been kicked out of Monaco, having gambled injudiciously. Sixteen times, he had had to flee Italy. In Paris, he met a man I'll call Caravaggio, a name you won't forget is made up. Born somewhere, one parent or neither Moroccan, Caravaggio, unlike Le Général, was accustomed to the Paris suburbs. He explained his métier of squatting with an opportunism that was no cause for shame. He was in prison when he saw a squat depicted on TV. There's something I can do when I get out, he thought. It appealed to him more than any livelihood for which his experience might have qualified him. In squatting, one did not risk serving time, and he had wanted anyway to pivot. He needed a place to live.

These men made themselves useful to each other. In the highest style they maintained a squat in the neighborhood of the Place de la République remarkable not only for the centrality of its location, but for the paintings that came, under their management, to decorate its considerable façade, courtesy of the graffiti artist Kouka: tribal warriors, wielding spears, a leggy Quixote on every oblong window. Le Général subsequently opened a squat in an eastern suburb and dubbed it Mirabeau, work he thought of as a service to the poor; the poor moved in.

In November or December 2012, Caravaggio or followers of his or someone made their way into the building on the Rue de Mouzaïa that would become Le Bloc. I heard they found an open door. One of them, alternatively, shoved a hand right through the mail slot.

Animals had overtaken the offices. The building smelled, to its first squatters, of cat. In a basement they found archives, strangers' papers and a stash of rubber gloves and paper masks. The last occupants, health workers, had stockpiled these items against an outbreak—of "bird flu," Caravaggio inferred. Days passed before they matched all the keys they found to locks.

On December 31, 2012, the squat Le Bloc opened to the public, a New Year's party. I heard it was packed, crags of beer cans lasting weeks. The walls sweated, one squatter told me. Another contended they cried. I wasn't there, and neither was Le Général—unfortunately he was once again in prison.

¶ Buildings stand empty for any number of reasons, some impermanent, and the conscientious French squatter, a reader of the online guidebook *Le Squat de A à Z*, would inspect a target carefully, noting the state of the windows—boarded-up, broken—as well as any other felicitous sign. A full mailbox, an unkempt garden. A heap of dead leaves before the door portended well. It was textbook to check out a target at multiple times of day, favoring a wintertime dusk, when tenants reliably announced their presence by switching on the lights. With holidays, though, that got tricky. It was possible, too, that people did tenant a building only to keep to some secret back room. A squatter acting on the guide's advice might wedge papers into a doorframe and, returning, see if they had fallen. Squatters in France read *A à Z*; squatters elsewhere read other guidebooks. In a 2017 history of squatting, *The Autonomous City*, Alexander Vasudevan, Oxford geographer, cites the German *Handbuch für Hausbesetzer*, "Handbook for Squatters," and *Survival without Rent*, "a 1986 how-to guide published by Lower East Side squatters" in New York City.

To ensure a building was vacant and amass intelligence about its proprietor, a squatter asked around the neighborhood. They obtained information from municipal offices under pretexts like that of a film shoot, *A à Z* suggests, or a capstone project for architecture school. For privately owned buildings, unsettled inheritances were ideal. So were abandoned work sites. Construction and demolition permits were known after two years to expire.

The well-informed squatter, hazarding an entrance, began by triple checking that the premises were empty. They rang the doorbell having prepared, just in case, some excuse. "Idiot kids," *A à Z* suggests, "playing an idiot game." Door open, they dropped any tool they had used. A friend on the outside, having read the guide also, would be there to retrieve it. Inside, a blinking red light might mean an alarm system had triggered. Even then the squatter could make their escape before the signal was relayed.

They would return with a toolkit: hammer, nails, screwdriver, screws, file, chisel, cordless drill, chain and padlock, the iconic crowbar. They brought food and water, sleeping bags, lamps they might elect to mute with cloth, whatever they deemed suitable for a barricade. First of all they changed the locks, to prevent the proprietor entering.

It would be difficult to add to this publicly available account without sounding, unpleasantly, like a cop doing opposition research. In the interest of irrelevance I will note that when, one night in August 2013, squatters gathered in a park opposite a target in Fontenay-sous-Bois, their bikes, falling, crushed a mass of mint, which gave off a smell so sharp it felt at least to me like an alarm. When, in December 2011, squatters entered a building in central Paris, they found an empty yogurt cup; one of them declared then to the others, to the rest of us, that it signaled a guard's passage. This reconnaissance of squatters put them in the position, surreal in a dense city, of sifting through debris for signs of life.

Classically they entered by night, but daytime break-ins were possible. They wore work blues. A prize was anything signifying abandonment: a rash of mold, a 1994 calendar. Of their entrance, careful squatters left no trace. If found to have damaged the building, as they all knew, they faced criminal charges. They risked jail time; in point of fact they would not benefit, when sued for eviction, from procedural delays. When squatters did enjoy protection, this was not for squatting's sake but for that of a sanctity French law assigned to any person's home. If they had stayed forty-eight hours, the building was their place of residence. As litigation dragged on, they kept living at the squat. No squat was permanent, but the law also authorized a judge to postpone an eviction for up to three years; this held especially in cases where eviction would disturb the peace (concern for public order being thus "the last rampart of a squatter's right to housing," writes Thomas Aguilera, a political scientist). The period of this grace, shortened since, contracted and expanded even then with the vicissitudes of French politics, depending on whether the issue of the day—terrorism, immigration—called, in the legislative opinion, for a strong-armed approach. Loopholes constrict, for example with the 2015 passage of a bill introduced by a senator who was also mayor of Calais, a municipality notoriously burdened with a makeshift camp, the Calais Jungle. Several thousand refugees had taken shelter there, and the mayor wanted them out.

Inside, the squatter went to work—quite often with a team. They hunted around for keys, if any internal doors were locked. They fixed up the building's wiring, installed lamps of their own. They tacked up Christmas lights, printed fabric, stylish posters, anything suggesting a home. Very quickly they would have to conjure this impression of a home. They carried in dressers and filled them messily with clothes. They brought dishes, piling them in sinks. Being quiet, they came and went minimally, accepting no visitor, ordered in pizza so as to save the time-stamped receipt. In March of 2013, squatters breaching a building in eastern Paris held one of their crew by the soles of his boots as he covered over a skylight with black felt, a precaution. Already they had blacked out every window.

When police inevitably discovered the squat, squatters would have to persuade the authority that they had stayed forty-eight hours. With the prior phase of squat life, which squatters called the "submarine," I came to associate smells and tastes: the stale air of a borrowed sleeping bag, instant coffee, ham and packaged carrot salad, slippery *pour apéro* peanuts, weed, whiskey, sugar candy.

A à Z is poker-faced. "Squats rely, in general, on spaces left to ruin by the bourgeoisie, the State, or the capitalist system," the guide notes.

Pursuant to all this, it notes that if, after forty-eight hours of occupation, squatters are sick of waiting, they may call the cops on themselves, pretending to be a neighbor.

¶ Scholars of French squats evidenced distaste for certain questions about the scale of the phenomenon. "No one is capable of giving a serious count," the sociologist Florence Bouillon said in response to a colleague's question after a conference in 2010. Nearly a decade after the engineering school Ponts et Chaussées, basing this on data from police, had indicated there were eight hundred "collective" squats in Paris and two thousand total in Île-de-France, the Paris region, no more convincing tally was forthcoming. But the numbers seemed to Bouillon overestimated. For want of further study, they had gained traction. Aguilera, the political scientist, cites Ponts et Chaussées's count for Paris though he notes that the figure seems, to every official he interviews just as it does to Bouillon, high. Despite this, Aguilera is willing to assume his own counts are, by contrast, low, making the assumption that many squatters wished, for their own reasons, to stay hidden and referring to parts of this population with a touch of self-congratulation as "invisible."

Squats could be defined simply, as occupations of buildings, yet the political scientist Cécile Péchu in her 2010 book *Les Squats* quibbles with Bouillon's definition, a state "of living illegally and without contract in a vacant space." Péchu, focusing on social movements, finds greater interest in the squat as an action, that "of illegally occupying a space in order to inhabit or use it collectively." After studying the French group *Droit au logement*, Right to Housing, activists who coordinated groups for moves into vacant buildings alongside other protests, Péchu concludes that the squat is exceptional as a political action, a mode of protest, in that it "constitutes, de facto, an answer to the demand it makes."

As to the question of who lived in squats, Péchu reproduces a 2004 table by Hans Pruijt, a Dutch sociologist.

Pruijt, acknowledging a "diversity" of squats, breaks it down according to the inhabitants' goals: "Providing housing for needy people" ("Deprivation based squatting"), "Creating housing for themselves, while adding to the affordable housing stock" ("Squatting as an alternative housing strategy"), "Setting up an establishment" ("Entrepreneurial squatting"), "Preserving a cityscape or landscape" ("Conservational squatting"), and "Building up counter-power to the state" ("Political squatting"). All but the first type—"configuration" is Pruijt's term—he describes, surprisingly, as "middle-class." Aguilera, for his part, makes use of a schema of Bouillon's in grouping Parisian squats into three categories: *activité, politique, urgence.* Squats of "activity" contained artists, partisans of a counterculture they fussed over busily. "Political" squats by their existence staked a claim, and "emergency" squats gave shelter to those in need. Occasionally one of these academics conceded a given squat could belong to multiple categories, a walkback that seemed insufficient. If all squatters lived in squats, which made for uncomfortable dwellings—drafty, chancy—what could it mean to separate out squatters who were really needy? Couldn't artists, by very reason of their vocation, quite organically find themselves poor, even unhoused? If an artist were unhoused, then, for them, which definition would be viable?

Modern French squatting follows from a 1945 ordinance. In the wake of the Second World War, it allowed municipalities to requisition vacant buildings and use them as emergency housing. Governments were reluctant to do so, and Catholic groups squatted in buildings to try and bring them around. As the century wore on, Parisians occupied buildings in an effort to obstruct the centrally planned development of certain neighborhoods. Some squatters, after the uprisings of May 1968, stood not only against a hegemonic urbanism but also for a counterculture, experimenting among themselves with social arrangements. Some were artists: but, as Péchu writes sternly, picking up with the sociologists' project of sorting squatters into artists and the serious, "artistic identity was not central: these activists thought of themselves as squatters first of all." Not until the 1990s does "one witness," Péchu writes, still a bit mysteriously, "the opposition between political squats and artistic squats."

In only some of the literature from 2010 (Bouillon's talk, which followed her ethnography of squats and Roma encampments in Marseille, not overly sunny as a picture) was there any worry that squats in France would go the way of, say, a substantial Amsterdam scene after Dutch law made squatting a crime in that same year. Also in 2010, the Spanish legislature harshened sentences for trespassing; a 2012 law would criminalize squatting in England. But just then French squatters, and in particular the Parisians, enjoyed a special tolerance, however tenuous. Subsequently a 2015 law that legislators said would protect against terrorism inhibited squatting, adding to the burden of the Calais mayor's law; a 2018 law did away with a two-month delay between court order and eviction as well as a ban on eviction in winter. In 2010 Aguilera had been able to refer to the French housing crisis as a headline issue. Jeudi Noir, an advocacy group active between 2006 and 2014, proselytized about the cost of living while carrying off spectacular occupations: on the Avenue Matignon, down the street from the Elysée Palace; in an *hôtel particulier* on the Place des Vosges; on the Rue de la Banque in central Paris. Politicians paid campaign visits to these squats, and the cold light of destiny still fell upon the squatters. By 2018 one of the founding members of Jeudi Noir was running for mayor credibly while several others, after damages were awarded to the proprietor of a building they had occupied on the Rue de Sèvres, were carrying debt.

Cities were fickle in managing squats, occasionally striking bargains with the occupants and bringing buildings up to code. In 2002, the City of New York sold off, for a song, eleven of twelve Lower East Side squats that had come into its possession. The Urban Homesteading Assistance Board, a nonprofit, got them for a dollar apiece on the condition it take out loans on the squatters' behalf to pay for repairs. (In the twelfth building, the *New York Times* reported, "squatters ... could not come to terms and resisted the city's overtures.") In that same year, the City of Paris acquired a building of some fifteen hundred square meters at the capital's geographic center, paying 4.57 million euros. It would spend another 5.6 million on the building's renovation. Artists had established their squat in this building, later known by its address, 59 Rivoli. In 2000 they had welcomed in, according to the ministry of culture's count, forty thousand visitors, making theirs the third-most frequented "contemporary art site" in Paris. Bertrand Delanoë, the Socialist Party candidate, promised the artists he would, as mayor, buy their building. He won against the odds.

The city, during his mandate, renovated the building, and when artists moved back in they signed a contract. It was, in this case, a *bail civil*; the more popular choice, for regularizing squatters' occupations, was another device, the *convention d'occupation précaire*, which resembled, in most ways, a lease—legally there had to be an outside reason, not one simply of a landlord's whimsy, justifying its precarity—and was referred to imprecisely, by squatters and by others, as a *bail précaire*: a "precarious lease." The artists would pay a nominal rent. They would refrain from sleeping onsite. Every day, every workday would be an open house; the studios would be open studios. 59 Rivoli would exist as a showroom, with no trace of homelessness, and in subsequent years it would not embarrass these artists to call their project an "after-squat." Particularly appealing to international tourists they soon entertained, this time by their own count, seventy thousand visitors annually. "Every artist dreams of moving to Paris," Christophe Girard, then the city's deputy mayor for culture, told the *New York Times* for a 2010 "Travel" round up of Parisian art squats featuring 59 Rivoli, the puff piece of which, presumably, every deputy mayor for culture dreams ("In Paris, Art Fills the Void").

City Hall kept track. A 2012 audit, conducted internally, revealed opportunities for the municipality to refine its strategy for managing the 59 Rivoli artists while valuing the rent abatement it gave them at 278,200 euros per annum. It had spent, the city reminded itself, a painful 1.49 million euros more than planned on the renovation. It noted, in the course of its audit, that the claim of third place in a contemporary art popularity contest was *abusif*—used in French for "overdone"—given that Palais de Tokyo, the museum for contemporary art, took in sixty thousand visitors a *month*. At least one person in the city government had soured on 59 Rivoli by the time Aguilera, researching his thesis, conducted anonymous interviews. "It was just because it was a campaign promise and we'll never again do anything like it," this person said. And yet, Aguilera observes, more like it was done. Between 2001 and 2010, according to a "confidential" source of his, the city spent eleven million euros in renovating about a dozen buildings that artists had occupied as squats.

French law defines the precarious lease negatively, as a

structure allowing for the bypassing of obligations associated with actual leases. It was in every one of its guises an at-will agreement. Though not always reflected in the language of the document it was understood from experience, among squatters in Paris, that entering into such an agreement would mean that no one could sleep in the building. (Occasionally, in violation, people did; the city stressed an imperative not to let squatters, when the line for social housing was long, cut to the front.) A *convention* conferred on La Petite Rockette, a group that had voluntarily left its squat in favor of a space being brought under contract, clarified the signees' liability for "security and surveillance." They had to respect their neighbors' quiet enjoyment of property that they, the neighbors, owned or rented. The ex-squatters would carry on in community-facing activities. They offered, among other services, a collection for recyclables. But ten people had lived at their squat, some of whom, as characterized by Martin Bobel, a member of the group, were really needy. The city rehoused only two of them, he told me in a 2012 interview. The others left for other squats, the odd apartment, the street. "Out of the two people, one died," Bobel said. "So only one person was rehoused by the city."

Squatters considered artists who signed these contracts "sellouts," to use a term from the art world. In the language of labor movements, they were scabs. The invective was bottomless. Artists squatted out of bad faith, seeking to please the city, its deputy mayor for culture, the minister of culture, *the police*, all the while lording their gift, a conversance with authority, over squatters less comfortable with any number of things: self-branding; the labyrinth of French official culture with its interlocking institutions, pomp, its École des Beaux-Arts; and, not least, the French language. Artists gave a bad name to squatters of all other walks. Bobel, though not himself an artist, held a degree in "cultural engineering"; he told me in 2012 that the contracted status suited him. (His accreditation is common enough in France. A government website geared at high schoolers eyeing careers describes "engineer of cultural services and patrimony" thus: "France is a gold mine in terms of cultural richness.") "We're going to be better performing," Bobel said, "and we're going to produce much more in the future."

Aguilera, doing his interviews at the ministry of culture, provoked this outburst: "We can accept to negotiate with real artists who have real projects ... but not with those fringe elements that pretend to make art and culture!" The exclamation mark is Aguilera's, and he was there. Surprisingly given this insistence that the French state worked with "real" artists only, it was difficult—from the literature, from my own interviews—to infer any working definition. Art was an obvious good. On that, parties agreed. Since agreement was so universal, no occasion really arose for the perfect clarification of the term. A permissiveness, looseness to the definition characterized the discourse when it came to artists. Unusual in Bouillon's painstaking prose is a stray set of scare quotes. Artists' "refusal to 'exile' themselves to the suburbs," in this instance, causes them to work in squats. The quotes postpone the problem of the melodrama of the verb; this, in the context of research dealing with the serious problems of refugees, rings wrong. Artists' stories were swallowed whole. In 2009 Françoise Galland, a councilor for the twentieth arrondissement, emailed an inhabitant of local squat La Miroiterie with a declaration of support signed by that district's majority, a leftist coalition. "The predicament of the squat La Miroiterie, 88 Rue de Ménilmontant, is particularly worrisome," the coalition writes. "This is a case of an artistic squat." Asked, in a 2013 interview, if La Miroiterie "contributed to the community," Galland was nonplussed. "*Bah* of course," she told me. "First of all, it is an artistic squat." Still more curious was the response of another district councilor, Marc Wluczka. When I interviewed him, he brought up artists who had refused to sign. "Deep inside me, I think they're right," he said, practicing his English. "Official art is something that should not be accepted. It should not even be discussed. But that's my personal opinion. As a politician—well. I'm in the majority, so. I understand the political reasons, but in my interior self, I don't agree with them." He spoke as if to go on claiming distance from the mysteries of governance: "Did Picasso ask for the help of the state? On the other hand, Michelangelo was living with the money of the Pope. I know that. But he had a boss who let him do what he wanted."

Awe expressed on behalf of institutions was dimmer, self-regarding. The Palais de Tokyo, one of the French state's museums, upon its opening in 2002 on a broad Parisian avenue began by working up a controversy among squatters who were artists. They objected to its look, which might be described as post-industrial, considering it appropriative of what they, the squatters, had to live with. As the geographer Elsa Vivant notes, squatters were not the only ones to whom this museum appeared to be playing dress up. "Today the latest in culture doubtless couldn't emerge other than from a squat, or from an industrial wasteland, however artificially maintained in the middle of the sixteenth arrondissement," *Le Monde* commented. But, Vivant contends, it was to placate squatters, who were appearing with regularity in French and Parisian media, that in September of that year the Palais de Tokyo held the first in a series of art-squat festivals it intended to be annual. (They were annual, and they were brought to a halt after three years.) *Festival art et squats* was, predictably enough, controversial all over again. Some Parisian squatters felt pandered to, while others directed their indignation at squatters who'd agreed to work with the museum, considering this a betrayal of principles they shared. The Palais de Tokyo's online archives used to preserve a list, "Acknowledgments," with an atypical section entitled "Regrets," a cognate that can also mean "apologies." "At last," the museum writes, "all our regrets go out to those squats who were with us in this adventure from its first moments and have since had to close their doors..." The ellipsis is the museum's, a punctuation of survivor's guilt. "As we all know," this museum continues, washing its hands of some sin, "precariousness is an integral part of the daily life of squats, and one of the objectives of this project has been to point up the relevance of these spaces and permit, maybe, a glimpse at some solution..."

And yet it mattered very much to squatters if their output could be officially construed as art when, in those years, they understood authorities to give artistic squats a pass. Even squats that did not rise to the level of receiving a precarious lease could expect, by virtue of their artistry, better treatment. Authorities handled a squat differently if it contained artists, referring the dossier to the ministry of culture, which evaluated, in its own words, the "artistic value of the project," as Aguilera would note in a subsequent paper. His sample size was sixty squats; of them, police evicted "emergency" squats at a rate of 87.5 percent. For artists, according to this calculus, the rate was a mere 47.7 percent. Legitimacy in the strictest sense accrued to squats where art was made. Lawyers defending squatters, always against eviction, were careful to mention any artistic activity, trying always to buy time. The Miroiterie squatters were in their own drawn-out proceedings represented by the lawyer Florence Diffre, counsel for the squatters of the Rue de Rivoli before the city's intervention. She collected up CVs in building her defense of La Miroiterie, a move by then routine, the squat the artistry of which was evident even to its local politicians and had, besides, the special power of avoiding, for all those within, the plight of homelessness. In response to Diffre's or a later lawyer's call, Bernard Morlon, self-identified "autodidact painter" in residence, provided an artist's statement of six sentences, which are naïve, strikingly, and strangely tender. "At the beginning of La Miroiterie, we made mosaics with bits of mirror," he writes. "I made a butterfly that still decorates La Miroiterie. Having painted butterflies, I currently paint flowers."

I knew La Miroiterie. In French it is a common noun and names a manufacturer of mirrors; one had operated in the building. The mosaics looked like insect eyes. Factory of mirrors: I also knew Bernard. I can picture the butterflies he cut out of black paper. In watercolor, he painted a pavilion of glass. It had window boxes, from which a palm tree sprouted. At the building's base stretched archways, a sign: LA MIROITERIE. This was La Miroiterie in the future, I was told; one day, I received a color photocopy. It looked like a mall. But I admired the artist's gentleness, the mystery of his gentleness. An invitation he committed to paper moves me—I have saved a copy of that, too—for its formality, its simplicity. Photocopied on a thin, fluttering slip like a strip of film, this message hand-lettered on a field suggesting in its texture the last gasp of some toner cartridge convokes a *rendezvous*, "RDV," at La Miroiterie: a party.

A higher culture did come out of there, supposedly. Bands from abroad would play the squat in summiting the top of their field, punk rock. I lacked the expertise to evaluate this claim, but I met a well-placed musicologist who was working to archive the concerts.

Visual art in squats could be shrewd, political. Installation revealed in the rudeness of materials something of the squatter hardship. Other squat art was sincere, crafty: I am thinking of a single God's Eye, done in yarn and spindles. Not all artists working in squats endeared themselves to me as Bernard did, but several, laboring in the throes of some obsession rendering them "outsider" in market terms, displayed, in their labors, a pathos I found affecting independent of the result.

Still more squat art left the observer, or certain observers, or me, with little to love. This spurious work was slapdash, not even baptized by suffering. At the squat Le Bloc, where many artists worked, a man spray-painted fire extinguishers so they looked like rockets or, in one case, horribly, a used tampon. Why did he want to look at that? Had it been sexist, an experiment in empathy? One reeled at the waste of time only to wonder, startled, what side one was on. Presumably he had found the fire extinguisher in the building, in this resourcefulness resembling other artists at the squat. One Bloc squatter requested of every artist there they decorate a linoleum ceiling tile just for him. The building itself, in its multiplicity of afterlives, appeared in a certain light as the strongest work present. Every object, not just fire extinguishers and ceiling tiles, offered itself up for repurposing. That the squat might conceal, in its recesses, illicit substances, other trespasses, gave every work an edge of subterfuge—it doubled as a decoy.

In these interactions of Parisian squatters and

authorities, a hole had opened in the place of "art." What did it mean? The hole was a door, then a window. A familiar definition—describing something redemptive especially of a lost soul, the artist's—was one I, in my own young life, had heard; because of these Parisian politics it took on, in the city's squats, a capaciously literal truth.

Truth felt in any guise welcome. In squats—vast, cold—one gave quarter to worries of a certain family. Their effect was crowding. The anxiety established itself firmly enough before any research was done, housing in Paris being however, at last count, the most overvalued in Europe. A perverse, obvious effect was real-estate speculation. Some percentage of Parisian lodging as high as 14 at that time was vacant, given over to investment or to second homes even as the need, unmet, increased. In France in 2010, the year I began this reporting, there were nearly twelve thousand evictions by police, the Abbé-Pierre Foundation found; that number had been growing every year. Ten million people were subject to housing fragility of some sort. In other countries there were many more. It was easy to worry, visiting squats, what I could do. Writing did not seemed as if it helped.

By contrast art served, in the days of the precarious lease, an unusually radical purpose. Persuading a judge to delay eviction, it kept open a refuge in which those left homeless for any reason were able, temporarily, to live. Literally art was, in this context, that which allowed the squatters, the artists, to go on living. Here was an example of art making itself useful. Useless, it was useful all over again. Art bought or borrowed time. That's what it was good for: a front. I had been wondering. Here, at least provisionally, was an answer.

¶ Living in Paris I was visited by the worry that besets every foreigner. Despite fluencies that I was cultivating in the language and Parisian lore there was, remained, some barrier I couldn't see. This barrier would keep me naturally from accessing the city's essence. This wall, however transparent or invisible to me, would keep me ignorant of secrets that I could not know existed.

Then news broke about the city's plan to build a clear glass wall around the Eiffel Tower.

It would be bulletproof. Following shootings in 2015, tourism had fallen off; in 2016, the drop—one million fewer visitors—was said to have cost the city 750 million.

The house where I grew up had big picture windows that dumb birds sometimes hit. I imagined the Americans, dozy after so many Nutella crêpes, ramming into that glass wall in the same way. That's how I felt as an American in Paris. Someone would say, this is dangerous, and at that, I would wonder. Really? Let me get a closer look. I don't count. I'm just passing through. I'm here to observe, a writer.

Thud.

¶ *Esquisse pour une auto-analyse*

When I first moved to Paris I spent eight months in an apartment only ever rented for the short term, furnished. There were two beautiful bedrooms of which mine was the lesser, plainly intended for children with its twin beds and window on the street, not the courtyard. It was the one with a desk. Simple, broad, the desk was by the window. The street, in the Marais district, was narrow, medieval. Outside my window was another window. A man worked at his desk, wearing a long white coat. He let a little torch burn. At first I thought he was writing or drawing by candlelight. Later I saw the jeweler's sign.

Overall the apartment was beautiful; I could not have made rent independently. The place came with a sleek, glossy refrigerator, paintings in their inoffensiveness practically abstract, old-fashioned windows so charming one did not begrudge them the draft. Even the bedding and towels the landlord had left were nice. I had two duvets because of the twin beds, which I pushed together. I would, in the course of the eight months, lose one of those duvets in a squat. A squatter told me I could stash it someplace, I'd bring up later, claiming justice, which won me no sympathy. People knew better than to leave things around. I didn't.

My roommate had made some kind of a promise to the landlord about the coffeemaker. It, too, came with the apartment, and it made espresso, each time consuming a capsule it disposed of voraciously, boring a hole in the lid, at last coughing up the casing, which settled, rattling, in a clear repository. In my landlord's and my roommate's understanding, feeding this coffeemaker capsules manufactured under a brand other than its own would, in the long run, cause it harm. I bought capsules at the grocery store, where they were cheap. My roommate corrected me and, when I let his turn come up, very properly crossed the city to the brand's store.

I can say he came from money, a phrasal verb without any sense of motion. Americans, we had graduated that year from the same American college. I met him working on the campus literary magazine. His family, whose fortune had been amassed in the meat-products industry, would subsidize our rent. I would pay him seven hundred euros a month, plus utilities; the apartment rented at twenty-seven hundred. Against the fellowship sponsoring my project, which gave me fifteen hundred euros monthly, all of this felt, still, like a lot, and my dad, to supplement the stipend, wired me sums it did not occur to send back. Friends visiting me in Paris during our first year out of college were the sort of friends who ate at restaurants. "The amount to them is nothing," one of these visiting friends said impatiently, referring to my roommate's parents' money, and she was right, so the trick was to change how I felt about their help. This seemed as if it ought to be within my control, as my own feelings were the problem.

In place of beans, French people ate lentils. Peanut butter, like tofu, was hard to get. At markets I bought persimmons, which had as merits being cheap and that I'd never tasted them. They stung my mouth, tannic, but I loved the color. I made a pot of lentils, inviting my roommate to have some, and soon enough he did, standing at the beautiful refrigerator. Neither of us spoke French that well. We had each other.

When his parents, delegates of the larger family, did visit—they stayed at a hotel—my roommate would instruct me not to tell them anything about the content of the journalism project for which I'd won the fellowship that let me live in Paris. I didn't tell them it was called "Squatting and 21st-Century Protest in Paris," a title I'd written cynically, applying in 2011, a time of media and scholarly interest in expressions of a body of youth empowered by social media to assemble; social media then seemed a resource for democracy. Much like Caravaggio hearing, at the university, of grants enabling the winners to do a project or do nothing in a foreign country, I had thought: There's something I can do when I get out. I'd worked on the application all summer.

So the name of the granting foundation was enough for these patrons to help in subsidizing my project, unless it was not and their son had talked them into it with difficulty that he, sweet enough to spare me, never made known.

We were twenty-two. The program, funded by the French and American governments, brought its fellows to a castle in the town of Chantilly, namesake of whipped cream, and gifted each of us a tiny whisk. They came in tiny paper bags. I kept mine on my desk, its packaging intact.

Another fellow had my same name but stood six inches taller. I found this emboldening. I loved to hear Jackie (her spelling; I was taught to spell my nickname with a Q) remonstrate with a roommate of her own about clothes that roommate chose. "You cannot go out in that!" Jackie said, with real alarm. It was a salmon-pink T-shirt, the neckline a V. Jackie's roommate's parents did something more artistic than my roommate's parents, businesspeople, did; Jackie's roommate, however, was applying to law school. But she planned to study intellectual property, to keep a hand in art, whatever she meant by art.

I had been interested in French squats for two years. I'd studied Spanish and judged French would come easily;

because of the similarity of the grammars, it seemed to. Testing this out, I spent the summer I turned twenty working on farms in France. My parents sprang for the ticket, considering the project educational. They could draw on a certain fund for the purpose of my education only; my mom, an economist by training, spoke often of having to spend it down. As for me, I would be paid in room and board. Privately I thought I'd get some writing done.

I went to work in the Pyrenees for a couple of British expats who needed my help in restoring a farmhouse that it was their ardent project to detoxify. With another worker, a twentysomething from Vancouver, I sanded and painted the attic. Though I was nineteen, I spent most of my time with the expats' daughter, who was, I think, five. Another task of mine was to mind her. We picked cherries. I heard from my family. My step-grandfather had died. My mother insisted I stay where I was, not join her for the funeral. It was important, she emphasized, to finish projects I began, and so I did. I traveled to a farm in Provence, having set for myself the goal of spending time "with animals."

My fiction was progressing very slowly even if I had a fine scene in which a young woman worked construction on an attic as she wept, so that plaster dust and tears combined to cloud her vision. My French, on the other hand, was awful. My host in Provence, a lively, frank woman who, having taught German, knew it to resemble English etymologically, squared that circle by addressing me in German very loudly.

Françoise and Nicholas were so in love, funny together though he was much younger than she and their age difference, when they'd gotten together, wouldn't have shown as it did now. Patently they had no need of help.

He tended a small, mixed herd of goats and sheep, pasturing them in an open field to which they followed him each morning and, late, squirting them with lavender, a natural antiseptic. She made the cheese, brought it to market, permitting me there to make change, which I did clumsily, unused to the foreign currency. The kids were all grown, so I slept in a bedroom. The ad had been posted out of curiosity about who'd come through. Both were autochthonous to that area, where their parents, I understood, had been farmers too, but their cosmopolitanism showed in an array of fraying political stickers that covered the wood of the bathroom door.

Nicholas guided the animals in rain or shine. But they were alone as a gray storm touched down and the herd of them, frightened, broke into a run, white bodies on the hill a waterfall. For sights like this, I didn't know how to thank my hosts. I picked them some of the flowers that were theirs. Françoise gave me a shirt, too small on her and nothing her daughter would wear. Her daughter had refused it already, Françoise assured me. So that was my first impression of the farmer's daughter. I will call her Anaëlle.

I planned to meet friends in Paris, I could I go up as soon as I wanted. I could stay, for free, with Anaëlle, who lived there. "It is just a squat," Françoise said, using that English noun, which French borrows. I never had any idea what she was talking about.

Anaëlle met my train, accepting the cool, heavy bag of cheese and home-brewed walnut wine her mother packed. Twenty-seven, she was squatting on her own in an apartment, a living arrangement I wouldn't again encounter. The door, heavy with three functional deadbolts as well as broken locks, opened onto the kitchen, where a metal, industrial-sized sink, the apartment's only sink, held toothbrushes and dirty dishes. There was a handful of mismatched plates, a hotplate and microwave, a grimy half-size refrigerator covered with magnets and bumper stickers and, on top, wide-bodied shells, which brimmed with ashes. Toilet and bathtub were in the kitchen, each encased by walls of plywood bound with string. To take a shower, one undressed mid-kitchen.

Her fingernails were black with grime. She was always working on her car, and still it did not run. A friend of hers, then, drove us to Père-Lachaise Cemetery, where Anaëlle found a freestanding map so I could pick out any graves I might have felt like seeing. The sun was strong. It caught in her blond hair; I took a picture. Both of us were blonde, medium-height, though Anaëlle's figure was wirier than mine, tough. We met up with her friend who'd driven us for drinks, eating peanuts, chucking shells under our feet. Anaëlle's friend shared he was thinking of moving to Romania while continuing to collect the French state's payout. In Paris, he was barely getting by. We parted ways, me following as Anaëlle found for us a nice organic grocery, where I watched her steal cheese to feed me. I was weighing my feelings of trespass and wellbeing as we reached Belleville Park. Anaëlle pointed out a distant, spindly building that of course I recognized, though I'd never seen the Eiffel Tower.

I wrote about that visit for the campus magazine, putting questions to Anaëlle in follow up. She included, emailing back, an almost equal number of questions she wanted me to answer about myself, something no source for any of my journalism before or since has done. For her own edification, she wanted to know, for instance, how much I, somebody, was paying for my schooling.

With a small grant from the college and a larger gift, an airline ticket, from my father, I returned to Paris during winter break my senior year, staying for most of that time in the dorm room of a friend. The rest of it, ten days, I slept in a squat in the twentieth arrondissement, Le Carrosse. I had found it on Google, I think called ahead. Artists had worked there in the past; by the time of my visit, as the squatters were facing down eviction, only a few did. The place had stayed open ten years, making it exceptional in Paris; squats more typically closed within a year, if that. Very newsworthy: I wondered if I had to sleep there. The professor supervising my journalism project, which would fulfill one of my requirements to graduate, wrote back with a story, the story of an American writer working on a book about Siberia. Constantly people asked the writer if he'd been to Siberia in winter, which he hadn't, and in that way he came to a realization.

The berth they let me have was a plywood platform built into the eaves of the building, which had been an auto shop. About fifteen feet long, it was only about six feet wide, and so I braved the danger of moving in the night and falling to land, crashing down on the cement floor of a workshop where a sweet-voiced young woman made theatrical costumes for no one in particular. My platform, outfitted with a scrap of carpet and a twin-sized mattress, was separated from another, similar platform by a gap and the head of a ladder that led downstairs. My neighbor kept this hole covered with cardboard, concentrating the warmth of his space heater. I had a space heater, too. It worked inefficiently because the platform had no walls. I positioned it between the mattress and the drop. A rich, funky smell hung about that platform. I attributed it to a pile of clothing. Streetlight, thin and milky, seeped through windows cased in bubble wrap. Doves lived in the roof and cooed at all hours. Words were spray-painted blue and yellow on the peeling wall beside the mattress. *SURTOUT DE MERCI MESSIEUR*, they read. *ESPECIALLY THANK YOU, SRS*. I read this repeatedly, trying to sleep.

The bathroom at the ministry of foreign affairs, presumably one of many, was high-ceilinged with creamy, gilded paneling, a pouf. With no window, it felt absolutely private. Jackie and I were putting on lipstick. I was also wearing a consignment-store blazer, "pencil" skirt, a pearl necklace given to me on the occasion of my graduation by a friend's grandmother in a gesture I had found inscrutable. Another old lady, French, came out of a stall and elegantly asked Jackie and me what we studied. "Squats," I said. "Nuclear policy," Jackie said, delighting her. In a photograph from the event posted to Facebook by someone else I am visible to the right of Laurent Fabius, then minister of foreign affairs, about to send troops into Mali. In profile at a podium, the angle is not flattering to him. Loose skin bunches under his chin.

My roommate and I were in silent agreement that paid work could never fulfill us, though we had different reasons. In college he'd done all the reading, using a ruler to leave his underlines, a discipline I had admired in him. Now he never complained of boredom, only spoke with brittle optimism about his self-improvement projects: getting Nikes monogrammed, reading *East of Eden*.

I followed up with the Carrosse squatters, evicted as I was finishing my last semester. At a loss, that loss, I went with Jackie and two other girls to Bruges, the Belgian city, taking a train that cut through foggy countryside. Jackie's stuff was in a duffel bag recognizable as designer, with an arresting pattern. Her roommate's, she explained. I remember the road's loose curve where the city, such as it was, petered out, at one edge the glow of a windmill.

A restaurant friend visited. My little sister, a college student, came over winter break and slept next to me in my bed for two weeks, and I was so happy, I made us kidney beans. I'd warned her I'd likely be busy on New Year's Eve helping to open a squat. The holiday was a popular time for it. The city's festivities distracted police; a squat could fill immediately were a party thrown. I accompanied the Jeudi Noir activists as they set up camp in an office building on the Rue de Valenciennes, near the Gare du Nord. Eventually the housing-rights activists living there, working assiduously, would obtain the city's promise to buy the building and put in public-housing units.

By then I had befriended a woman who lived at the squat La Miroiterie. I will call her, because the quality of her name she mocked was its petit-bourgeois fanciness, Marie-Laure. She worked tending bar at the market Enfants-Rouges, near where I lived. I loved its heaps of herbs and steaming couscous, strings of lights. Occasionally I met her there and together we took the bus to the squat, a direct line. La Miroiterie, an old squat too, was like Le Carrosse a famous squat of Paris. The achievement of its punk scene became a talking point that fall as Miroiterie squatters petitioned the city, imploring it to save them from eviction.

To me Marie-Laure spoke darkly, vaguely of her family in the country's north: real French fascists she'd explain, especially the men, father a soldier, grandfather a collaborator. She was a believer in clean breaks. Now thirty-seven, she had left that family for good at twenty-two, in Paris beginning her career in marketing. She had a sister of her own, unable to understand the part of Marie-Laure that was "rock and roll," Marie-Laure told me. Her smile caught, had a crag. I liked the glamor of her black eyes and hair, black T-shirts stretching femininely over her torso, jeans that hit unfashionably low; she was tall, smoked a lot. A ginger cat with tattered ears installed itself in the upstairs room where Marie-Laure was living at that squat, two buildings on a courtyard. She hadn't wanted animals or children, preferring her freedom; the cat had found her. Marie-Laure had named it Orange. "The cat is wild," she told me, "but it knows where it is safe." For me she saved her stories of horror at the squat, of punks "with long knives" or the girl who'd shown up naked, shivering, in the courtyard, whom the squatters saved. Because La Miroiterie's artistic identity was foundational to its political campaign as well as its legal defense, because of my own research interests, I asked Marie-Laure, just like that, if she was an artist. Anyway she got the question all the time. During concerts, when she tended bar, I helped, snacking from tubs of candy set out on the counter that reeked of old beer. Structural hunks of the concert hall were visibly unsound. Bags of glass dust and dangerous chemicals were said to lurk in a back room, relics.

An artist lived downstairs. He was British, and as I spoke with him in English I was surprised to feel exposed, articulate again. I lacked the critical framework to appreciate his art, noise music recorded under the names of Andy Bolus and Evil Moisture, but I liked his presence, which was gentle, and a set of thoughtful interactions with the rotting building. When it snowed he spoke of walking carefully backward so that tracks led toward the squat, a trick. Once an old woman, knocking, told the squatters she'd gone dancing, young, in a basement ballroom. Andy looked for it, shifting debris that filled that courtyard, trashcans and rusted shopping carts, in the hope of finding a trapdoor.

I listened rapt to Michel, who organized many of the concerts. He was a sixth-generation Parisian, he said. His father, an Egyptologist, had been away on business often. Left alone, the boy took up excavations of his own in the city's catacombs, a warren of tunnels spelunkers explore, their ports of call illegal accesses. For these excursions Michel had adopted the surname Ktu, a contraction of Cthulhu, the name of a kind of monster in an H. P. Lovecraft story. Michel Ktu the *cataphile* had a looming, lined face. "*L'underground, c'est moi*," he said. An ancestor of his had died, he said, in defending a barricade of the Commune of 1871, which was, I was learning, a temporary people's government following a Prussian siege and the deposing of Napoleon III. Its last defenses had fallen in the neighborhood of the squat, Belleville, an area rich in revolutionary history. "I am the stones of the city," Ktu told me. He spoke of a painter named Daniel Pipard whose house La Miroiterie had been before it was a mirror factory. There Pipard had hosted parties featuring stars in the firmament of Belleville legend, among them the singer Edith Piaf, who apocryphally was born, Ktu may have been the first to tell me, in a doorway on the Rue de Belleville.

The *New York Times* would be running a story on La Miroiterie. Focused on the impending eviction, it would chronicle, for local color, the squatters' resistance. Marie-Laure let me know, and I hid from her that I was furious; why did she want to talk to them? I emailed the professor who'd supervised my school project, complaining to him that, if an article about La Miroiterie was to be published in the *New York Times*, I was the one positioned to write it. As I am unnerved to remember, he was sympathetic, suggesting I make something of a tricky situation by getting the other reporter to interview me as an expert. I didn't think I had a sound bite in me. But I would have to publish something as, given the newspaper's interest, the story was publishable, and though months had gone by I'd come in the first place for a story.

Despite the investment in La Miroiterie of some hordes of musicians and concert organizers, and rather than to any of the rest of five to fifteen live-in squatters, the labor of interfacing with journalists and with the lawyer seemed to fall to Marie-Laure alone, as often it would to women in squats, but we also had, perhaps, an understanding. Paris has an aspect that is *villageois*, in French a compliment, and within this village La Miroiterie's eviction became, briefly, a cause célèbre. Marie-Laure would be interviewed for a show to air on France Culture. She wanted me to come. We took a suburban train to the gilded sixteenth arrondissement, finding, opposite the Eiffel Tower, a looped white building, the national radio. It went fine, though I watched Marie-Laure carefully as, going home, she fell silent, at last texting the squat's lawyer at the time, Sylvain Dreyfus. *En route vers la gloire*, a friend texted her. Dreyfus was an important name in France as she had told me, the American. She closed her eyes. I saw her rest against the window of a darkening compartment as we were carried east.

My roommates' parents were in Paris not just, or primarily, to visit him. They were benefactors of an exhibition that would open at the Louvre, a collaboration between an American museum of which they were, voluntarily, patrons and the French institution. A friend of my roommate's, another classmate of ours, came separately. Some misunderstanding had transpired. My roommate's friend, even though he'd come all the way from the US, was not invited to events associated with the exhibit's opening.

(My own, private assumption, which might not have risen to consciousness, had been that I wasn't.) So together this friend and I visited the exhibit after it had opened, acting as if we were normal museum guests. The paintings having made the trip from the US were hunting scenes in which this other American, my classmate, appeared to sense inadequacy.

I was relieved to see him cheer up. He wished to tour a squat where I was working; I knew, without knowing why, that Marie-Laure would love for me to bring him. They got along really well, drinking in an upstairs room we called the workshop. Canvases were propped against the walls, layering side tables. The old floor held up with a tremor. We found ourselves in leaving pausing, the courtyard bursting with graffiti as this classmate took my picture posing with the mural that was most obscene, he had insisted. He posted the photo to Facebook, which mortified me obscurely—I didn't know what my problem was—and, stranger, made me feel I had committed something like betrayal. Of whom or what, I was unsure.

There was another squat I visited, Le Stendhal, named after the street on which it stood. Like La Miroiterie in the east of Paris, it sat lower on the hill underlying Belleville. One of the housing-rights activists I'd met in getting going had introduced me to the squatters there. They were closer to my age than the Miroiterie squatters were, in other ways sociologically similar, college-educated; I overheard one of them scolding another for missing messages in a Google "group" they used to organize. Some native Parisians, they were housing-rights, DIY, bicycle activists, miscellaneous idealists. Their eviction order would come due that spring, but they knew of a vacancy. The collective totaled about twenty squatters, a few of whom lived in a secondary squat, a satellite, on the Rue Orfila. They all wanted a part of the privilege that settled in squats on those with a hand in the opening, perks like first pick of the bedrooms. Each addition to the opening team would, however, extend the time to break in, multiplying the risk.

So my request to come along was difficult but, for some reason, granted. We went over Easter weekend, on Friday night knifing apart thick fabric, baling it. Supplies fit in a truck, which we pushed to get going. The night was dark. Someone within had left a ground-floor window open. Another positioned my foot: "Hurry up." Behind us a window blind was finishing its struggle in the half light. It fell. Yellow streetlight landed there. We found a room in which to sleep as another teammate, bringing up the rear, used bike tires to hang a ladder just inside the front door of the building. If intruders came, we'd hear them.

I got used to the sounds each of them made in sleeping. A bruise was forming on my hip from the thinness of the sleeping bag, the floor. A squatter who was a theater worker, feeling sick, napped elsewhere in the building, reentering the room where the rest of us were living just to swig from the whiskey that sat on the table and gargle theatrically. Someone else had brought Easter candy. We discussed the internet's manipulation, a tool they'd need called a "triangle key," *The Great Gatsby* as another of them was making progress, often, in a project of his own. He was designing a game in which the players met characters who told them what to do. Complying, you moved over islands in a blue sky patched with clouds. The islands were green, pastoral. The squatter was not only coding the game but writing the text, designing those characters. He was, during this submarine, working out bugs. He showed me a character, its arm a fat baguette. That was a bug. Behind it, though, the islands drifted appropriately among the clouds this squatter had invented. I asked, "Is making games your passion?"

"Making worlds, yeah."

A few of the other squatters held degrees in sociology, meaning that approximately one-fifth of the collective was, on the basis of this training, accepting of my research as they understood it. Others, however, thought about journalists much as did the "anarchist-autonomous" squatters who opened their squats in Paris's eastern suburbs. Though the *totos* were anarchists, they did abide by something like a policy, refusing interviews, preferring to share their own news, a practice referred to as "auto-diffusion." The tendency toward obfuscation at Le Stendhal ran deeper than my intervention, as I was relieved eventually to understand: I didn't have to take it personally. Two of the squatters were called Roch, and both, apparently, chose not to share their last names—not with me, not with anybody, or so it appeared. During the submarine, I heard the game designer reasoning with one of the Rochs, saying that while the other squatters usually referred to the Roch at hand as Roch at Orfila and the other Roch as Roch at Le Stendhal, with both Rochs living at the newly forming squat, the collective would need some other way to differentiate them. "Why should I concern myself with what you say about me when I'm not there?" Roch said in answer. "I'm not paranoid or schizophrenic."

My article about La Miroiterie went up, and I sent the link to Marie-Laure, who texted back to say it had betrayed her. She didn't say why. I paid a visit. Bands played La Miroiterie three nights a week. Usually I went in through a gate on the street without paying, saying to the people tabling that I'd come to see Marie-Laure. This time, however, I did pay. Marie-Laure, at the bar, wouldn't meet my eye. She had explicitly encouraged my reporting about the squat, and yet I was evicted from La Miroiterie. I mean that figuratively, a bad analogy: experiencing none of the violence predicated on police eviction, I left. In the street, I saw Michel Ktu. He was acting normally, which surprised me, and then his girlfriend, who was young and beautiful, got out of a cab and said, "You've been writing some funny things!" I apologized senselessly and, as they began making out, left them, threaded Belleville hill down to the Métro.

My roommate moved back, flying home, his trunks following on a slow boat. It was summer finally; I moved farther out, to the nineteenth and a house share behind a bakery where two roommates, strangers, and I would pay just about five hundred euros each. A year younger than I was and five years older, respectively, they were Dutch-French and French, a girl and a boy, a student and fashion worker, each one a dream. I, though, would bring home flowers, which died quickly in a windowless downstairs room. The heat of the bakery, it always seemed, had stifled them. The baker, Véronique, was highly regarded in her field, even winning prizes, which made her exceptional as a woman. That was my understanding. She smoked and talked in the small, dirty courtyard that we shared. Flour sacks pooled loosely, water traced a black line to a drain. By night we heard the beeping of Véronique's machinery, a footfall of weasels, which lived in our walls, the shuffle of feathers as doves outside a certain window settled. It opened up over a low roof of corrugated tin, where I clambered with the idea of relaxing, reading, to watch those pigeons roost wherever metal spikes that clustered like the bristles of a hairbrush did not prevent them. At a party of Jackie's I'd met a guy; such meeting felt, by this time, distant; one morning he noticed the smell of bread woke him. It woke me. I hadn't been aware a smell could do that, but, as the man in my bed reasoned, a stimulus to any sense could: the clap of hands, a push... Jackie flew back, leaving me with myself. I found a job teaching English at a university, half a dozen ninety-minute classes weekly. This, furnishing a visa and some income, would let me stay. Our house sat higher on the Belleville hill than Le Stendhal, than La Miroiterie. Close by was the squat Le Bloc, which had first opened to the public that New Year's Eve. In 2013, I would visit Le Bloc regularly. From my new house it was a fifteen-minute walk, convenient.

¶ *The* –4

People stood out front as if waiting: smoking, talking. Of consecutive double doors, the first set bore a monogram in stenciled capitals: B-L-O-C. A grille resisted lifting, sticking. Just inside was a foyer, at the back of which stretched a crescent-shaped desk referred to by squatters as the Accueil, Reception. Watch was kept. Behind that desk a crank could operate the grille.

"This is a building of the people," the squatter Dominique, who had worked construction, told me, referring to its history as a public health agency and its suitability for heavy use. Hard floors swept clean. Banks of cabinets, their material a blond composite, lined the halls, which at rhythms of their own let onto rooms that had been government workers' offices. The doors of frosted glass shut with a clang. They kept in the warmth of space heaters. Open, they let smoke and music circulate; they aired disputes. A female squatter—for women comprised a minority at Le Bloc—drew my attention to gaps in the fabric or paper stuck up to cover certain of those doors. People liked to see feet coming in the hallway, company, warning. Each door wore a padlock.

Living quarters in these ways took up the aboveground stories, thirty to thirty-five offices a floor. Into bathrooms, which variously came with pairs or rows of sinks, sitting or squat toilets, and mirrors, squatters had built showers. At least one room per floor served as a kitchen, but all did not have kitchen fixtures. The kitchen on the second floor, though it was much used, lacked a sink. A squatter who lived on the third floor told me they'd had, on that floor, to padlock the kitchen. Reputedly clean, it attracted the messier residents of other floors. After they finished making messes on their floors, they came and made a mess on the third floor. Though he characterized the padlock as a necessity, it embarrassed him, as the proper role for a squat, by which he seemed to mean its default action, the direction of motion that matched it, was to open, he said, not to close.

Hallways wrapped the building, graffiti serving as street signs. In a stairwell, French words for "Live fast die young" marked off the third floor; a death's-head labeled the basements. At least one of the artists would speak, early on, of all signing pieces "Le Bloc" in the hope of getting work piling up to cohere into a movement, and while I don't think this plan gained followers, the will was representative; some artists developed a memorable brand: a skull-and-crossbones below which unfurled the legend, in English, LE BLOC SONS OF ANARCHY.

They had at least one motto: *Tu dors t'es mort*, "Sleep and you're dead." This was explained to me as a challenge, serving to encourage participants in a shared project of sleeplessness, and as a constraint on behavior, to dissuade them from falling asleep just anywhere.

On the ground floor was a gallery in a dedicated pair of rooms. Caravaggio had worked already with artists in residence at Le Bloc, and the squat's management was meant to take a cut of sales.

The first basement, called the *moins un*, was used by the squatters for building-wide meetings as well as public-facing open houses. It surrounded a patch of greenery, the base of an atrium within which a disco ball had been suspended. To its every side windows could open, a garden at the squat's core.

The –2 was low ceilinged, utilitarian. Ducts snaked, silver prisms. DJs set up there, parties spilling over, and I heard some people even slept two stories deep.

The –3 had been a parking garage, as had the –4, where

during the building's occupation runoff of its every leak would end up, black pools.

According to the documents of their eviction suit these squatters' entry had been forced. But judges tasked with the case repeatedly would fail to investigate the break-in. And the squatters maintained otherwise; similar to other claims made around Le Bloc, its correspondence to historical reality was not, for every squatter, of defining value. "A trade secret," somebody said.

Sometime in December their neighbors, perceiving the occupation, alerted police. A bailiff stopped by, taking names. Out of perhaps two hundred squatters (they gave higher estimates, too), thirty-six at the most were named as defendants. The bailiff, in the proprietor's pay, was motivated to give a low head count, as one of the squatters explained to me; this one, in any case, did. A far under-populated occupation was harder to defend, seeming less reasonable to the judge. As there might be damages to pay, squatters, for their part, considered it strategic to feature as defendants those of them who were insolvent.

In the onslaught of arrivals Caravaggio invited artists and then everyone. The building's occupants referred to its square meterage, a brag: "seven thousand," "eight thousand," they said, a figure that, reported in documentation of the later renovation, was, very precisely, 8,186. They developed a sense of themselves as historically important; when squatters called Le Bloc the biggest squat in Paris, one tended to believe them. When, somberly, a young artist called it the biggest in Europe, I understood she was still mourning the eviction, the year before, of the massive Tacheles in Berlin. (I was interested to read in promotional materials for a concert at Le Bloc the contradictory claim that Forte Prenestino, a squat in Rome and one band's home turf, in fact was the biggest in Europe.) About Le Bloc's early days, about its parties, I would hear even years later claims that struck me as outrageous; there was one about a sponsorship by Red Bull, the corporation, said to have installed dispensers for its product free of cost on every floor. Red Bull did not respond to my requests for comment; I was ready to forget this claim entirely but then found mention of Le Bloc in an article about Parisian nightlife on RedBullMusicAcademy.com, apparently a hub for sponsored content. The title of the French article dated September 2016, three years after Le Bloc's eviction, translates to "A Permanent State of Party."

Not every artist working at Le Bloc would sleep there. Many simply maintained studios whose disciplines would range. 3-D printers filled one; jugglers practiced in a basement. A craze built for a photography style referred to, in English, as "light painting" that, over the course of a long exposure, left the subject swaddled in strands of color swirling as if at that person's command. So they set about immortalizing each other. A sculptor made installations out of Le Bloc's trash. Preeminent were the graffiti artists, understood by squatters to be well known in graffiti-artist circles. Empty cans slotted into a grid were sprayed with paint, contributing another oeuvre. Despite the rate of repainting, certain murals were let be as if by implicit agreement. Despite the heterogeneity of expressive practices and a certain factionalism within the building, it was rare to see tags sprayed to deface a finished mural.

Essential, for any squat, was having neighbors on its side. Neighbors of all kinds were understood to side with artists. The squatters of Le Bloc, as early as January, distributed flyers. The -1 was partitioned into alcoves in which each of these residents exhibited, and it allowed even so for a view of the group: paintings, knots of musicians, "wellness" activities. An activity for children was set up. Fans trained on heaped balloons could make them skip; the kid sat in the middle.

Some from Le Bloc would ensure that it was registered, enabling the entity, and themselves really, to accept donations. Crucially, in collecting unsold food from supermarkets, this organization's members would be able to ask the employees for leftovers directly rather than dumpster dive. A squatter from the second floor went mornings, wheeling a shopping cart to be unloaded on a table in a hallway near Reception. Free for the taking: yogurt, which stays good long after the sell-by date; packaged meat and sandwiches; vegetables with skin in such condition it would give way at a touch. Heads of lettuce crowded a cabinet opposite the second-floor kitchen, peeking out.

So the *association* Le Bloc was incorporated after several months of occupancy in a "declaration to the prefecture of police," which squatters filed with that prefecture on May 28, 2013. Le Bloc, according to this appealingly breathless founding document,

> responds to the flagrant lack in terms of [sic] artistic fabrication; cultural, social, and technical exchange; Le Bloc must respond at top speed to the recurring and endlessly unsatisfied needs of local artists and technicians in terms of spaces open to implementation, to creation, to information technology, and to practices in every discipline of artistic, technical, cultural, and social research.

The prefecture of police, as was standard, promulgated this notice, duly publishing it in a registry that June 8.

Wednesdays in the second-floor kitchen, volunteers and at least one salaried worker making up a "Squat Mission" of the NGO Médecins du Monde ("Doctors of the World," spun out of the better-known Doctors without Borders), held office hours during which they helped the squatters with their chores of paperwork. A common problem was that of *domiciliation administrative*, the address where a homeless person could receive the mailings so important to the French welfare state. Addresses were available; you had to know about them. A foreign woman with a toothache received advice to have it checked out anyway.

Despite faith placed in the state in such cases, or because the squatters knew the processes of recourse intimately, they were triumphant in characterizing social services that they provided to those subjects the state would neglect, beating it at its own game. Housing was just the most obvious. They spoke pointedly of the irony clear in a health agency's shuttering of a building that so ably could serve as emergency shelter. That the agency had left behind its trove of private data, health records, seemed to these squatters final proof of a fundamental indifference of which they had always suspected their political leaders.

They had entered the building ahead of a date in December 2012 coinciding with the 5,125-year cycle of an ancient calendar, much in the news as a "Mayan apocalypse." The forecast was, for these squatters, the stuff of shared jokes. Le Bloc had begun at the world's end, they would say. The squat picked up where the world had left off.

More often they spoke of *competences*, what each of them could do. During the first of weekly meetings, squatters introduced themselves by, I was told, tallying their skills, suggesting to the group that any person interested in picking up a skill—screen printing, say—should come and see them. I heard a squatter worrying, conversely, that the community was unable to properly care for individuals who might, that squatter felt, require psychiatric attention. They lacked training, were "not social workers."

Among themselves, they encouraged sharing meals: they all liked to eat and drink well, and it was, in that same squatter's opinion, shutting oneself in that led to violence, madness, all that which began in overreaction.

Voices swelled in halls, the glass doors grating. Fluorescents buzzed and flickered.

Caravaggio, who spoke in the accent of the suburbs (a way of speaking he adjusted for the benefit of my understanding, automatically correcting himself when, interviewed, he used slang), at last told me his work at Le Bloc wasn't all "social" or charity. "If I hadn't opened this," he said, "I'd be in the street. And so would my buddy over there, and my other buddy"—the litany became joyful—"and this young man wouldn't have any place to work..."

He was fat, a round face split by his laugh. My tape is messy with the voices of some friends of his and fellow squatters as he gamely let them draw out his responses. We sat at a hallway table, these others helping advance a discussion of incarceration to which Caravaggio, getting laughs, contributed harrowing tales, for my benefit pausing to gloss differences between the French prison system and the American. Of bystanders, he demanded hashish or tobacco. When I asked about children at Le Bloc, he shouted obligingly down the hall: "Mehdi, is your little girl around?" Apparently she wasn't, but a man emerged, presumably Mehdi, and, letting out a wet laugh, started talking to both of us about something else: a history he shared with Caravaggio in "trashy" squats (*à l'arrache*) that meant the two men, finding themselves among "artists" at Le Bloc, were upwardly mobile, for them another trigger for hilarity. In the halls Caravaggio fielded and made requests, responding in Spanish to a woman who complained in Spanish that she had no money. Men interrupted our interview frequently to ask about a job on which, apparently, he was lead. Mosquitoes were breeding on the −4, where the pools of Le Bloc's effluent had opened up and stagnated. Someone had set down plywood, bridges. A wall was fleshy with the eggs. The men would haul sacks of cement to this, the deepest sub-basement, where it was dark as well as swampy, and fill in the plashes.

"I can come back later if you're busy," I said.

"No, no, don't worry," Caravaggio said. "You'll come with, and we'll keep going. We'll just be doing some construction work, and you'll ask us all about what it's for."

It was understood in other Parisian squats that within the superlatively populous Le Bloc, certain men enjoyed authority. Caravaggio did, for having opened the squat; so did others, for reasons less immediately clear. Useful to an understanding of Le Bloc is that many of the squatters found these men intimidating. All called them *tontons*. The reference was to *Les Tontons flingueurs*, a dated flick whose title is rendered in English as *Crooks in Clover* or *Monsieur Gangster*.

At Le Stendhal, gossiping, I brought up the matter with a squatter who told me delicately that while Stendhal squatters believed in direct democracy, Le Bloc had a more "representative" model. Visibly *tontons* commanded authority in settling fights. At one of the building-wide meetings that took place weekly they stood together to announce a rent hike, fifty euros a month to sixty.

Le Général said in the *tontons*' defense that breaking in ate up resources. Scouting vacancies, they paid for gas. They had to buy brooms, a video projector, those sacks of cement, Caravaggio told me humbly. Another *tonton* said that a police informant warned him how *tontons* would get in real trouble if ever they made money off a party. The cop would've hated for that to happen. "He was a subtle cop," the *tonton* added, not like other cops.

Caravaggio, orchestrating introductions—"In France we give *bisous*, kisses, even to the boys"—brought me to that *tonton*'s room, on the fifth. In the association's founding documents some squatter had bestowed on "Big Vincent"—the very tallest of Le Bloc's Vincents—a title. Caravaggio, for my benefit, used it, addressing Vincent as *Monsieur le Président*.

"You want to know how this place is organized?" Vincent said to me. "You're looking for a unicorn. The problem is that people here are marginal. They're here because they reject rules. That's fundamental. So it's impossible to make up rules specially for these same people."

"We make rules," Caravaggio said, "but a minimum."

They relaxed, eventually joking between themselves, men, about certain women at Le Bloc. I had a hard question, about the resolution of disputes. "On the subject of management," I said, "someone mentioned a kind of internal court."

"Oh yes," Vincent said quickly, "that's us, we get together at night, we go to the -4, and Le Général..."

I cut in, alarmed. "The -4?"

"But of course. You want to wale on somebody, better

do it down below. It's more discreet. It's every Thursday night, this get-together."

"He's joking," Caravaggio said, uncomfortable.

But I would have it confirmed by another *tonton*, by two *tontons*, that such a body did exist, created in response to complaints the squat's government was insufficiently transparent.

¶ *Curiosities*

The building's size was a point of pride that the Bloc squatters held in common, but it was not the only one. Caravaggio, early in our interview, rattled off the squat's constituent ethnicities, in his brag an echo of that value shared with corporations. They all made appreciative reference to Le Bloc's multiformity. These squatters' origins were various and included Algeria, Chile, Côte d'Ivoire, Ghana, the overseas departments of Guadeloupe and French Guiana—which I will also call by its name in French, Guyane, so as to avoid that possessive—Italy, Jamaica, Japan, Kazakhstan, Mauritius, Mexico, Morocco, Romania, Senegal, Spain, Togo, Uruguay, the USSR, and, even before my arrival, the US.

I kept hearing women at Le Bloc were treated well, a claim that gave itself the lie in its very syntax (in the cordoning-off of women and the looming question of the subject, a potential aggressor to whom cover had been granted). Still, though the *tontons* were not, in my woman's experience, bien-pensant regarding gender, one French artist transitioning while living at Le Bloc felt comfortable. A few of the others, given the chance to correct a bailiff on the matter of the artist's pronouns, did so with apparent eagerness.

Here and there lived an otherwise homeless Frenchman taken in by *tontons* some years previously on condition that he quit drinking and do the dishes. A petite, emaciated man with a beard ending at his chest and tons of bracelets, he was called Jesus.

One *tonton*, a thickset, dreadlocked Frenchman,

unnerved me by only very late in my reporting addressing me in English that was perfect, even posh. Of some other *tontons*, he said: "The problem is that these people have trouble communicating, so they're just going to get upset and smash people up, and I don't think it's the proper way of doing things." He had gone to boarding school in Kent, he explained.

A Frenchwoman in her twenties from the suburbs had grown up working with the Red Cross—her mother ran a local chapter, she explained—and raised money steadily, at Le Bloc also, to fill a shipping container she would send to "Africa." These parties didn't happen at Le Bloc, but she threw fundraisers.

A more senior Frenchwoman, a painter, explained while clutching a portfolio of her work that a grandfather of hers had helped lead the French Resistance during the Second World War. His children were needfully split up and hidden. The squatter's mother, given away to a provincial family, was brought up to make a living by competing in motorcycle rodeos. In consequence the other siblings, placed in higher-class homes, came to reject her. The squatter, who was living on the second floor of Le Bloc, told me that not long before she'd met a cousin of hers, a rich man, because he was trying to buy one of her paintings.

Not sure I believe any of this, I noted.

Myths of Paris came to roost at Le Bloc as they did at other squats, as if squats were the city's unconscious. Three boys nineteen years old arrived from Italy to launch careers as painters. Le Général provided secondhand canvases, white paint with which to blank them. The teenagers had stolen previous canvases from 59 Rivoli, they told me. At Le Bloc, they slept in one of the ground-floor galleries; it looked as if a family of swans had molted. While their French was just OK, the English spoken by these Italians was very good: after they told me they wanted to live in Montmartre, haunt of the cubist Pablo Picasso, I asked, I thought reasonably, if they wanted to recreate *la bohème*. "Not recreate," a boy said. "We are *la bohème*."

A Mauritian man living on the fifth floor was a kind of lapsed philosopher, having been through too much schooling to content himself with any job; a woman about my age, white, French, explained she stayed at Le Bloc having failed a course of study in the philosophy of art. A white Romanian woman my age was applying to the Beaux-Arts, also a talented acrobat.

From memory it was on the second floor where two men I'd met at Le Carrosse had come to live, one middle-aged, one older. They had lived before at Mirabeau, the squat Le Général had opened. The old man, who due to a bad leg couldn't work, was Algerian and had come to France years before for fear of events he explained with a single word, "terrorism," nearly the same in my language.

On the third floor lived a Moroccan musician, a performer in the Gnawa tradition. He had few possessions apart from his instruments, the most important of which was the gimbri, a tall, three-stringed lute of camel skin on which the man lavished attention. By hand he sewed a strand of cowrie shells onto its strap, sequined and red.

Also on the third lived "the Russians," as they were called in aggregate, though one had been born in the part of the USSR that became Belarus; I had known them, musicians, at Le Carrosse.

For a few days a man from Germany slept in a basement, apparently uninvited; he regaled me from the very first question with tales so violent I wished I'd asked nothing, about fights, acts of sabotage associated by him with some kind of punk scene. A musician and artist from Guadeloupe who was Black referred to the German as a "white Rasta," because of his dreadlocks.

Many squatters referred to the inhabitants of the fourth floor, which was majority Black, as "the Rastas" though only some, perhaps, identified that way. (One who did gave me his business card; he sold food. Others sold posters, for example. A band from Jamaica visiting Paris stayed at Le Bloc, also Rastafarians; reggae groups performed on the -1.) Vicious rumors would spread about a Guianese man living on this floor who'd take it upon himself in meetings to question the *tontons*' management, calling it racist. He was said to have padlocked a shower—he may have been the one to build the shower—and sold, around the squat, copies of the key. Also alleged was that on that floor rooms were rented out to new arrivals in France, Senegalese men maybe, many to a room, as it was said, who couldn't access other housing when they wanted, the story went, for immigration documents.

Because of the seriousness of these allegations, I looked for the men, and yet I didn't like finding myself in that position, of hunting. (Separately I met at least two Senegalese men living at Le Bloc, one called Suleman and another, Action, his DJ name; both had, I thought, immigrated long before.) Very late, as the date of the squat's eviction—December 6, 2013—was approaching, the fourth floor emptied out. Standing in its eerily calm hallway with my research question I called a Bloc squatter who had also lived at Le Carrosse, a Japanese musician, a trumpet player whose passport, even that, had expired, and learned he, at least, had left Le Bloc for this reason.

The beauty of Le Bloc was not that it took in everyone, but that it took in anyone; a failure was that it could not take in everyone. In October of that year, a ship sank off the coast of Lampedusa, Italy, a large number of passengers dying. Press reports identified them as undocumented migrants from African countries and, after that fashion, too late to do them any favors, set them down in history. Casualty counts—"more than 100," an "estimated 300," "at least 130" with "200... unaccounted for"—did not discourage, by any burst of clarity, the public complacency. A few dozen or hundred got away from the wreck. I stopped by Le Stendhal around that time, where an artist from Taiwan, someone else who'd overstayed in France, marveled at the difference, stark enough, between her own predicament and the one in which the passengers had found themselves. "I feel very guilty, because I know a lot of illegal immigrants who risked their lives to come here," she said in English. She spoke little French and confided in me on the basis of our shared language, one strangeness we shared. "I just took a flight, and I stayed because of my curiosity."

¶ Luís, sixty, of medium height, white hair, a handlebar moustache yellowed as if by sun asked, as the interview began, if I would mind his smoking, a courtesy not ordinarily extended at Le Bloc. He thanked me though the room was his and took my lead, joining me in laughing. Above the neatly made bed, postcards and a seashell rested on a shelf; pens, Coke, and a small sack of cat food were arranged on a desk.

The biographical details he shared were of a melancholy specific to our setting: and that's how I ended up here. Born in Madrid, he'd lived in seven Spanish cities, once crossing a swath of countryside on foot. A child, grown, was working in Moscow. A brother had died in a car crash. Luís, who had lived with an uncle and slept in the entrance of a bank, read widely, having studied psychology, and worked intermittently, some jobs becoming specialties of his, for example the building of "expansion joints for highways and airports," a long phrase he repeated in those words. The boss would not renew a contract. He could not have found another job in Spain, above all because of his age. He took a bus to Paris. It had been four years since then.

In Paris, where he had slept in Métro stations, moving among them with the goal of avoiding other street sleepers, he had experienced certain station controllers as strict. In Madrid, municipal showers ran hot and cold as soon as someone homeless got in. In Paris, no soup kitchen or baths were open daily, and it became another madness to keep track of the schedules. Luís's assertion was not only of those details but of his own capacity to notice, to resist their making a fool out of him, to be, if anything, picky; in any case the frustrations of homelessness did not end there. Social workers had quirks, one of which was always to ask about the quality of the client's stool, which in a member of the homeless population was uniquely poor, the predictable outcome of bad food, sauce without onions, stale bread distributed for free.

"Sauce without onions?" I asked.

"Sauce without onions," he said. He had a liking for statistics, regretted having found no statistic on the loss of hope. Still, when in the subway an announcement was aired of a "passenger accident," he felt sure in his judgment: suicide, another of the homeless. Even if its services were, in Luís's view, crazy-making, the state continuously paid for them, by which he inferred they benefited politicians, perhaps providing what he referred to as "good publicity for society," advertising messages that valorized society like: you won't go hungry, you won't be cold.

Three men, filmmakers shooting a documentary about Le Bloc, knocked and took from me the key to a room there that they and I shared for purposes of our research.

The door shut, making its clang. Luís, soft-spoken, sat at my side, as the dimensions of the room necessitated. I noticed a smell of canned red sauce.

Receiving the *revenu de solidarité active*, an unemployment benefit then a little more than 450 euros monthly, he could afford cigarettes and groceries of his own, which he considered more healthful than the *récupération* of food collectively available at Le Bloc. Strangers had entered his room in his absence three times, breaking its little lock. They took only his laundry detergent. Laundry he did elsewhere. That a washing machine overflowed chronically suggested to him intentionality on the *tontons*' part. Although Luís had, at Le Bloc, sought refuge from all things "social," these powerful squatters seemed to him experts in the domain of the social. Like the state apparatus, they kept in motion, he told me, a "psychological war."

He kept to himself and worked to keep the ground floor clean. Though the cats he fed were not his, he didn't like to see them eat garbage. In a bowl set out for them he had found human excrement, he said.

A few possessions he had left for safekeeping with a friend: a fridge, a debit card. "A very honest guy," Luís said. "I'm lucky."

He gave "Spain" as the location of haunting, dreamlike sights all rich in inference. Ghosts of fascism stirred as if out of dormancy. On a sidewalk he had seen an older woman being marched along, conceivably against her will, her captor wearing the regalia of the regime. Through a window, someone on the inside detailed to Luís their fear of leaving. A Kosovar man, a friend and excellent chess player, avoided churches even as many men homeless as he was found that they made for good places to sleep. This man caved, set foot in a church, and was not again seen. Hospitals in Spain were Catholic, were connected to the Catholic Church in hidden ways, and in such supposedly life-giving places new mothers would learn their new children had died. A mother or a father would ask to see the body. Nurses would explain that to accommodate would just upset the parent. Luís was surprised I hadn't heard of a phenomenon to which he referred repeatedly, using an unvarying expression. I did learn later of its basis in reality: "The stealing and selling of babies by the Catholic Church." Other prefab expressions: "a factory of crazies," by which he meant the state's social services; the "leaving of reality," when interface with services had resulted in insanity; and, as a catch-all, *trucs sociaux*, "social stuff," which I misheard, through Luís's accent, as *trou social*, "social hole," which led me to metaphors.

Because Luís so clearly had a story to get out, I was

surprised to hear, after an hour and a half, that I wouldn't be permitted to publish any of it. He used that verb, *permettre*. I reopened negotiations, explaining I could leave out material Luís considered sensitive but did want to draw on his phenomenology of homelessness. After some confusion, Luís led me to understand it was for my sake, not his, that he was discouraging me from writing. In trading on any of his information I assuredly would risk reprisal in the form of firing from a job or worse, but Luís was "lost" already, "condemned to death," the diocesan evil merely waiting for these pressures to bring about a suicide, manipulating them idly with its long arm. Against the fate he maintained a daily practice of mind-strengthening exercises. "Up till now I haven't lost my mind," he said. "I am well acquainted," he said, "with the system that it is forbidden to know."

By "system" I understood Luís to refer to the Catholic Church and various accomplices; for my purposes the term encompassed, also, the extent of an exposure to humiliations reserved by societies and states for people already living out-of-doors. A third system was Le Bloc, where my experience of life intersected with his and where Luís considered the *tontons* deliberate in imposing a social order.

It was interesting to meet Luís as a journalist, from which perspective the pertinence of his paranoia, entailing the condition that I not mention him to a past employer, otherwise an obvious route to verification, was that it granted him something like exclusivity. Paranoia was the refusal of corroboration. To thwart those who would surveil him, Luís avoided using email or cellphones; I wouldn't be able, later, to ask him for clarification. He told me he would never, could never give away the locations of the places he had found to sleep. At another point he said that out of all the Paris Métro stations, Télégraphe was warmest, deep under the Belleville hill, and he slept there soundly.

Journalism, meanwhile, exerted a force of its own on Luís. From a pocket he drew an *El País* article dated the previous month and, in three motions, unfolded it, showing me. Fascism was exhibiting symptoms classic of its onset, he invited me to notice: the government was censoring leftists, Jews, and Gypsies. "No," I murmured. But sure enough, a headline read: "The Government cancels aid to leftist and minority groups' publications." I would take a closer look outside Le Bloc. At issue was the withdrawal of a total of six hundred thousand euros in state funding to a clutch of magazines, some serving readerships that were trade unionist, Jewish, or self-identified Gypsy (*Gitanos*, one of the magazines). The journalist, Anabel Díez, was writing with ostentatious fatigue about one editor's invocation, in response to the budget cuts, of Martin Niemöller's famous poem about the Holocaust ("First they came for the socialists... trade unionists... Jews"). In fact the journalist was pointing up an absurdity that to her had seemed self-evident in likening such an event to the great tragedy. Luís, in some demonstration of journalism's dangers, had not taken her that way.

Into his French he sometimes threw a Spanish word, unwittingly it seemed. One substitution he made systematically, using the Spanish *yo* for "I," not the French *je*; about life at the squat, he said in French, "*Yo* reject it totally but *yo* am happy."

After the eviction I would have no way to find Luís. So that he could find me, he asked if there was a café I frequented. I told him to leave word at Les Chics Types, Avenue de Laumière, for a blonde American girl—me, by that time twenty-three.

¶ I met two of those filmmakers for coffee and saw that they had aged. They were five years older, we were; my hair had, it seemed, turned brown. So engrossing were events at Le Bloc that those of us who showed up out of curiosity, thinking of documenting them, could end up doing so extensively: in this obsession, I was not alone. The filmmakers, however, had set aside their Bloc project. Their producer, after one hundred ten hours of footage had been taken, had not been able to get them paid.

One of them, also an actor, had chosen a café in Belleville—his neighborhood, their neighborhood, and my old neighborhood. The carapace of Le Bloc was near. On the terrace we sat to crowd a corner table where clear tarps met, rustling at the edges of our vision as the actor spoke quite freely of his passion for the project. Fascinating to this actor was an influence he had observed cameras to have on the squatters. Individuals used on-camera interviews to improve their standing in a hierarchy at the squat that seemed to him otherwise unyielding.

The project of squatting—making lives in a building where there had been nothing—did to my mind work as a metaphor for that of filmmaking, that of making writing. Possibly it was for this reason the squat had allowed for a narrative treatment. Our work seemed additionally justified by long campaigns of self-articulation underway within the squat, which offered commentary on Le Bloc—artists' contrivance of brands, the sculptor's bricolage with found objects, Le Général's adoption of such a nom de guerre—since their film shoot, like my notebooks, served as a stage for these performances. And yet any renown that might have redounded to the squat as the result of our own artistry would come too late to help the squatters, to save them from, in all bluntness, homelessness, the cold of the street.

The filmmaker was referring to a hand in the action at the time.

Despite this, I said in conclusion, pushing at my French, I didn't think either of our projects had changed any squatter's situation really, materially.

That had been important for me to get out. But, about the filming, he was adamant. "It did."

¶ Music Rooms

A smell was typical of Le Bloc, stale, hoppy, that mixture of tobacco, hashish, and, because there were few refrigerators, ham and cheese, cut by a tanginess, mandarin peelings. It deepened in the ground-floor music room as other squatters enforced their rule that the windows of that room stay closed, so that the riffing of the players would not disturb them. I knew those instrumentalists from Le Carrosse, Russians—men on piano, shakers, a whining trumpet—the Japanese trumpeter, a Togolese musician playing along on guitar or drums, resorting as if in extremis to vocalization. On some beat, he shouted in English, "Tomorrow!" Oleg, coughing with laughter, convinced a pit bull to lick the cork. The old piano's pedals wheezed like bedsprings.

Valentin Nassonov's accent was thick. When he said *élève*, it came out "elef." Born in Novorossiysk, a city on the Black Sea, he told stories for toasts, a custom, he said, among Georgians, "So they can learn a little something in their lives."

His own sense for drama connected so closely to his physical beauty it was hard to tell which attribute preceded the other. Forty-nine, he looked older but wielded superb control over the expressions of a heart-shaped, feline face. His hair was silver, eyes black, and the elegance at Valentin's command was like that of a black-and-white photograph. He spoke in koans, announcements, snapping open charm to watch the quality unfurl like a flag.

He could not return to Moscow. People there were worn-out, mercenary. He called thirty of them to ask if he could stay the night and all refused.

And so exile, too, was self-imposed, a matter of principle, leaving openings for heroics. Asking not for bottles of wine but boxes, which held more, Valentin cloaked these requests in the elegance that was his. To friends he would elaborate a scheme for saving the box liners, inflating them with his own breath. They would form a raft. He vowed to pilot it across the English Channel.

Anastasia loved this story and the man. She and Valentin showed off their love, which had deepened since the days of Le Carrosse, nuzzling and speaking, for Anastasia, exuberantly. She leapt up and went to get her son from school, returning with the boy—just nine—and sticky day-old cake, a deal.

French was Anastasia's language. She read only slowly in Russian, the language of her parents. And yet her French retained, I thought, a latecomer quality, as if adopted in youth or in ways of her choosing, the vowels lush. "We have no culture or country," she instructed me. Filled squats were the reflection of their occupiers. "A squat is a mirror that intensifies. What can you bring? What is your truth?"

When we were alone, Anastasia spoke earnestly. Other times she liked to tell all the squatters I was a spy.

Nights, she went home. An argument about the economy swelled, Valentin bursting it. "Now," he said, "we are going to sit and drink wine and talk. Not political talk, but talk about the happiness of man."

All around was red wine in cups of thinning plastic. Rinsed, they wore down.

A woman lying on the table, stretched, was someone I would never see again. She hated Normandy, which she called morbid. So much cemetery tourism. She found much to hate about the city. "There are no stars in Paris," she informed us.

To me Valentin turned only to lean away, forming an

assessment. "You remain a little vague," he said, "someone of the air."

By day easily led into an argument over the metronome setting he faced, on its other side, the Togolese guitarist, call him Guy. Between us Guy would intimate that Valentin required wine to play, playing unreliably.

But he was generous, Guy, pedagogic in sharing such observations. It is some testament to the state of my French or a youthful approach as I began my project that at Le Carrosse he had invited me to call him Guy Guitar, wrote it in my notebook for me.

He was older than the others, had nine long years on Valentin. I called him *vous* until late in our acquaintance, sensing this might please him, the mode of address out of use around the squat. Guy was reserved, tall, gray, with, high on a cheek, his scar—a tribal marking. He reproached me just for asking about it when, in his experience, white Frenchmen, because he was African or Black (his French unaccented), attributed it without his input to a fight.

Like Anastasia he lived nearby, in the twentieth arrondissement. Nine-to-five, however, he spent at Le Bloc, every day packing a container with couscous, which, after emptying, he'd clean with a piece of bread.

A small room at the corner of the ground floor farthest from Anastasia's workshop was his office. Warped, yellow paperbacks framed Guy on three sides; opposite him, below the single, high window, was a couch. This was the last room before a side door, and strangers settled there occasionally. Guy tolerated them, himself working steadily, smoking, taking notes, playing guitar as if softly murmuring. He was working on a novel about Le Bloc, which he described as sociological. It would deal with Le Carrosse, too, and at Le Carrosse I had paid twenty euros for an earlier novel of Guy's about a squat, which depicted, I hadn't yet read it, "a comfortable death."

"Ah," he'd say. "You're back for more."

I watched rattails rise from the cigarettes Guy rolled. He closed his eyes as he exhaled, sending the smoke through his nose. He could express with this look pleasure or a weary pain.

"There are many artists who are violent," he would say. "You can write that in your book. They don't like to admit it, but there are many artists who are violent."

Spring came, and windows showed sparks leaping in the courtyard, men soldering. A head appeared in a window and, wanting it closed, began shouting. What I caught was a complaint about "resonance."

Valentin left the room and returned. "Don't play piano with the windows open, because there are psychopaths who live all around." He said this loudly as I wrote it down. "They search for a pretext to throw us out of the most beautiful room in the house. They are jealous because we are happy in this room as they are over there sniffing their—"

Anastasia punched me in the arm. "You have written a chapter!"

I decided to stay the week at Le Bloc. I would round-the-clock observe, and the Russians were to be my hosts. Anastasia had promised a workshop cot if a room was not forthcoming. After more rounds Valentin showed me to the Russians' spare room on the third floor, his room perhaps, when he was not at Anastasia's. I had a small bag with underwear, granola bars.

Russian spines lined the bookcases, the walls were lined with Orthodox icons. Clocks kept slightly different times and ticked as if in answer to each other. He indicated the single bed that had a T-shirt for a pillowcase, attending to the curtains. He kissed me goodnight on both cheeks. Then he showed me how to wheel an office chair behind the door to lock it. I mentioned having read those books at college. "You can read by the light of morning." He waved at the stairwell across from the door. "Be careful," he added. "Keep yourself hidden, because usually, they are a little crazy."

I went to wash my face and use the Turkish toilet, returning to find Valentin still outside the room. He demonstrated how to tune a radio in case I wanted music. He re-emphasized the chair against the door. He said, "If anyone gives you any trouble, tell them to talk to Valentin." He kissed my cheeks and left. The chair fit snug under the handle.

Voices rose in the hallway. I heard Valentin's accent: "Shh! There is a princess sleeping here." I heard retreat. I called an American friend to talk about the book I wanted to write about squats in Paris.

I could call her because it was only 9 p.m. in New York. The pitchy voice I knew was soothing. I started to whisper, she was not going to believe where I was sleeping—

I dropped the phone. The door had been shoved open, chair skidding away. There was a man-shaped blackness on the far wall that had to do with shouts outside, with laughter.

He was gone.

I put the chair back in its place.

In time, the red wine worked. I had weird dreams and woke from them alert, even lost, experiencing no peace between sleeping and waking in which to recall their content.

I got dressed and visited Guy in his office, morning light, as he was working with absorption on a story about a man into whose head a horn was growing. I pictured a ram's horn, twisting in. Artistic invention, and that alone, could cause the pain to subside. Guy hadn't decided which kind, if the outlet would be story, sculpture, but had in mind that this character would fail to complete a project, and as if in punishment the horn would remain. In the end the man, accustomed to the horn, would wonder if he'd dreamed it.

Later that day I was asked to vacate. A family of Russian musicians, passing through, had need.

I didn't have the chance to meet them, cannot verify.

Ideas about the United States circulated more or less recklessly at Le Bloc and around this time four or five American girls about my age materialized. How they had found the place was not clear. They credited their discovery to openness of spirit, which had whisked them across the continent. They had visited Israel. Everyone in Israel had dropped acid, participating in "nature parties." The women seemed to have a bit of money and were stretching it. The one with business at the art squat was Erica, who painted. One day I watched her. She painted quickly, layering color on wood.

Erica seemed anxious as I watched her paint though generally was open with me, once offering Mexican food her friends had prepared. She may have believed we shared a predicament. She tried to summarize the squat. "It's Paradise and Hell at the same time," she said. "It's hard being an American girl. I swear to God. People take care of me. People want to fuck me."

She said she was a textbook Taurus, loyal to a fault. Everyone asked for her help. Sometimes she wanted to tell them all "get outta here"—her Boston accent. I happened to find myself at Erica's side the day after bombs exploded at the finish line of the Boston Marathon that spring. Guy Guitar tickled bongos as Erica spoke of an ex-boyfriend.

"He's still working at the Cheesecake Factory," she said. "His mind is not open. He was like, 'Yeah, I witnessed the Boston Marathon bombing, and it was traumatic, but then like two hours later I was eating a quesadilla down the street.' I was like, 'How can you even say that? It's not funny or polite?' And I didn't miss him at all." From Guy she accepted a spliff.

Weeks passed, and I heard the squatters evicted the American women. I was told they went to Barcelona.

One just had to know about a pair of doors within the bank of cabinets that lined the ground-floor hallway that they opened not to shelving, but another room—Anastasia's workshop, of which this hidden access helped establish its overtone, like a joke's, of a place where clandestinity had played itself out. Who wanted to find it? I opened up those doors to knock on a further door of frosted glass.

"*Entre*," she would cry. I found her bending to adjust a sculpture. She put on a reggae song, "Jacqueline," for me.

I loved to watch her work. There she made arrangement of a sculpture underneath the window. Sun glazed her shirt white. White paint streaked her jeans in the direction of the motion of her hands. She was fitting a mask over a dummy's face and playing Strauss through a cassette. She draped a blanket on the dummy. Its pile caught the light.

I recognized another sculpture, found by her at Le Carrosse.

"You are the wandering squatter," Anastasia said.

As I made for Anastasia's workshop, Valentin waved me over. I started to tell him his presence was better than his absence, something he liked to say.

Valentin motioned for quiet. He was standing at a closing door. Its closing engrossed him. He was listening to the rusty hinges. He closed his eyes in pleasure. The hinges whined, and Valentin made gestures of conducting an orchestra. As the pitch rose, he shrugged both shoulders and puffed out his chest as if the sound were entering his body to inflate it.

He opened his eyes and exhaling, gave me a look of surprise. I wanted to remind him he had invited me to listen.

The more I asked Guy, the worse conditions became. Supposedly a lawyer charged with the squatters' dossier had asked them to stop throwing parties.

We sat, a hot day, at Reception. At opposite ends of the desk played separate radios, competing vigils. Teenagers with the look of the neighborhood, boys in soccer shirts, dropped in, and, as they made for the stairwell, Guy shouted after, asked who they'd come to see—

"You've seen the extent of confusion, Jacqueline."

I was still living in the center, in that beautiful apartment, and the place I found to go as the temperature permitted was a park, the Anne Frank Garden. Green spaces were rarer in the inner districts, space of any openness was, and within this garden's rings of trellises were characters belonging to Paris's perimeter, the section of city where I got in the habit of looking at people.

A metronome ticked on.

Growing into my role, I one day read back a witticism

of Valentin's—a quotation to be verified. He stared impassively. "You have understood everything," he said.

The Russians and Guy and the Japanese trumpeter lost their dominion over the squat's ground-floor music room that May or June. It had been a good spot to sit and drink as the disco ball dappled our faces. If there had been noise complaints, Guy preferred to blame a group of grasping gangsters who had conspired to replace even musicians with squadrons of young men and 3-D printers. The printers were self-replicating. Music was not profitable. "At least," Guy conceded, "the loss of this music room has put an end to the story of drinking and drinking all day."

So in July I sat with Anastasia in the hallway. She liked to say her art was how she lived, that night by moving out a table to the hallway. It was a special night, celebratory; a friend of mine would stop by later. Anastasia smoothed a tablecloth to set in place a fat, glowing candle, green-painted bottles, a rose in its vase. A Styrofoam bust, a model of the Eiffel Tower that, short a foot and its head, remained a pure symbol. She hammered in nails, mounting a capacious, complexly molded golden frame.

People passed us toting cameras. These were tourists. They photographed Anastasia's scene, politely aiming below our faces. Le Bloc advertised its tours by posting on a Facebook page the residents maintained. Guides made extra cash. Guy despised the practice, not only for this soul-selling aspect. "Like a museum," he said.

"My life is my art," Anastasia said to the tourists. She invited them back to hear Valentin play. They agreed, Valentin rushed to change into a white collared shirt, but no tourist returned.

She sprang to fetch a camera of her own and took my photograph. Reaching for the Styrofoam she made it pose. "Here," she said, "an interlocutor." She joined me. "We're at work," she said.

"Yes," I said, "both of us at work."

A saturnine man in a T-shirt passed by, and she asked if it was all right about tourists returning for Valentin. The man turned his head without slowing down. "That's not what bothers me," he said. "What bothers me is I could die right here in the hallway and no one would come to find me."

Anastasia rose to follow him, their voices fading.

Another squatter, Sylvano, came to visit her and Valentin. He wore a Hawaiian shirt and appeared as if he had been shot to bleed hibiscus blossoms; bruises bloomed. I asked, "What happened to you?"

"It was a guy who owed me money," Sylvano said.

No one else laughed.

The other guy was younger and had seized Sylvano's neck. He had been fasting. "You're lucky it's Ramadan," he said.

"You're lucky I'm drunk," Sylvano said.

We sat around with two more Russians, guests of Valentin's. Dmitri had eyes the color of a polar bear's and a guitar. He sang around a cigarette as Valentin, his eyes closed peacefully, blew into the trumpet. They played Russian folk songs, children's songs, these were unhappy. Anastasia ran a cord from her workshop to power the tape recorder. "We are going to make beautiful archives," she announced, for another passerby had asked. Dmitri unwrapped a chocolate bar—from Moscow, we learned, and frothily dark. We drank rosé and Côtes du Rhône, ate slippery peanuts and sunflower seeds. The rosé was warm and tasted like rotten strawberry jam. Le Général joined us, wearing slippers. Climbing atop an old piano, one of several that lined that hallway, he contrived to smash the rod of a fluorescent—mood lighting.

Presently Valentin put down his trumpet, looked outside—that door gave onto a driveway, dumpsters—and shouted, "Someone is dying!"

I ran to the inlet of pavement, which was wet from an afternoon storm. Others followed, saw a squatter carting pizza boxes. Music falling sounded vaguely like a muezzin. A triptych of graffitied boards leaned toward trees that leaned toward Le Bloc, drying. No one was dying. We went inside.

"It is a bird who has died," Valentin pronounced.

That week someone in that building, likely visiting, had pushed another down the building's stairs. This second had kept rolling in an attack that had gone on. A coma victim, he was staying at the hospital. A younger relative had done this as I heard from many, a nephew. Valentin, that night, was first to tell me.

Anastasia lit thin candles as the sun set, melted them onto a washing machine. She placed a felt hat to shelter the Styrofoam bust. Valentin snapped into anger. "When you play," he snarled at Dmitri, "play a song from the beginning to the end, as though it were the first time in your life you were playing it and the last. Exercises, you do at home... No, play something romantic, Dima."

He removed the mute from his trumpet. Dima sang in Russian, phrases rising like suns. Valentin put wine in my glass. Sylvano, drinking opaque liquid out of a plastic bottle, arrived again from the direction of the dumpsters and let his helmet swing. When Dmitri had finished the song, he forcefully said, "Translation in French." This was provided. We asked if any Russian songs were not sad.

"Dmitri, they are asking the question," Valentin said, "are there any Russian songs that are not sad?"

Dmitri left off playing, told us no. He leaned his guitar against graffiti and took peanuts.

I watched Anastasia's candles burn. A nail stuck out of a thick white one. The flame was going to consume the wax until that nail tinkled, spent, onto the tabletop, in with the shells of seeds. There was an edifying step built into the description of the French word for sunflower, *tournesol*. The language was sometimes harsher and sometimes more delicate than English. Dmitri, then, asked what I was doing. Anastasia always introduced me as a secret agent.

"You know, the only sociological studies done on social groups with cultural projects similar to ours have been done on terrorists," Le Général said. As for history, the only history he cared about was the history of suburban projects like the one he hailed from, which had been razed. In return, he would have liked to raze Versailles. Recent events were complicated to discuss, he said, asked about the violence. He reached above his head to tug the golden frame. It leaned askew.

These people who had become my characters—could I join them in their expansiveness? The next day I asked again, and Le Général confirmed what Valentin had told me, though, in my understanding, he wasn't there to see it either—Guy wasn't, either.

"There has been a little bit of, ah, let's call it familial violence," Le Général said.

Valentin rushed me to the −3. Like the −4 it had been used for parking, the third basement. The floor was muddy. It smelled like a lake. The air was cooler than that of the summer day. Valentin offered a sweater. He was chivalrous and exuberant about the space, which he called a secret to be kept for the musicians. He was drinking white wine out of a plastic bottle and insisted that I join him. "Drink!" He sat on stacked, splintery palettes. My perch was a sideways filing cabinet. Dry branches were hanging around us. Gleaming in a pool of weak light was a huge white plaster head, like Easter Island.

Far off in the gloom, a man was moving. Usually he tended the bamboo plants that sprouted up around the disco ball. He had strapped a paper mask over his mouth.

Otherwise Valentin and I were alone. He played without muting his trumpet. He played brightly, popping out loud notes. Putting down the instrument, he said, "Well, good. *Bref*, I'm good here. There's no one for me to bother."

He described the way the space held onto sound. "You can find this in the mountains. Echoes. The sound you can have"—he whistled softly, waving a cigarette—"it touches the sky."

I could see him, why not, barefoot on a foothill. Through shouting he had learned how mountains sounded. Lost years were spent in searching for a space that would take so well to music. He had dreamed, while serving in the Russian army, of a sound so memorable he'd told me of it when I met him.

His imagination urgent, he would carry couches down there, a piano. "You have inspired me, like a muse." But I didn't think I figured in his bliss. I knew he was lying and I would not take it personally.

A memo had been posted up to workshop doors where I had seen it, signed by authoritative names—their authority was recognizable—proclaiming about "violence" that it was punishable by "immediate eviction."

One day the drink with Valentin was thick, sugary tea, a

Thermos. He had resolved not to turn to alcohol so early. He knew the mosquitoes to lunge as soon as he lifted his trumpet. He had played with a jazz band in Moscow, after his military service.

The band had toured in Switzerland, which, following the August Putsch, evicted them. Anyway they could not stay. The pianist returned to Moscow with the bass player, the drummer. The horns forded a river, they tried to join the Foreign Legion. They were given seats at the conservatory in Strasbourg, France. They would conquer that city's jazz circuit, very soon the hottest act in town. Of his time there Valentin retained the bright memory of a dinner or soirée, one of several in the home of some great lady, a Georgian duchess maybe, where a man of means but his lesser in charisma finished a speech that Valentin, with little French, failed to understand. He could understand its fatuity. The man had left an opening. Valentin could summon to mind exactly one French saying. "One mustn't exaggerate," he said. That evening it met with delighted laughter, success that Valentin, in his youth, in the confusion, found incredible.

He left Strasbourg for Paris considering fame his due. In Paris three jazz clubs banned him for fighting other musicians, French ones. These French played for money, for glory.

Valentin, in that sub-basement, played for God.

It was a disclosure he could accommodate, then, by humbling himself, becoming coquettish. Fumbling with a tobacco pouch, rummaging in the shredded tobacco for a square of hashish he felt like Cyclops, hunting for Odysseus.

His son's mother was, he explained, a screenwriter; she had taken dictation, but he caught her making changes, and he wanted things his way. He would drive as far as she would make him drive, without complaint. Reasons, often, would prevent their son's leaving with him.

Guy defined the strangeness of exile in terms of a distance separating him and his child, French, a daughter, grown. Although he rarely spoke personally, one day he spoke of her, saying she worked as a photographer, had visited Bali. Funny, he said, how one could live with another person, have her for a daughter, and fail to understand her.

"Something I didn't know is that, for the past forty or fifty years, there have been babies born in squats, and they have grown up knowing only squats," Guy said.

Anastasia added more of the bottles that she painted green and foil pill packs. She lit incense, thrust its sticks into a wall where a rash of holes broke out. Other displays collected as if against her will. She had to corral a bunch of bedposts in an umbrella stand. Heaps of German-language books would settle, for some reason, in the hall, and she took to pasting up their pulled-off spines so that her workshop wall would look as if it had absorbed their shelf. A French flag draped high in the space, its central panel gray with dust, time. She found a handheld American flag, which she kept for me.

Though he called it a music room, it differed from a room in that it lacked walls, and Valentin complained of what he saw in the old parking spots, traces of passage. A Russian newspaper he'd left had disappeared. Speaking of such breaches in a proprietary way could hold a certain pleasure.

The summer progressed, and Valentin, as I looked on, confronted Le Général over twenty euros he, Valentin, was owed, he said, in compensation for practice time he'd lost to a film shoot taking place on the −3, to pornography as Valentin described it angrily.

The airing, settling, and inventing of petty debts were all common sights at Le Bloc. I went down to the −3 just to see, and, there in reality, some guys I didn't recognize were winding cables, lifting spotlights. It seemed they were ending a workday.

"Le Bloc is not a dream," Guy said. "It is camouflage for people and their *business*."

The term of my fellowship ended.

Notices went up, late that summer, on the doors of my new building, so that you read them in leaving.

NOUS AVONS LA TRISTESSE DE VOUS FAIRE PART DU DÉCÈS BRUTAL DE PAUL BORNET LE 14 AOÛT 2013, they read—announcing a death. There would be a funeral: UNE CÉRÉMONIE AURA LIEU MARDI 20 AOÛT 2013 A 16H AU CRÉMATORIUM DU PÈRE-LACHAISE. Apparently the deceased had worked or lived in the building where I was new. With my roommate from the Netherlands I tried to work out if any of this meant the death had been, literally, brutal—a murder?—or was simply standard phrasing in the French of ceremony. It was polite to call all deaths "brutal," the way everyone sorry was "desolate." Or else the victim had been hacked apart near where we slept as violence came and went.

I left Le Bloc to find Anastasia and Valentin on the patio of a bar across the street where Valentin sometimes played. They called out to me and I joined them, friends asking where I'd been. I had returned from Dieppe, a seaside town in Normandy. The boyfriend of my new French roommate ran, in some way, an arts festival there.

The weekend had been tiring; I hid this from Valentin

and Anastasia. Exhaustingly I'd liked on sight one of the artists, had found his work intelligent, a dark-haired man. Late we'd taken vodka to the water then undressed in the roommate's boyfriend's kitchen, people sleeping throughout the creaky beach house, the artist sitting heavily on a stool, head in hands. I looked more closely and saw that he was sobbing. This person shared that he had separated from wife and daughters. "I am skin," he said in English. "I am empty." I asked if he wanted tissues or a glass of water. He wanted to sleep next to me and I found him mid-nightmare, clawing his hands, violently gnashing his teeth. There was no stilling him. I rolled away. By morning he helped himself to his feet by pressing a hand on one of my thighs. Le Général had a name for me, and I could worry I was her, *la petite psy*—the little shrink. Used to soliciting everyone's worst, by now I had asking all over my face.

The artist had worked at a squat, it came out earlier that evening. Years previously, in Belleville. Learning of my research, he asked if I had heard of it. Evicted long ago, it was called La Générale. This declension of the Bloc squatter's nickname confused me. Making sense of what the man meant consumed all my attention, I was unable at the same time to appreciate the vulnerability he was assuming in attempting to translate his glory days. He criticized the city's lease and the artists, if they could be called artists, at 59 Rivoli. I didn't think nostalgia could account for the full force of his enthusiasm. At La Générale, he said, no artist had failed to produce real work. What they made there had been, he said, insisting, real.

We took vodka to the water stumbling, tripping over pebbles. He added that he hadn't slept with anyone, not since his separation. He said English words, "Like a virgin," singing them, writhing, the American reference made out of convention for me, because I was there.

Valentin regarded me coolly. "I have been everywhere," he said. "Rome. Britain. Brittany. But the most beautiful sea is the Black Sea. The water is not salty, so you can open your eyes underwater. And if you have a little scar"—he showed me a cut on his thumb—"after fifteen minutes in the Black Sea, it heals right away."

On the far sidewalk, an old man lurched. His gait looked painful, shoulders hunched unevenly. "See him?" Valentin said. "I've known him a long time. He is an accomplished Russian painter. I have one of his paintings." Recently, however, this man had been prescribed psychiatric medication, because he was "too impulsive," and taken it.

"Now he wanders like a vegetable. All day, from one *porte* to the other." The man was approaching the Porte des Lilas. Contemporary city gates, exits and onramps to the highway, they opened onto all that lay beyond. Would he ever make it out of Paris?

"*Bref*," Valentin said. "Life is sad and short, but it's an obligatory passage."

I examined his small, black eyes. He was holding the joke in his face, his eyes brimmed with it. I burst out laughing. Valentin looked startled and laughed. I ordered a platter of ham and sausage and shared with Anastasia as he began at the keyboard. Rising, he talked up one of the squat's hallway pianos to the man who ran the bar, made him an offer. Then he picked up his trumpet and sent sound into the street.

¶ I met up with Aguilera, the scholar; he had written a letter in support of my fellowship project, sponsoring me. With worry, he asked, "Are you still doing fieldwork?"

I created a distraction by becoming indignant. "I am working on something *literary*."

⁋ The places in the nineteenth and twentieth arrondissements where the occupations of Le Bloc, Le Carrosse, La Miroiterie, and Le Stendhal all transpired can, if connected as points on a map, form a quadrilateral that takes as its southernmost extremity, for a more attractive, balanced version of the shape, Le Stendhal's first location, Number 50, Rue Stendhal, instead of the second, Number 5. Le Carrosse always sat at the right-hand corner, the eastern—on the Rue du Capitaine Marchal, called by the sleepy name of "Bua's Path" well into the nineteenth century. La Miroiterie serves as the left-hand, western point. Le Bloc is at the top. The lines forming that top—drawn from La Miroiterie up to Le Bloc on the left, and from Le Bloc down to Le Carrosse on the right—are each about a mile long. The polygon's bottom sides—from Le Carrosse down to Le Stendhal on the right, and from Le Stendhal up to La Miroiterie on the left—are each about a half-mile long. The shape is that of a kite, upside-down and crushed, this trapezoid as if upright in mud after a crash landing.

Sections of its built environment equidistant from the center were incorporated into Paris more or less contemporaneously; they look alike, notes the historian Eric Hazan, comparing city walls to "the growth rings of a tree." (He tallies six walls over eight centuries, counting the Périphérique.) Settings of two of the four squats demonstrate this effect even within a growth ring (as the land below all four was incorporated into the city at a stroke, in the nineteenth century). Situated differently—Le Bloc astride its slope, Le Carrosse more modestly in the local tangle around Edith Piaf Square, where she's figured by a statue, dancing—the buildings share a similarity in their neighbors. Near each are the architecturally lovely *Habitations à bon marché*, the city's first social-housing projects. Unusually in Paris, their façades are brick, of the golden-salmon color that spreads to everything an hour before dusk, and the detailing is art deco, many of these buildings having gone up in the twenties on land that used to lie within the the no-build zone.

In both locations, a trifecta of boundaries—the marshals' boulevards, the Périphérique, and, between them, the tramway that curves around part of the city—makes for a challenging crossing. Just past it, in Gallieni, in Lilas, a big, relaxed mess of a bus depot flops down (city over with, Paris pretense fallen).

Along one of the slim roads that connect Le Bloc and the towers of the Place des Fêtes, a wall is papered over in posters. Authors, a group, sign off with an address, 45 Rue du Pré-Saint-Gervais, which places them at the top of my polygon. The Arctic Flowers, they identify as anarchists, and one of the posters convenes a neighborly meeting to discuss a TV documentary about the history of anarchism, a documentary the Flowers criticize "in the context of a long-term reflection that we are conducting around the question of the diverse forms that the liquidation of revolutionary heritage takes today"; across adjacent copies of another poster, this one invoking the uprisings of 1968 ("put an end to commemoration, put an end to liquidation"), someone has scrawled in marker, *PRAY TO JESUS CHRIST / OUR ONLY SAVIOR / AMEN*, giving a sense, not only of lively public debate, but also of the neighborhood's prevailing theologies.

Calm settles a few yards away, where the top-right leg of my polygon crosses the Rue de Belleville. To one side of a gate vines cling, budding red; to the other, a plaque dates Belleville Cemetery to 1808, proclaims it the second-highest point in the city after Montmartre, and notes that some remains of "republicans" "massacred" during the Paris Commune at Rue Haxo are interred there. A second plaque makes a claim in contradiction to the first plaque's that the spot is the very highest in Paris (129 meters above sea level). Nearby, one of the oar-shaped mayoral markers, abstaining from debate, offers instead that Claude Chappe, the inventor, in the waning days of the eighteenth century chose this site for his telegraph for the simple reason of its elevation. Area residents, called Bellevillois, suspected Chappe's intention with the telegraph was to communicate with the hated king, at that time imprisoned, downhill in the present-day Marais. The marker notes that the Bellevillois then organized the direct action of burning down the telegraph. Chappe installed another, the cost absorbed of doing business there.

Cemeteries recur, the dead making claims for themselves. (No cemetery exists in the inner arrondissements, the city center.) Charonne Cemetery, runty satellite of Père-Lachaise, sits at the bottom of my polygon, which also includes all of Tenon Hospital. Staircases of stone help to form the points and, given its elevation, lead down from this piece of land. One runs breakneck from Le Bloc, falling to a boulevard. At the end of Rue Stendhal lampposts preside over a gentler set, pink-flowering boughs brushing them. My southwestern side overlays no street precisely but is nearly coincident with the Rues de la Bidassoa and d'Annam, between which a perilously steep staircase makes for a suitably forbidding boundary. Named after a river helping to form the Spanish border, the Rue de la Bidassoa continues, stringing along a plastic clown-car carousel about which nothing is beautiful, joining the Rue Sorbier where it hits the Rue de Ménilmontant. There, below the left-hand corner of my polygon, the light changes. Children cross the street at a run, the first ones stretching to touch a bright mosaic, work of the Parisian street artist Invader. They slap it, proof.

Before 1860 this area lay, for the most part, in Belleville ("Beautiful city"), in those days France's thirteenth most populous commune (city or town). (Some of it fell within the hamlet of Ménilmontant, popularly and administratively considered part of Belleville though it had, and perhaps still has, a distinct, slightly sleepier character.) On January 1, 1860, by imperial decree, Belleville, along with ten other communes touching Paris, became subordinate to Paris, a district of the capital. On that day the city's population leapt up to 1.6 million from 400,000, its surface area more than doubling. The man who, having staged a coup, could sign decrees so ostentatiously imperial was Louis Napoleon, the lesser Bonaparte, hapless nephew of a short conquistador—the one who inspired Marx's remark that history repeats as farce. With the coup, he became Emperor Napoleon III. When the farce of his Second Empire plays the stage of Parisian memory, one archvillain is Georges-Eugène Haussmann, the baron whose other title was prefect of the Seine. Appointed by the national government, then as at many times during Paris's history in charge of managing the city, Haussmann thought of himself, from his own memoirs, as a "demolition artist." Annexation was of a piece with the development scheme by which he also infamously rebuilt, razing tenements and much else to put in boulevards, monuments, parks, and the six-story buildings called Haussmannian. Modern banking was in its nascency, and ballooning loans were taken out for everything. Arbitrary, ugly, scary, the process of

Haussmannization made the city strange to its inhabitants, as Walter Benjamin writes in the papers collected in his *Arcades Project*, a fragmentary city history. "The inhabitants of the city no longer feel at home there; they start to become conscious of the inhuman character of the metropolis." In the time of Haussmannization, according to the French historian Jacques Rougerie, "the center of gravity of revolutionary Paris" shifts to Belleville.

Ordinance banned pollutive industry within the city, and perimeter towns like Belleville, industrializing, grew dramatically, due in part to in-migration from the provinces, to that of workers. (Factories were sited to the east of the city for the reason of prevailing winds.) Between 1831 and 1856, the Belleville population (Ménilmontant included) was multiplied many times over. Ex-Parisians made up much of this number. They were priced out, homes leveled in the renovation. The percentage of residents born in pre-1860 Paris was outstandingly high in Belleville: 45.8, according to a count in 1872. This half of the town had left Paris unwillingly, Rougerie writes. They understood themselves as driven out. But annexation didn't appeal to them, not even as a way to get back in. Rather, officials polling the population in 1859, as another decree required of them, learned that "most" Bellevillois respondents were "hostile" to annexation (the historian's word, not the pollsters'); after only about one hundred of Belleville's (by then) sixty-five thousand souls had been asked, the line of inquiry was abandoned. Besides a loss of autonomy in governance, townspeople in the newly annexed districts could worry about a city tax. Belleville faced a third threat, unique to its case: Haussmann would split it in two. On March 7, 1859, the Belleville city council "very respectfully" and publicly expressed the local preference not to be split in two. But this was done, and since annexation Rue de Belleville, the town's artery that was then called Rue de Paris, has divided the nineteenth and twentieth arrondissements. Haussmann sought in overhauling Paris to preempt rebellion—avenues like the Rue de Pyrénées were made wide to deter insurgents from barricading themselves in, unless they were made wide as "necessitated by the crinoline," voluminous frills having come into fashion that century—and the splitting of Belleville has been understood in similar terms, as an attempt to shore up social control. For many twenty-first-century Parisians the name denotes only a Métro station and its environs, a Chinatown. Administratively, Belleville is one of four precincts into which the twentieth arrondissement divides; only a corner of my polygon overlays it though the Rue Pelleport, meridian of Old Belleville, is also the meridian of my polygon. And this new Belleville is smaller.

What Haussmann might have liked to subdue suggests itself statistically in Gérard Jacquemet's landmark study of the "thugs," "beggars," "arsonists," and "cutthroats," as newspapers so pejoratively characterized the locals, of nineteenth-century Belleville. It also had its feel on the ground. The construction of the Thiers Fortifications made Paris an exception among European municipalities. City walls around Vienna, around German cities, were being at that same time taken down; the French peasantry, meanwhile, resented those ramparts for they would make Paris the prize, and the countryside was as if surrendered in advance. Within this newest ring where the village would "stretch downward" had extended, memorably according to Bernard Rouleau, another historian, "a very picturesque zone": "wine taverns behind burlesque signs, bric-a-brac sellers, old shoes, old laundry, metal scrap, shady hotels, unmarked businesses, sheds exhibiting taxidermied monsters, performing dogs, sword swallowers, men selling clothing on trestles, all torchlit. Another world, a permanent flea market, spontaneously formed on the edges of Paris and which annexation would upend." Wine cost less outside that wall where tax was levied, and in Belleville as in other suburbs, taverns, *guinguettes*, catered to escapist Parisians; Hazan evokes "one of the most famous *guinguettes* of the age, that of Mother Saguet": "For twenty sous you got two boiled eggs, a sauté chicken, cheese, and as much white wine as you liked." The specialty of Belleville's establishments—the *Boeuf-Rouge, Coq-Hardi, Sauvage, Epée de Bois, Galant Jardinier, Carrotte filandreuse*—was the green wine of grapes grown on the town's slopes. Alongside effects of the city tax developed, in Parisian literature, the thesis that compression within its walls necessitates release. Hazan quotes from Victor Hugo, who anthropomorphizes houses that jostle, competing for air. They get past the city wall and dash across the plain.

¶ *Building Management*

While the French spoken at Le Bloc was slangy or, like mine, accented, halting, Le Général's was delectably correct. Evidently he delighted in it. Deep in his mouth, seen in a laugh, fillings glistened. Silver rings, bracelets, and a chain-link necklace glinted amid smoke that he sent circulating, a hashish spliff's. On a cap of army green he brandished patches shaped like medals. I would find him in a ground-floor office where he dispatched duties to Le Bloc's *association*; he was Secretary. A din rose from desktop fans as he fielded requests for space, hearing by his own account from two or three creatives every day. A graphic designer had brought in a mockup of a pamphlet about the squat. A wish of Le Général's was to see, for example, a Bloc manifesto in print. "A limited edition." On a slow day he browsed listings of military equipment, inviting me to admire an insect-eyed speedboat. Scribbles covered the walls, iterations of the inside joke, in French a *private* joke, *Si tu dors t'es mort*. "Sleep and you're dead," Le Général said.

Le Général rarely slept. He never dreamed. He made use of all those prison sentences to network—the experience a crash course, each time, in "administration"—and catch up on his reading, his thinking. He had devised capacious theories, many dealing with technology, evolutionary biology, overpopulation, the American and Jewish peoples (I had the sense he trotted out those for my benefit; I am Jewish), and social programs. His own work was a service to the poor. If "the economic incentive" were to go up in flames, "half of all Americans wouldn't know what to do anymore." And: "Look what I've done already, without money. Imagine what I could do if I had a little money."

He had surfaced, he claimed, from four months in prison, where he had written some eighty pages of autobiography. Besides con jobs, activism with the *indignés* and all of that work as an electrician, locksmith, a forger of IDs, the stint of homelessness he claimed in Monaco, those other squats in Paris and Rouen—a hometown in which he took glowing pride; home to Joan of Arc, it always did well under siege, he'd say, staving off Germans and Vikings—he had sold sandwiches, in a past life, out of a truck at the Rouen Armada, netting two or three hundred thousand euros in ten days. "Oh, all kinds. With vegetables, without vegetables..."

That summer he lingered at Reception wearing a hoodie and clutching a mug printed with the same brand, in English—SONS OF ANARCHY LE BLOC ORIGINAL—looking like a corporate boss.

"I'm a consultant," he explained to me. "A poor consultant."

He had fixed up an adjacent room, soundproofing it for use by one or a few of seven daughters that he had, he said. They lived elsewhere, but one day, there was a ten-year-old spinning his chair. She fit on the seat. She had a round face like Le Général's and shiny, caramel hair.

Le Général was peering into his computer. From the speakers wafted soft explosive sounds, a game.

"*Enchantée*," the girl said, glancing up from a smartphone.

"She is American," Le Général advised her.

I nodded, smiled.

"Ah, Jacqueline, an American in Paris," he would say, as I followed him in the hallways.

As a child he had been assigned to a psychiatrist after

disappearing for three nights. "They thought I had problems," he said. "But I didn't. That was just according to whoever makes the rules for society."

This was an infrastructural story for Le Général, one he often told. He was classed as a runaway child (*enfant fugueur*), passed off to social workers, to juvie, unfairly in his evaluation.

He had been reading comic books in the cellar. "No one went down to the cellar to look for the comic books," he said.

When Guy alleged that weapons were trafficked at Le Bloc, the only way to investigate the matter at all safely was, it occurred to me, to ask the squat's secretary. Indeed, Le Général didn't seem to mind the question. "We no longer take out our guns," he said expansively. "Now we have pepper spray, which allows us to subdue tension." (I did hear, after the eviction, from someone who was sprayed, not by Le Général.)

I asked about a *tonton* I'd seen break up a fight. (The man, who told me he did not give interviews, was understood to be by trade a dealer.)

"Delegating the use of force to a single person works," Le Général said. "It's democracy."

"So he's, a little bit, the policeman of the squat?"

Le Général laughed, scandalized. "Don't tell him that."

¶ *August*

It seems I didn't note exactly when the doors to Le Bloc finally did break. They could still close, by late that summer. They could open; the effectuation of this change of state had taken on its own, unassimilable character. A squatter would prise open the inner set, after which they pulled and wound by hand the cord dangling behind Reception, which operated the grille. The doors on the street, which slid apart, had to be kicked.

Guy claimed summer was dangerous: August was, the dog days were. Residents would go away on vacation, letting unknown friends occupy their rooms.

"It has really deteriorated," Guy told me. "When a squat is in the middle of rotting, this is what happens."

"These are not the people who will build the society of tomorrow," he said.

In cracks lacing the roads of eastern Paris the sealant was sticky with heat. At Le Stendhal, a drip of chatter issued. They could try and open another squat in August, when buildings in the area would empty of those neighbors likely in any other month to raise the alarm. But the squatters, some of them, would be away from Paris, too.

One, who went by the nom de guerre Renard, "Fox," slumped on a couch. "I am as motivated as an oyster," he said, and I asked if that was a French thing.

In the squat I had helped that spring to open they planted vegetables (on the shed roof, an old toilet for a planter), and the squashes were in bloom; marigolds bloomed. On a table was resting the vivid yield of zucchinis. Renard, though, nursed a concern that air pollution had contaminated this produce.

In the kitchen was a whiteboard that had been titled FOUND OBJECTS. The title had been struck through. LOST OBJECTS, the whiteboard read.

A computer belonging to the resident who coded games was stolen. He, José-Xavier, told me in the kitchen that he had done everything wrong. "I didn't hide my computer." (He was speaking English, which he spoke very well.) "Normally I hide my computer. I had the light off. Normally I leave on the light."

The Taiwanese artist, I'll call her Odette, came into the kitchen carrying a single wooden maraca.

"And I was in the workshop!" José-Xavier continued. "I'm never in the workshop."

Odette unscrewed the head of the maraca, poured in some rice, and with a strip of balloon reattached it.

"I was working on my window," José-Xavier said.

"So this person knew you were in the workshop," Odette said, and shook the maraca.

José-Xavier wondered aloud if they could build something like a tripwire that would cause a floodlight to switch on. People were always climbing onto the roof to water the plants.

An artist who had lived at Le Carrosse texted, asking me to call him as soon as I could. He had to borrow twenty euros. We met at Gambetta, a terrace table.

Panhandlers came up when our coffee got there, enough to warrant comment.

"You can't give them anything," the artist said, after I had. "It's a job."

He was positive, however, encouraging, about my writing on Le Carrosse. A summer trip I had planned struck him as an opportunity to achieve the distance I would need.

Squatters left Le Bloc in throngs to go and open other squats, Guy said. "Le Carrosse was calm compared with this."

Guests came to stay at Le Stendhal, Swiss, one traveler painting his tag across the walls. *HYPER,* it read. The more permanent residents warned the tagger after "four or five times" that if he did it again they might kick him out, José-Xavier relayed to me apologetically, adding that they couldn't have even one person tagging the squat, because then everyone would want to.

As the outcome of a mismatched jurisdiction the case of Le Bloc, heard that June, would be retried in November. Because people lived as well as worked at the squat, a *tribunal d'instance*, not a *tribunal de grande instance*, would have to hear it. In any event, the judge was not able to "draw a distinction between artists who don't live in the building and those who live there full-time," the decision explained.

For Guy, walking me through these authorities' maneuvers, the relevant question was one about punishment. After a judge ruled as to the validity of an eviction the prefecture would wait, to carry out this order, on the landlord's word. There were ways, such as identifying safety risks, to avoid a wait. Violence within could prompt this authority's acting. "If there is one death," Guy said, "immediate eviction."

At Le Stendhal Odette spoke of trauma inflicted while still living in the family into which she had been born. She didn't know if the trauma was special or normal. "Maybe I just need to grow a ball," she said.

"A ball?" I asked.

"Some guts," she said. "Take it in a macho-person way."

At Le Bloc, Guy and I discussed our methods for note-taking. After his eighty-fifth notebook, Guy said, he had stopped numbering them.

I was on Number 16.

The language department at Assas convened us all, eventually, for training sessions. There I made two friends. Each of them lived near me in the nineteenth. A few years older than I was, Irish, both were named Brian, and they had moved to Paris under beauty's spell, having quit a banking job after reading, in each case, a different American author. For one Brian the fateful book, read at his desk, was David Foster Wallace's *Infinite Jest*. For the other, it was *A Moveable Feast*; at the invitation of this second Brian, I accompanied him on a Hemingway-geared walking tour of the Left Bank.

It was very hot. The sky was blue and flat and there was no shade. The tour guide, an Englishman of middle age in hiking clothes, appeared to resent then-young Hemingway for his writer's cool, which struck me as a—I'd brought my latest—*bizarre way to feel toward someone dead for many years*. This guide drove home to us that, despite Hemingway's picture of bohemian poverty in Paris, his wife Hadley had had a trust fund. "He wrote the book at the end of his life, when he was losing it a little bit, and that's why there are all these contradictions," the guide said of *A Moveable Feast*, and dispatched James Joyce's *Ulysses*, also composed in Paris, similarly: "I've tried to make it through *Ulysses*, and I fall asleep. Do you know why? Because it's stream-of-consciousness, and that means twenty-four hours, nonstop, every thought in his head, no editorial."

The church we stepped inside was dark and cool, a relief.

Brian was also writing in Paris. As we walked he asked me if I wrote about myself. I took a stab at describing a technique of narration that seemed to me "ideally unobtrusive."

In response, Brian volunteered that he wrote about himself exclusively and I realized I had said too much, a kind of lesson.

¶ During the night that last night of August a Le Bloc squatter died. Documents from the eviction litigation show that, like most of the defendants, he had joined the suit belatedly, that summer. Ludo, the nickname in circulation, was a short version of his first name. He had come from Nantes early in the summer to ingratiate himself, the others at Le Bloc appreciating his helpfulness; now, they remembered him for it. He kept night watch, was chivalrous "with the women," came to someone's aid in a rigged fight although he was not broad. He took out the trash. Few were friends with everyone as he had been. "They belong to the place," the English-speaking *tonton* said. "It means they have nothing else."

I hadn't met Ludo. In reviewing photos I see he had a delicate, pretty face with a thin, sharp nose and big dark eyes. Circles under eyes, hair to his shoulders, arms crawling with tattoos. It was summer the entire time he lived there.

One of Ludo's friends had warned him, ahead of going on vacation, that if Ludo went on living as he was living the upkeep might in the end kill him. Ludo gave this friend a gift, a skull, a candleholder. Skulls, common in tattoos and graffiti at Le Bloc, referred to the community, not death necessarily. Ludo told him, "When I die, you can light this": a joke, the man said. He had been left to wonder what to do.

This friend of Ludo's and another described their experiences of the death in the same way. Each had worried about Ludo and, despite the burden of this worry, gone away on a planned trip. They didn't blame themselves; each felt accessible a wish they'd kept a closer eye on Ludo.

I was away, too. When I got back to Paris, I joined Guy on

the -1, and he told me about the death. Mosquitoes from the -4 found us. I could see welts rising on my forearm, pink and white.

"You can't play with life, because in the end a person dies from that as well," Guy said. "We've played with life, forgetting there is also death." He used *on*, "one," and could have meant "you," "we," "I," or, as now strikes me as likely, "people here."

We climbed the stairs and sat at Reception. Both double doors were open, airing out the building.

¶ *Ludo*

"For a time Le Bloc became his church" was the recollection of a squatter named Fred.

"What was it?" I asked. "A slowing down, a sense of scale?"

"Above all a deafening," Fred said. "An astonishment. I don't know what else to say. *Bien heureux, bien heureux jusqu'au bout, un clochard céleste.*"

¶ *The* –1

For their open house that September, the artists of Le Bloc made Ludo T-shirts. *LUDO LOVE*, the walls read.

At Reception was a collection box, for Ludo.

At a weekly meeting in that basement their lawyer Julie Convain gave a presentation. Expressing the hope she could get them another year in the building, she would need residents to write, she said, testimonials about their "artistic activity" or "precarious status." She met applause and went on as if emboldened, "inspired" by "that squat by the Louvre," 59 Rivoli. She had heard of squats with precarious leases and considered the achievement within reach.

Le Général cut her off dramatically—that wasn't what they wanted—and, below the sound of laughter, asked her something privately.

"Besides a precarious lease, there's not much else," I heard her say.

In a later meeting people asked if there would be, for them, any prospect of rehousing. That went only for squats under contract. "We're pirates," some elaborated. Talk turned to a pileup of dishes, the second-floor kitchen. The meeting was ending; a *tonton* shouted above the rumbling crowd that if anyone had anything to add, now would be the time.

A woman stepped up to introduce herself. Visiting Paris from somewhere in Chile, she was there for a marionette festival.

A man clutching a French horn without valves stepped boldly into the dwindling circle, the arc he'd left goading him on. "I am a miserable guy," he cried, "and I know it."

"With a lease," Le Général said, "you can't paint on the walls. You can't smoke in the hallways. You can't live on the −2. You can't live in your workshop."

Anastasia, in her workshop, was stuffing long socks, making limbs out of them. They looked as if dragged up from undersea.

The Soviet system in which she was born had not valued the owning of property. So, at Le Bloc as at Le Carrosse, an acquisitiveness of hers that was only human could find its fullest expression in "harvesting." "I am happiest in harvesting." Home was provisional, in her understanding. Her family had thought of France that way.

There had been, she reflected, "little Anastasia who knocked at the door to Le Carrosse," and there she was. People asked if she lived off her art. She would tell them her art was her life. "Is that not the achievement of a dream, when you manage to connect art and life? Or I should say, when you make of your art your life. And you, at your level... *fin*, what am I talking about. It's enormous. It's so enormous I feel like keeping it a secret."

As I was getting this down she quietly moved behind me, picking up her camera, and took my picture.

"You wrote about the squat of K—," Oleg said, "and Le Carrosse. Those squats are long gone. We have already begun to forget them."

Le Général's first son, Oan, was born. An old Celtic name, Le Général told me. ICI BÉBÉ DORT, the door read.

Oan's mother, who lived there with Le Général, used a bottle to feed Oan, at two months fat, quiet, with a rash above the eyes and silky eyelashes. Le Général snatched the baby up, cooed proudly his way just to reinstate Oan in his mother's arms and show me into the next room. Supposedly on leave from administrative duties (though that morning had found him fishing in the second-floor kitchen trash for Bloc-related dossiers, he said mysteriously), he was working to build a loft. A fan was canceling the voices of the hallway. Carpets curled, awaiting installation. Huge stripped doors against a wall were salvaged from that Fashion Week. As the room would be the baby's he planned to paint it carefully, spray it with antibacterial stuff. Overhead was a skylight. If the squat stayed open he'd shatter it, build a "cabin" up there, and go sunbathing.

"Right now he has a relatively calm, familial air," I told Guy.
"Yes," Guy said, "we're hoping for good."

¶ *Traces*

Mirabeau, the squat Le Général had opened in an eastern suburb, was tiring to visit, messy and lonely. I was sent there after moving to Paris by Guy, encountered by chance at a Miroiterie concert. After the eviction of Le Carrosse, before Le Bloc's opening, Guy had practiced at Mirabeau, a former office building as it seemed mostly to be. Anastasia made work in a backyard where there was a row of red sheds like stables. Even as I was reporting at Le Bloc I went to Mirabeau occasionally, visiting a former inhabitant of Le Carrosse. A Moroccan man, he had lived in Spain, where his daughter, a little younger than I was, still lived, and in France he worked construction. Hassan could see I too was someone's daughter, the daughter of someone out of whose sight I had removed myself. He spoke of missing his child and gave fatherly advice, one effect of which was that I sensed I could not in good conscience stop visiting. He encouraged me to exercise, avoid being in a hurry to get married. "We get older every day, but life goes on," he said.

He waved at the window of his room, one of the offices, in which we saw, beyond the yard, a building lurid with graffiti. "Le Général wanted to get in there, but police came right away."

In the yard was a card table, on it potatoes and bread. There was a mattress on which a girl lay reading. There was a metal trashcan, in it leaping flames. There was a bone-white dog, in a dog bowl on the steps cooked pasta.

Hassan had worked a job helping an office to move. He related this and made me gifts of objects in the room. There were offerings to be procured at the work site, a printer, lamps. We had the same phone, a BlackBerry. I could have the case off his. His daughter wanted an iPhone. He wanted to move to the countryside.

Hassan's neighbors in the squat, a Barcelonian, a graffiti artist whose hometown I took no note of, showed off a marijuana plant they cultivated in a closet. A fan and sunlamp crowded it, a little thing.

"Yes," they said, "but it will grow."

Hassan drove me as far as Gambetta, to Paris. The building that had been Le Carrosse was almost on the way. We got out to take a look. "Hasn't much changed," said Hassan. "We'd have to see inside."

From Gambetta it was a five-minute walk to Le Stendhal, where I still dropped by sometimes. Odette was making, for everyone, vegetable soup.

When Le Bloc's −1 turned over it hosted a rare solo show of works by painter Morgane Merrheim, who lived on the fifth floor. Then living as a man she painted haunted faces, working so rapidly that those paintings, drying, dangled from the cabinets in the hallway.

She had something to show me. I joined Morgane in crouching to unroll it, wider than one span of arms: a painting of Pascal Hollemaert, who had been, I knew, a legendary boss of Le Carrosse. She told me happily that Guy had recognized the likeness in this gaping, cubist face, pinched at the chin like a skull, eyes two shapes, mouth low on the face streaked with black and, as if clawed at, red. She had done it quickly in an upstairs workshop at Le Carrosse, using her fingers, a wash of coffee, at last pastels.

Guy appeared as I was cleaning up my notes. "That one," he said, "that's the monster. He's told you about it? Well, yes, listen up." At that Guy walked off laughing, glancing back at me.

I heard it suggested in Anastasia's presence that Morgane print T-shirts and make a living. "Let him," she said, "die of hunger."

In the kitchen of Le Stendhal Odette appeared, frantic. "My mother has had a heart attack!" she said.

I looked around. No one else spoke English, and I couldn't quite find the word in French.

Odette clutched at her chest. This was it—I understood—the decision to leave France, never to return, or stay.

¶ *Paris Past*

Le Bloc was "too big," Anastasia said. "It resembles an airport," she told me, "or a university," voicing a dissatisfaction I shared, or felt on hearing it that I shared; I could not have named it. The will of Bloc artists to make themselves saleable, and an accompanying vigor, were in contrast to the ethos of Le Carrosse when we were there. The artistry of that squat had been to insist on its remove from society, in Anastasia's understanding as in mine. People there "cultivated their difference," she said, "like a secret garden," a line that had impressed me and for which I sought, in retrospect, something like evidence.

Years went by, and in an online archive I found a documentary about the squat, *Ceux du Carrosse*, victory dawning as I cued it up. Even the colors were bright. A man fills IV pouches with water and hangs them from the ceiling; they glitter, hanging there, like jellyfish. I was glued to a scene of a barbecue featuring music, merguez, rings of neighbors. These squatters, all of them gone from the squat by the time of my visit, discuss their eviction suit, making claims that are just metaphorically true and yet, in that way, unassailable. A woman, a painter, says rich people evict artists from squats while simultaneously buying their paintings. A tall man with jumpy, overlarge eyes is shown soldering and, as sparks arc, speaking of his family, "inveterate alcoholics," "real crazies." This is Pascal Hollemaert.

His legend permeated hidden seams of Le Carrosse to reinforce the squat like caulk. An electrician, he had wired the building, and in his absence power winked out daily under the strain of many space heaters. He sculpted metal—spiders; slender, tortured men—working that surface until it looked as if crawling with worms. The shapes not quite from nature, they looked natural at Le Carrosse. Masses of bike tires hung from a back-room ceiling like chrysalids. In that room was another collection, a number of televisions, for an art project I was told.

Squatters at Le Bloc had known him, and they spoke of Hollemaert in terms that were outlandish. "He was nuts, Pascal. When he got up in the morning he'd take an axe to the floor because he'd seen a ghost in front of him." "He would defend himself against the walls." "He wouldn't sleep for ten days." "When he said, 'Come to my room,' I said, 'No.' He said, 'You will regret this,'" one woman, a Carrosse squatter, told me after the eviction of Le Carrosse, adding: "That's the tendency, when you have someone who opened the squat: he begins to take himself for a tyrant." Another artist, working at Le Bloc, would speak evasively of Le Carrosse and, later, say they just could not discuss that squat, citing impedimental exhaustion. "At Le Carrosse, you really had to sleep on one ear," they managed, once, to claim. "You hit the other guy to say good morning."

According to this legend Hollemaert's efforts to control the squat consumed him finally. Or addiction did, or madness. He was said to have governed through the use of a length of wood, a kind of scepter, his baton. He handed it off to another squatter and pronounced that man the squat's new boss. "It's you," he said, as a third squatter told me. In the countryside Hollemaert was recovering; the others, when I stayed at Le Carrosse, expressed a hope that he would not return. One warned it would be dangerous, in conversation with Hollemaert, to make him remember Le Carrosse. But I thought of doing so. I wanted to meet this Hollemaert badly. I wondered what I would ask. I would have to ask for comment on the allegations, and I may have also sensed, by then, that he'd have something all his own to tell me—a missing piece.

¶ *Quiet Days in Clichy*

My friend Julien was having a bad year. He had had to sue *Libération*, the newspaper, for defamation; though he had won, the damages were modest; since the appearance of the contentious investigation, which had come out in 2011, he had had irrevocably to take his distance from a citizens' association called Macaq. Julien's work with Macaq had consisted in opening vacant buildings to squatting even as he was by day a civic leader: Julien Boucher, councilor for the seventeenth arrondissement.

No more. The journalist Willy Le Devin, by way of his main line of questioning about Macaq, reported that Boucher had charged a company card improperly, and in addition to being ad hominem the articles struck a salacious, emotional note. What journalists usually do with an anonymous tip is check it out; Le Devin had reproduced one such tip as part of the lede for his first article, attributing it to an inhabitant of a squat that Macaq had maintained on the Rue de la Banque in collaboration with Jeudi Noir and Droit Au Logement, the housing-rights groups. This squat was active in, according to the article, 2007. Le Devin got the call in August 2010.

"I'm in some distress," the caller began, only to pull themselves together with alacrity:

> "I'm calling to tell you that an association managing the squat at 24 Rue de la Banque funds itself illegally, subletting floors of the building to private companies. No one knows. Above all I don't want to give the impression of spitting in the soup. These people helped me and I'm grateful to them for it. But when you're publicly defending a cause like that of improper housing, you can't at the same time forget about ethics and go about things in such a way. That bothers me."

> The voice is quavering, halting in tone. "Please, don't ruin them, even if they can be, at times, rough. They told people living in the building: 'This must remain a secret. You really owe us, so keep your mouths shut.'"

Julien, at a hearing for the libel case, pulled me aside, explained that Macaq had employed the otherwise unemployable—explained this with identifiable noblesse oblige—and told me the anonymous source was such a person. What Le Devin had finally pinned on Macaq was a pattern of leasing space in its squats that had made it 15,500 euros in profit or, according to *Le Parisien*, 38,000 in just one of the years under review. Boucher, in the article, came quite clean, calling the deals "between friends"; proceeds went to cover utilities. A subsequent report found the association's bookkeeping was of "a very artisanal character" (*un caractère très artisanal*). Journalists emphasized that this subleasing was done in contravention of a contract to which Macaq's squats, including Rue de la Banque, all were subject—the precarious lease.

On the stand, Le Devin said that Macaq, DAL, and Jeudi Noir had been subject to hagiographic treatment in the press, making it "the moment for a critical investigation to fall on this movement"; correspondingly his writing owed its drama to the loftiness of the position from which it would, so to speak, kick Boucher down. Not only did Boucher, in his official role, belong to the Socialist Party, so did activists with Jeudi Noir; of particular interest, however, was the revelation that Boucher's own mother was closely acquainted with the Socialist mayor; Delanoë had known Boucher "almost since he was born." Reportedly he had even put in an appearance at Boucher's wedding and said to the groom, a bit formally in one journalist's rendering: "Your work, often rebellious, is generous and collective. Continue to put into play a creative disorder." It was with avuncular disappointment, then, that the mayor's office resolved to withdraw funding from the association and, effective March 2012, kick it out of a building at 123 Rue de Tocqueville that the city had placed at Macaq's disposal.

I first met Julien in December 2011, during the lame-duck period between the controversy and this reprisal: a man with an active smile, distracted—by a chirruping iPhone, by a fedora—but fundamentally at his ease. When I showed signs of having understood something he had said in rapid French he shouted out in English, "Yes we can!" The occasion was a Jeudi Noir meeting at Julien's apartment, a squat with resilient good cheer of its own; the building's ground floor was dark and muddy, opening into a wet ditch, but this man's place smelled of fresh paint. Well heated, it had bar stools, a surfboard-shaped kitchen counter, sleek sound system, a black light, and, deep within, fancy showerheads, which he had just installed and was happy to show off. Rain fell, and because of a leak, it came down in the bathroom.

In a subsequent interview, Julien told me Macaq and Jeudi Noir were not "habitual" squatters; unlike "anarchists," they were unafraid of using their connections to execute on plans. Such connections were a source of comfort to police, he added, and for my research gave me a cop's number: "No texts to his cell phone. No email. Nothing in writing." Bon enfant, Macaq operated only in squats that agreed to precarious leases, and yet even this was to provide the investigative journalist with dirt; the leases, Le Devin notes, "formally forbid all commercial activity." By the fall of 2013, when I was deep in my reporting at Le Bloc, Julien had stepped down as Macaq's director and all but retired from opening squats.

Something happened then to call him out of retirement. He was needed. And for some reason, he called me.

That year, four women in flight from Ukraine had made it to Paris, where they'd been met with a collective hero's welcome. High-profile cases, they were granted refugee status. Inna Shevchenko, Oxana Shachko, Yana Zhdanova, and Alexandra Shevchenko, called Sasha, were early or founding members of Femen, the group behind a smattering of protests across the European continent one signature of which was that the activists, all women, appeared topless. Collectively these women had lunged at Putin, Berlusconi, and the patriarch of the Russian Orthodox Church, survived humiliating treatment at the hands of Belarusian police, spent a month in a Tunisian jail after demonstrating there. They stood against capitalism, "dictatorship," anything they liked. The Ukrainians spoke little French, and there was an uncanny muteness to the protests, an unresolved, even irresolute quality, the two breasts like unblinking eyes. Undefined, they received, in Western media, definitions out of their control, and they were harnessed to causes other than the ones of their first choosing. They had on arrival in Paris moved into the Lavoir Moderne Parisien, a theater in the eighteenth arrondissement. They amassed a following of French girls, whom they set about training. The *Monde diplomatique* journalist Mona Chollet, writing in English, similized the red-white-and-blue poster of female nudes they'd hung out a window in full view of the neighborhood, a Muslim neighborhood, to the "public pork and wine picnic-provocations organized in exactly the same place by far-right extremists in 2010."

This was a very good point, and not immediately comprehensible, I do not think, to the newly arrived Ukrainian women. They had developed a contextual anticlericalism alongside their critique of corruption in government, a pre-Maidan government of troubling closeness to Putin's Russia as well as the Orthodox Church. Western journalists misinterpreted these activists' position on sex work as abolitionist in the way of Western anti-porn feminists when that issue was the activists' strongest, their premier, most clearly sourced. The objection they had to the conscription of Ukrainian women into this industry, specifically its international-tourism wing, was a protest against globalization and the ransacking it had entailed of the post-Soviet economy. The fate of their peers, a fate they refused for themselves, was to service foreigners at home or, as cheap exports, abroad.

In France they were showily famous, the images those of flowing, beribboned tresses, the Ukrainian peasant's crown aflower; of warrior stances, every mouth open in a scream; and of, of course, the "boobs," a word they used in English, which they were learning rapidly. Though a French postage stamp was modeled on the Femen faces they were unappeased; in February of that year, 2013, they stripped down to jeans invading Notre Dame, where they set to thwacking bells and had to be removed, alas forcibly. This was "in celebration of" the homophobic pope's retirement from office. "Sarkozy used them to show that he was very liberal after all," Marie Dosé, a lawyer who represented one of them, told me in an interview.

In their Parisian exile, however, the Femen popularity declined. There was something mercenary about the French girls, their recruits; it was never clear why they were doing what they did, and yet they disavowed any merely aesthetic motivation: they were not artists. The pundits were split: constituents of a "secular left," with which some of these French identified, encouraged

Femen in an anticlericalism targeted with growing frequency at Islam while other writers in Paris called them "fake." A schism in the group itself ensued, and the French press picked up on this eagerly. From the beginning, the Ukrainians had received death threats and for that reason took it personally when, in 2013, a fire caught in the theater where they were living. They had to move. They had few resources. The director of the Lavoir Moderne Parisien was friendly with Julien Boucher; they had summered in the same small village.

"This is Jacqueline," Julien said, at a planning meeting, "an American journalist who has the habit of opening squats with the Jeudi Noir and who is a very good friend. Jacqueline, come sit next to me."

Julien had brought up Femen in an interview to which I had subjected him ("feminists" being what I'd jotted down in ignorance). "They risk something," he had volunteered. "We"—Parisian squatters of another sort—"risk nothing."

Other than that, I hadn't heard of Femen. I did some research.

To ride in a white truck of supplies and furniture I got up early, meeting Julien and other men on the Parisian outskirts; our target was in Clichy, a suburb to the north. A few, I understood, were promised rooms. One of these, in the passenger seat, reached an arm out the window to quiet, idly, a ladder trussed at the truck's side.

We stepped down for a coffee. He rolled a sleeve to show me fine white scars. Branislav Petrić, a sculptor and student of art history, living in a car, was thirty-nine but looked much younger; a Montenegrin born in Bosnia he identified, if anything, as Yugoslavian. It had taken him a month of basic training to learn that he would rather kill himself than kill. It had been enough to seem to want to die; that army couldn't tell the difference. A friend had kept watch as he cut his arm.

The metal gate swung open. Leaves piled, rotting, in a courtyard. "An alarm will go off, and it'll be loud, so cover your ears," Branislav said, and helped me, in the silence that was so conditional, over a windowsill. Julien had left for work. Plaster peelings mixed with feathers on the floor. Cables stuck out of the walls that gaped with holes all fringed with fibers from which cables had been yanked. Metal blinds let in the sun, discrete white lines. I cupped a palm over my flashlight. "Come with me," Branislav said, "you're going to freak out."

It was a barnlike hangar, partitioned barely. Platforms of light wood jutted, rimmed in silver railings and served by treaded staircases. Metal beams joined these like spokes. The roof, glass ribbed with iron, was angled like a church, pulling attention. I dreamed of standing in a giant, delicate machine, guts of a clock that I could stop or break, the reverie was striking, at a touch. I bounced on my heels experimentally. Thin metal amplified the sound.

In the adjacent building an alarm was tripped—that high-pitched anapest. Men took it out.

Another followed, formless waterfall of sound.

Femen arrived—in leather jackets, leopard-printed sneakers. They helped clear insulation from the hangar, plaster fragments. The plaster crumbled at a touch, was brought outside. The day, changing between rain and fog, felt antiseptic, scouring.

"They're adorable," Julien said to me, head in a fuse box. "Real activists." He tugged at wires, pulling away a few like leaves from a bouquet.

By night we lined hallways with candles, wore coats. The heat would not work. We sat in the dark so as not to draw notice. Over a hot plate in an area where the power had been already restored pasta cooked, carbonara. Inna Shevchenko drank seltzer, not alcohol. Passing an iPhone she showed us the national stamp, the face on it printed with features like hers. "Already I am the new Marianne, but I don't speak French," Inna said in English. Her bright green eyes almost closed as she laughed. She described duties that were hers with resignation, grace, a beauty queen's: travel wore her out, but she got to meet interesting people.

To me, Branislav said he reserved the right to rebut what I eventually wrote.

I asked what he anticipated rebutting. (I was still trying to figure out what I could write.)

There was the real, he said, pinching my arm—I felt it—which hurt, and then there was reality. "I must explain it to you. Reality is the story, the narrative, there are many versions."

He led the party to the hangar, where his sculptures were arranged. Out of granite he made shapes that were softly curved, like seedpods. Closer up they were revealed, embracing people. He spoke of a pneumatic drill, his treasure. Granite was expensive—a limitation. Given a conservatism this alone may have imposed he simplified the heads, making the foreheads short, the noses angular. The grain showed over time on sculptures left outside as dust and grime collected in their tiny, concave places.

Here and there were relics, old phonebooks. The air was

bad, I thought, catching up fibers of the insulation we dislodged. A sink out of use was striped with gold-brown molds *like Jupiter*, I noted.

"The real is a series of things escaping narration," Branislav said. "Yes, one can explain in a film someone's torture in a prison, but one must torture the spectator for them to experience it. The banking system is a fictional factory that produces fiction. It works just well enough that when we stop believing in it, it stops working."

Julien plunked down a boombox. "It's for the cops," he said. "You have to put on France Inter. They love that."

"For us," Sasha Shevchenko began, unpacking, "we were worried, like, who is Julien, maybe he wants to lie to us, use us." She took out a toy unicorn, set it on the sill, and let me know Femen had been taken seriously in their homeland, taken for terrorists.

By morning I saw that on the floor where I had slept there was a little wooden fan, poking into me.

Julien wanted me to move in. He thought I'd be a good influence on the Femen.
  "It wouldn't be right for me to take up space in a squat when I have a salary," I said, a little piously.
  "You can go out to eat all the time," Julien said.

With Branislav I took a break from setting the scene, I switched on my tape. His thesis dealt with a role played by risk in artistic creation. The word came from the Greek for a cut, he said, meaning Latin. Though cuts were clean breaks, or because breaks were frightening, a risk most often had to be taken without its rising to awareness. Putting one's life into one's art was an attitude more than it was an intention. A paradox Branislav had identified in the practice of art was that many risks taken by artists revealed themselves only after the leap.

Crashes captured by the tape were all improvements to the building. One of the French Femen interrupted to remark that we weren't helping. Branislav had an assignment on which he had to score 18 out of 20. It was to make a mock press packet for an established or "emerging artist, still being born," and Femen would be a suitable subject.

"Except we're not artists," she said. "We're activists."

"I'm the one who decides who's an artist," said Branislav. "That's my field."

¶ Le Bloc's neighbors had complained of noise and seeing drunks in public. "If housing is a right, well, so is property," the state's lawyer said. There had been, that July, the assault on the stairs: "an altogether worrisome event." There had been an assault with a knife. The building was meant for greater things, destined to become social housing. That struck the squatters as ironic, and some of them laughed aloud.

Convain, their lawyer, had copied into the document that would serve as her argument or *conclusions* twelve extracts from constitutions and European law as well as examples from jurisprudence. As is typical in France she did not, on the day, read them all off. She did list artistic practices in the building, calling their occurrence together "relatively unique in France."

"Quite modern," she called it. One Madame Fournier, a member of the Paris City Council, had in June offered a usable statement about the squat's artistry, evidence: "Despite the size of the building and the complexity, then, of managing the site, the approach taken is of a high quality."

In comparison with all that law enshrining rights—the law at its most moving, with a different, human charge— there was, in Convain's rhetoric, something of a letdown. Electricity was up to code. No one used the elevators. She enumerated the fire extinguishers. "One saves people's lives with this initiative, in spite of everything." As for the July assault, she said, it was a familial affair, the squatters' term for it also, according to Convain something that could've happened in "any HLM"—any housing project (the poor and their troubles).

Anastasia and I were among the last to leave the room after the hearing that November. Emphatically she addressed Convain and the judge, telling them that at Le Bloc, *récupération* went on every morning. The judge shushed her. Every day at Le Bloc, Anastasia insisted, people ate for free.

One resident, pale, frantic, and called, like the old artist, Dominique, kept at their lawyer, uttering mantras for her to will true: "If you say there's a delay, if you say we can appeal, that reassures me. You can tell them certain negative elements have left."

To the judge Convain had indeed said that the residents were open to any compromise.

For my part I was straining to convince Caravaggio, now at Reception, to take me along when he broke in someplace else.

In reply, he insisted I take off my glasses and had a good, long look as I stood still, hating him. I just wanted an answer, a verdict as it were, and I would have to wait.

Le Général walked me partway home, smoking in defiance of a drizzle. He relayed news that Guy had told me: Mirabeau had been evicted without warning. I would hear from Hassan he'd been out working, had lost everything. This eviction, forceful, had been in retribution for the weed plant, which police found, or so Le Général said. "There's an old saying," he said. "I think it's Jewish. Don't shit where you eat."

Rain poured, drops meeting the pavement like marbles shattering, though of course they made no dent.

¶ *Charter in Poems*

The Universal Declaration of Human Rights, which the UN General Assembly adopted in 1948, affirms the right of each person on Earth to carry on at an adequate "standard of living" (in French it is "level of life," *niveau de vie*), including housing. The declaration is not considered binding as international law; in the US, specific jurisprudence, one reads, has established that it is not.

Convain also copied over part of Article 11 of the 1966 International Covenant on Economic, Social and Cultural Rights, a UN treaty. Signatories recognize the human right to, explicitly, an "adequate standard": food, housing, clothing, and something surprisingly time-based, "the continuous improvement of living conditions."

She copied over Article 8 of the 1950 European Convention on Human Rights, which stipulates states must not interfere in an individual's right to lead their own "private" life, with exceptions: if the law allows, and if such interference should prove "necessary in a democratic society" for reasons that are (to a layperson) broad, their list (to a layperson) long: "national security, public safety or the economic well-being of the country... the prevention of disorder or crime... the protection of health or morals... the protection of the rights and freedoms of others."

She copied over part of Article 31 of the European Social Charter (1961, since revised), whose parties "undertake to... promote access to housing... reduce homelessness with a view to its gradual elimination" and to make housing costs, in an apparent oxymoron, "accessible to those without adequate resources." A treaty making reference to this charter as authoritative went in, too.

Convain also excerpted Article 34 ("Social security and social assistance") of the Charter of Fundamental Rights of the European Union (2000, new one in 2007), which states that "the Union... respects the right to... housing assistance," softening it significantly with the kicker: "in accordance with the rules laid down by Union law and national laws and practices."

I had observed her in her efforts to collect, in addition to the artists' dossiers, evidence of requests her clients had made in vain for units in social housing. The document of Convain's argument also cites a 2007 French law that—following the 1982 Quilliot Law ("The right to housing is a fundamental right"), the 1989 Mermaz Law ("The right to housing is a fundamental right," again), and the 1990 Besson Law (expanding on the imperative of its predecessors, making it active: "To guarantee the right to housing constitutes a duty of solidarity for the whole nation")—instated an "opposable," or actionable, right to housing. Residents of France who find themselves indecently housed and whose petitions to the government go unanswered can take up this failing in an administrative court, suing the state.

When, about the *droit au logement opposable*, housing-rights activists told me, "It doesn't do anything," they referred to the distance this law kept from lived reality, a distance that could appear cruel when one's status as housed was at issue. The filing of a dossier did not materialize a place to live. It worked slowly, if it worked. Years later came the studies with their finding that it hadn't worked at all.

¶ In Clichy, the Femen activists and Branislav were safe. I had missed it, but police had come. The squatters had called them. The leader of the police had been a woman. The activists had appreciated this, and they had found it enjoyable to listen in on Julien as he explained the situation. "She had on a little smile," one of the French girls told me. "She knew she had to be serious."

In their understanding the commissariat had been apprised of the need for Femen, who were famous, to stay safely in the building. The police were told "there was a geopolitical context."

"And that was the decision of this beautiful woman," said Branislav, "the most beautiful woman in the world."

¶ A sign on Le Bloc's broken doors said not to push too hard. In Anastasia's workshop I found her, Valentin, Oleg, a third man, all eating hamburger pizza as it stained the box. That man was French, an artist Anastasia had allowed to share her workshop. He was moving out. Framed works of his were visible, mottled under bubble wrap. Anastasia had created voodoo dolls, arranged them in wait. She had moved out much else. A shopping cart stalled, filled to triple its height. A cymbal hung high. Out of that stuck a pig's snout, pink costume. It was midnight. I had eaten. Valentin asked me to play the piano for them, close my eyes and feel the keys. He leapt up and leveled the accusation that I was doing so badly on purpose, to show I couldn't play.

With no choice he played himself, ambling, delicate. A young man I recognized as one of a group newly arrived from Uruguay came in, drink in hand, and stood listening.

We were joined, too, by the musician and artist from Guadeloupe. Jean-Luc Georges Irenée, drawn by the music, clanked softly as he moved around Le Bloc, always in a leather coat of metal trim that reached his knees.

Anastasia fell to packing paintings, ripping masking tape to make a lot of noise as Valentin played loudly, setting his feet to tapping in boots, shrugging one shoulder high while sending the other, the left hand in search of a note.

At last, he smacked that hand down so all the low notes sounded, standing. "Excuse me," he said, as if indisposed. "If you go all the way to the bottom of the depths of this enigma"—coming to the table—"you will see just how deep it is." He tossed back his head and laughed. Anastasia slapped his back. Jean-Luc noticed the red eye of a tape recorder, hers. "We've done so much," he said, "so many beautiful moments that were never recorded, it's too bad—"

"As soon as you have a new place you'll forget the old one," Anastasia said.

"But this place is special," Jean-Luc said.

"Oh yes—it's tough! Tough, tough, tough. But it has had *such* energy."

"Our problem here is that we let in parasites," Jean-Luc said. "If you put down a pizza and look away, people eat it." He had not ruled out attributing this influx to the judge, calling the "parasites," "the carrot they hold up so as to make us evict ourselves."

"I invent sentences," Valentin said, "sometimes fifteen a day, sometimes fifteen thousand a day."

"Nights are a little bizarre," Jean-Luc said. "By day, you have people who are normal; by night, people who are not normal."

"Stop telling scary stories," Valentin said. "Don't you have a funny story? Play the piano, Jean-Luc—maybe for the last time."

A duty of Jean-Luc's to keep night watch now bound him to check in on a party in the basements. In the stairwell climbed white kids my age; one let a beer can drop.

"It's as if the boat were sinking," Jean-Luc said to me, "and there were pirates coming on board to steal what they could before it sank."

Downstairs, a *tonton* I recognized was taking the arm of a woman I knew only slightly, a dancer, and drawing her into a room, for some reason scolding her. For her it seemed a matter of dancing to resist, to demonstrate her resistance. She drank, suffering from episodes of, apparently, estrangement from the world; she yelled at you. (She yelled at me; I couldn't force an interview.) It was understood the *tontons* had evicted her. She had no place to go, she stayed.

Spotlights in the second basement turned a fog opaque. I saw the fog machine; there was another, very ambient humidity. A hole in a wall joined two rooms like a cave. A man asked if I was doing sociology and, without waiting for my answer, made a gesture of waving away a bad smell.

The DJ table was a gleaming heap of speakers and loose motorcycle wheels. Lights plugged in there arced, flashing, below the ceiling. The programming was for thirty hours of sets, a third-floor resident informed me. They had just begun and would go on "until Monday."

In the soft light of a hallway couples embraced, every so often one of a twosome taking the other's hand to lead them a few paces this way, that way.

On the -1, by the bar, a man I didn't recognize was drawing on the floor, a calligraphy all his own that he was happy enough to explain. He also was complaining his drawings were being stepped on. That was so like Le Bloc, he said. I filled out loops that he had left to make a sitting cat, its back to us.

The artist's work absorbed him.

Le Général stood in a doorway. "It's the weekend," he told me. "Don't work." In his own work he never rested (he informed me, now that I had given him the opportunity). His legs were sore from circling buildings, peering in windows. "Spycraft, Jacqueline." With other *tontons* he'd occupied a building just to be evicted. It had in Le Général's understanding housed a manufacturer of luxury materials, leathers. Glass walls divided up the offices, "like prison": out loud he imagined the workers, together, separate. He worked through the night. Very early, in "an explosion of light and color," power ran. A door closed automatically to trap all members of the expedition. But the building was heated, beautiful, and they managed to change the locks. Then, at 10 p.m., "real-estate people" came by. They could do nothing but bluff, telling the people to call the police. Police, when they came, did not believe the squatters had stayed long.

At the bar, two men brought up Ludo. "He was a guardian angel," one of them told me. "Fatigue, an honorable death. Dead! And we're still here."

"Well," said the other, "we are tired."

◀ *Place des Teufs*

As my involvement with Le Bloc deepened until, in November, I decided again to sleep there, I would often cross the Place des Fêtes ("Party Plaza"), where, before the classes that I had to teach, I caught the Métro. A neighborhood of residential towers topping out at twenty-eight stories this is, within Paris, a point of population density. There are however at its center stretches of concrete where no one lingers. Children play at the edges of a fountain in which that month no water ran, a spiral down.

In 1861, the year after Belleville village was incorporated into Paris, this square's identity and function were, if not perfectly preserved—the municipality at first declined to fund the customary *fêtes foraines*—memorialized, brought in line with an official nomenclature. After the installation of Haussmannian kiosks, its limits not so meaningfully redrawn, a square was christened with a preexisting name. Around it were found, of the old village, lime trees, low buildings. The altitude was a buffer efficacious against Parisian modernization. For decades, Belleville remained "the village within the city *par excellence*, perched 120 meters high, feet in Paris and head in the countryside" writes Patrick Bezzolato in his history of this arrondissement. As late as 1887 the Place des Fêtes served as a fairgrounds. Neighbors complained of a "roar of wild animals."

After what the twentieth century did to this locale, Hazan no longer deigns to call it Place des Fêtes. "If you ... reach on foot the immense tower blocks constructed on what was once the Places des Fêtes, it is clear that the managers of domination had a score to settle with Belleville." That the renovation was undertaken by powers that be as their revenge on this Belleville for its role in the Commune was, back then also, a rhetoric of protest. For historian of the *banlieue* Annie Fourcaut the renovation "symbolizes the reuse of themes of Haussmannian modernization"; the towers were, for other historians, *cités-dortoirs*, built to suit a new class of commuters, outsiders, a dormitory town. The 1967 plan had left central Paris and the gilded west untouched; it savaged the east. Six thousand five hundred residents of the Place des Fêtes evacuated; only two hundred returned. Though many units of the towers are public housing, only 10 percent of the neighborhood's residents, writes Bezzolato, were re-housed. But the neighbors organized their own campaign, in the eighties persuading the city's mayor to "re-renovate." The architect in charge of the project, Bernard Huet, would comment that, in working to bring out the local identity, he was confronted with a mystery. This memory that was his to channel resembled something "almost literary" in the sense that, while not a "historical memory," it was one to which "the inhabitants [were] relatively attached."

> Old Paris is no more (the form of a city
> Changes faster, alas! than mortal hearts)

These lines, from Charles Baudelaire's poem "The Swan," are taken as the great articulation of a people's trauma following the Haussmannian blow. Baudelaire, Benjamin teaches so patiently, "was forced to claim the dignity of a poet in a society that no longer had any dignity to offer. Hence the buffoonery of his attitude."

I went along with *récupération* as the day was dawning to climb, alongside shopping cart and squatter, to the Place des Fêtes and its chain supermarkets. Of each of those apartments just a single window, sometimes, shows; the curtains, of clashing fabric, give the towers the appearance of quilts. The smell of bread poured from vents of a store. Skinned rabbits stretched out; men set out cheese and seafood on massed ice, lifting fish as cats lift kittens. In the tunnels were the newspapers available, as every day, for free, flimsy enough to serve as barometers for a public kind of feeling. The platform where I changed for a train to work smelled sulfurous. An island had formed in Japan after volcanic eruptions, I read. Rock had come up from the seafloor at a thousand degrees Celsius and stayed. The ocean threatened to retake it. Bucolic names of suburban stations came over the intercom, breaking like waves. Full of wonder, I tore out the item, added it to my notes.

At times I wondered whether, due to my enclosure in Le Bloc, continuous note-taking, late in the game my decision to sleep there, I had achieved an appropriately heightened state, sensitive as a baby.

What would a real-estate agent call it? An experiment in co-living in the ruins of a city. Against the threats of teardown and eviction, reporting had at least the dubious ability to say how things had been.

Graffiti within Le Bloc were multiplying at that eleventh hour: Anastasia asked if I had noticed. Our filmmakers had drawn on a wall of her workshop. "Even they need this," she said.

¶ "I'm a little disconcerted," Dominique, the old artist, said. I had found Valentin's room empty and orchestrated an interview. "It's hard," he said, "because when people get to the point of integrating into Le Bloc, with all the challenges of asserting yourself, getting over a phase of homelessness and into the squat, that's already a huge step. It's really a lot of time before they learn to live together, and the payoff happens after... With a decision like this, the whole edifice crumbles. *Hop*, emergency, *hop*, everybody's back to their own business, their fears, getting their life in order, holding on to their papers, everything resets."

Caravaggio came into the room, took a frying pan, and left.

I asked Dominique about Ludo.

"It's true that this huge performance squats offer can also devour," Dominique said.

"It's a question of scale," I offered, a line I often heard at Le Bloc.

"But that's the squatter's mission," he said, "to create possibilities." He stood gathering his hat in his hands and thanked me for our talk.

¶ One response available to the inhabitants of Le Bloc was regret: for the effort they had spent in dignifying, with any principle, the discomfort in which they lived.

"Nuisances to neighbors," the judge wrote (in the *Ordonnance de référé*, "interim order," dated November 13, 2013),

> linked notably to the organization of a rave, to multiple cultural events, to the presence of great numbers of people deep under the influence of alcohol or of other intoxicating substances in public near the squatted building, which seriously inconvenienced the neighbors, lasted from December 2012 to August 2013...
>
> Concerns in connection with the right to housing and care for every human being cannot, in any case, justify the violation characterized by the taking of another's property...
>
> What matters, then, is to put an end, urgently, to this manifestly illicit nuisance...
>
> There is no call to remove from the suit N— B—, L— H—, and J— M— B—, who remain occupants in the capacity of their artistic activity and must assume responsibility for their personal engagements.

In France it was unusual to evict in winter. A policy called the Winter Truce protected tenants who'd fallen behind between November and March. The rule was often honored for squatters. Meanwhile the "another" here (*autrui*), owner of Le Bloc's building, was not an individual but the state in whose name human rights were guaranteed.

Their lawyer Convain had asked only for more time. But the eviction ordered was immediate. There would be a fine of one thousand euros for each day its inhabitants remained in the building past the date that would be set for their eviction. There would be a grace period of eight days. The verdict, again typically in France, did not specify when those days would fall.

The next night I found Le Général piling into a car with Caravaggio and three other men of Le Bloc. I rapped at the window—pushy. Le Général gestured that he'd phone me.

At Reception the "policeman" was shouting, saying with violence the week would be "tense" for everyone, "tragic." Even if "the best dancer in the world," he yelled at her, the dancer was only "human." "You have no monopoly on all the world's misery," he yelled.

I kept a record of lines like this in the thrall of something like justice. Justice was, in English, a term for a judge, like the one in the reality of whose decision all of them, from then on, would live.

On the -1, to music, Rastamen swayed, one of them absently spray-painting (the peaceful whistle of the spray, the can's occasional rattle in a shaking fist). Morgane's exhibit was over. Across the walls were sprayed a lot of anarchist A's and the epitaph RIP LE BLOC.

¶ *Boulevard Haussmann*

A certain peace, in the absence of its major personalities, settled like weather over the squat. I did hear that *tonton* on the third, telling the dancer in a shout he didn't want to see her in the aboveground living quarters.

I thought I would get some interviews done. To the Frenchwoman Stella's room, on the fifth, I brought bags of herbal tea, my digital recorder. We sat around a wooden spool, something industrial, with Caravaggio's girlfriend, who didn't want to be named.

Stella, for the sake of the group, would not be moving into the new squat, not right away. A squat in its infancy was fragile, these women agreed, the cohesion of the group within crucial. Stella had been dating Morgane, one of the privileged artists who had followed a *tonton* to Le Bloc after making art in prior squats of theirs. No longer, and Morgane was being difficult.

Caravaggio's girlfriend got a call, something about candles. Hanging up, she made quick, jumbled reference to caring, in the building of Le Bloc, for a puppy. "They've cut power," she said then.

Continuing brightly in the interview, both women told me they labeled food they didn't want stolen with notes that conceivably a man could have composed. One good one was "If you touch this, I'll cut off your finger," Caravaggio's girlfriend said. Stella had brought home a nice cut of meat on which she'd thought to write, "If you eat this, I will eviscerate you and send your entrails to your mother."

Masha Guttsait joined us. It was instructive to speak with those of them the mission and its activity had left behind. To Masha, Caravaggio's girlfriend explained that, given where in the city the men were, it was unlikely they would be evicted that night, a Saturday. "There's the Galeries Lafayette," she said, naming a department store. "Tourists everywhere."

"They'll do it at five in the morning," Masha agreed.

"You have to block off roads. They can't block them off there." Caravaggio's girlfriend went to get something and returned. "It's a castle," she said.

"Don't talk to me about it," Stella said pleasantly.

Here and there were cans of paint and butcher paper. Stella had made a painting out of one wide wall. We discussed the relationship that she had left, the construction of belonging in a squat out of bricks of one's own labor, hard work Stella had done. She would not have traded her life at Le Bloc for any other. She had learned practical skills as well as how to make herself exist. But she had found it dizzying, in a community intended as an alternative, to fall into every trap society held in store.

Caravaggio's girlfriend offered that while women at Le Bloc, unlike the men, could make reputations for bedding as few as two partners out of the dozens of squatters, they didn't fare as badly as their type in other circles did. "People will still talk to her. They won't stop trusting her."

She took a call. She returned to Stella and me. Caravaggio wanted backup. She didn't feel like getting arrested. Caravaggio wanted everybody.

"I'll come," Stella said.

"Me too," I said.

"You don't mind getting arrested?" Caravaggio's girlfriend was surprised.

"I'm ready," I said quickly. "I don't have my passport or visa with me, but I have copies. Hold on, I have to pee."

The tape stops there.

We passed Crimée, Jaurès, Barbès where below tracks

of an elevated Métro a makeshift market, I thought, had atrophied; it left negotiants to haggle over, soon lost to sight, bags, bags of flyaway plastic. The cathedral Sacré-Coeur flashed in a window. At Pigalle, the streets cleaned up, chalkboard menus legible. The deep dark of the late November night was incomplete: there were insectan stem eyes, an old-fashioned Métro sign. A veil of Christmas lights for a McDonald's. A display window as if aflame, putting a woman in silhouette.

A blade of the Moulin Rouge rotated to slice the sightline of a cross street and was gone. Caravaggio's girlfriend made a calculation: "With thirty people there, they can't arrest us all."

Stella made a turn; we were traveling downhill, into the river valley. The streets quieted as we crossed from the ninth arrondissement into the eighth. Gilded cafés, awnings and the slender legs of terrace furnishings really gleaming: The Royal Trinity. Au Petit Riche was another, on the sidewalk before it some oysters on ice. A man whose job was tending to them, to the oysters. Japanese restaurants. Big-name banks, grilles with flourishes. A turn and, framed at that street's end, façade. A church.

Police might leave, the women reasoned, leaving alone the businessmen, the tourists, so as to come back in the morning. We knew of a ban on eviction by night.

A right onto Boulevard Haussmann. Two men, Black, lifted velvet ropes to let women in heeled boots past them and through the doors labeled CLUB HAUSSMANN.

Plasma-screen TVs for sale. In a window they all played the Eiffel Tower, sparkling. It was a test pattern.

The otherwise vacant building that squatters from Le Bloc had entered, and where they had even stayed the night, was six stories of limestone and finely wrought iron, a perfect specimen of the Haussmannian vision. We took in the delicacy of the ironwork, the swoop of arcing doors of heavy wood, where a guardsman in a reflective vest was standing, and a peeling sign: MONTE PASCHI BANQUE. It was one in from the corner building. Across the street a comparable site was an Apple store, arranged like a shrine. Grand matching buildings worked together to define a clearing of wide road in which nestled, lavishly, the jewel of Haussmannian renovation: the Garnier opera house. Just south of it stretched the exquisite arcades of wrought iron and glass, the Vendôme plaza, the Tuileries; to the west lay the Madeleine church, lay a little-known Perfume Museum.

Police cars had double-parked, blinking.

Le Général approached us on the sidewalk, hands in pockets, a cigarette dangling from his lips. He made no sign of recognition, only said under his breath: "The other side."

Briskly, we walked around the building. "*Oh là là,*" Caravaggio's girlfriend said loudly, as if to confuse anyone potentially on our tail. Cars streamed by.

Caravaggio was addressing police in a ring with another squatter from Le Bloc, Marty McFly, named for my country's cinema.

We loitered, pretending not to know them, at a stop for the 54 bus. The women with me lit their cigarettes against the cold.

An old lady got off. "Excuse me, do you have any idea what's going on here?"

"Oh it's not *serious*," said Masha, waving her cigarette. "There's always something going on."

Through the smudged glass of the bus shelter I watched Caravaggio address the cops, McFly gesticulating in the service of some point. He dropped it and stalked over.

"CRS got here"—riot police—"authorized for violence... *C'est foutu*. The owner said, I am a capitalist and you're not gonna spend a year in my house..."

Out of a second-story window leaned another woman, the philosophy of art student. As many as twenty squatters from Le Bloc were in there with her.

"This cop told me, if you know people in TV go ahead, call them up, I agree with what you're doing."

I texted a friend, a stringer for *Le Monde*, and wouldn't hear back.

Into the building through its archway filed twelve gendarmes in shin guards, clubs slung across their armored bodies. Each of these men in crossing the threshold removed his headgear. Above the doors one *tonton* was leaning out a window. There were more cops on the inside.

Caravaggio was causing the women around me to giggle. "He looks good in that leather jacket," they said.

Two more columns, twenty-four gendarmes, went in. One of Le Bloc's best graffiti artists, Doudou, came over to say she had taken a ton of photos.

Le Général passed again pretending not to know us, this time wearing a backpack, toting a duffel. He turned back. "Jacqueline! You got here too late." We kissed each other's cheeks in greeting.

Troops were assembling, CRS, carrying clear shields.

"Watch out," yelled a squatter, mocking, from the sidewalk. "Fight hard!"

CRS piled into the building.

The rest of them came out of the briefly open squat lugging duffel bags, sleeping bags, mattresses. "A beautiful thing, France," they shouted back. "Beautiful. It's cold out, we put people out in the street."

Two more came out, carrying a fridge.

Valentin was wandering the sidewalk. "We got out

alive," he said. "There's that."

Morgane emerged from the building and told me that even its carpets were clean.

"At the beginning," Valentin said, "when I got here... I told the cops... I introduced myself as a kind of higher-up brigade chief. They let me in for ten minutes, and then they threw me out."

The last ones out were laying down their mattresses. "You have to go in through the roof!" they shouted. "Careful! They're on crack!"

A policeman asking around for identity cards, switching tactics obviously, said that he'd heard they were all a "collective of artists."

A Frenchwoman of middle age, wearing a pink scarf and sparkling earrings, with aplomb was addressing police, "I live just across the street, and I think it's a shame. They were in there for a month! It's scary to see you all turn up like that."

Valentin, too, was addressing a cop. "Your presence," he said, "has surpassed our every expectation..."

Morgane and Masha led him away.

"I wish you good luck," the woman said, making an announcement. "I'd have liked to have you for neighbors. It's a pity we meet like this."

Gendarmes left the building maintaining their column, at last breaking into a trot.

The granddaughter of the leader of the French Resistance was using a mini iPad to snap photos.

Revelers dressed for the Saturday night gave a wide berth by walking in the street.

A rumor circulated on the sidewalk that Le Général was, somehow, still inside.

"Party's over!" yelled Caravaggio's girlfriend. "We're all outside!"

"Who are we missing?" someone else asked quietly. "Le Général? Is he the only one?"

I looked over the shoulders of police flanking the doorway, across paving stones, a sharp-tipped iron fence, to see a courtyard: columns, potted trees. Semicircular windows let in golden light, which pooled with corresponding precision.

"Can you see?" a policeman asked me sarcastically. "Would you like me to move?"

Their neighbor had returned with tiny plastic cups, coffee, which she offered to the squatters.

"Did the sheriff leave?" a member of the CRS force asked—of whom, I took no note—just to be corrected: "Le Général."

And there he was, ripping open a baguette brought by the women, stuffing it with halal turkey we'd picked up.

Le Général said again that I was late—the CRS had cleared out; men in armbands, guards, were taking their places—and invited me to follow. For a moment, then, we stood before the opera house, which had been, I would learn in reading, Haussmann's most expensive building. We could see the east façade, built to fit entire carriages. Charles Garnier, the architect, assembled a defense for using gas lighting onstage that might be described as flamboyant; he "more than anyone" studied the possibility of electricity, as he wrote, and finally thought it too new. Gas was also Haussmann's darling in those days—giving Baudelaire, the city's poet, high occasion for the expression of his horror. Garnier left no centimeter of the opera house without embellishment—"Make me a Bernini, but in bad taste," he wrote to one sculptor—and it gleamed with live fire.

"You want souvenirs, Jacqueline?" Le Général held up a ring of keys.

They were thick, silver. As we headed back toward their building in the midst of its eviction, a middle-aged man stopped Le Général with a question about the operation's final aim.

"We open it," Le Général said, "and then we live inside."

There was an edge to the man, who introduced himself as the property manager.

"I am a cowboy," Le Général said, using that English word. "I've been living in the margin of the margin of society since I was a child."

"But you can easily see," said the property manager, affecting amusement, "that this is a ridiculous and inefficient life."

"I go from place to place," Le Général said, "from lawsuit to lawsuit."

"But what's the final goal?"

Le Général waved at the sidewalk. The people were relaxing on their mattresses, one guy eating from a sleeve of cookies. The people looked tired.

"It doesn't benefit humanity, only a small group..."

McFly showed up, livid. "But you have money, and you're sitting on a statue!"

The property manager was equanimous. "I find this thinking short-term," he offered. "It's divisive."

"Before, I made a lot a lot a lot of money," Le Général said.

"I just don't understand why someone as intelligent as you isn't putting his energy elsewhere," the man said, and mentioned a historical figure, Abbé Pierre—"A bourgeois," Le Général retorted. The manager asked if I was taking notes.

"She's a journalist," Le Général said, "who has followed me for two years. I will go on."

The Frenchman, who declined to share his name, evinced delight. "We'll go on, you and I, through our parallel worlds."

A little brown dog was wandering and set its paws on Le Général's shins. "What do you want?" he asked it quietly. "You want a joint?"

In the Métro someone sleeping between seats was giving off a smell. McFly, despondent, sprayed a window with his tag. He had found a list of emails in the building, a souvenir for him, a printout. He showed me photos:

Bloc squatters, posing in bank vaults. (Caravaggio and some of the others had gone to open another building already, McFly said.)

A stairwell like a nautilus shell.

Pea-green, Versailles-style paneling. (The others described walls of marble, of velvet.)

From a window they had seen clear into the opera house—some had. Watching for a moment, savoring the sight, not anodyne. Then they let the others know, others pausing in responding to the summons that was worth their time. Spellbound, they all watched the dancer—leaping, dipping, stretched, as if dancing just for them, and in a way she was, rehearsing. They would have understood her movement as going with music, some music they could not hear.

The Abbé Pierre's name is well-known in France today, denoting the foundation that collects to provide for the homeless and to increase, more generally, a national standard of living. Its namesake, a celebrity priest, in the winter of 1954 made his appeal over the radio to the sympathy of all French people, lionizing a homeless woman for dying on the Boulevard de Sébastopol while still clutching, according to him, the order for her eviction. Five hundred million francs came in donations, an episode called by journalists "the uprising of goodness." A standout gesture for its level balance of generosity and self-repudiation was Charlie Chaplin's. He gave two million, calling it payback, or back pay, due to the clochards who, as a group, had made him a fortune in serving as the template for his character. All this mob sentiment rose to the attention of Roland Barthes, who wrote in his *Mythologies* about a "public" who "no longer having any access to the experience of apostleship" could be found "clearing its conscience with a glance at saintliness's storefront."

Before losing sight of their white woman neighbor at Opéra I had watched her, in the full flush of do-gooding, making a spectacle out of her own fraternal feeling. Lightly she scolded the property manager for his insistence on the eviction of apparently "good people." Had they been "Romanian," she said to him congenially, that would've been another story.

Valentin, back at Le Bloc, couldn't help mentioning the bike against the door. "Make your barricade," he said repeatedly in wishing me good night. "Make a good barricade."

In the morning my neighbor Jaouad made coffee for me with pepper and ginger, a way his mother in the Atlas Mountains had of making it to keep the drinker warm even outside. "Don't think too much," he added. "You're always going off into your thoughts, your book, asking why, how, asking about other people's problems..." At his door leaned a pole longer than the door was tall.

I had my second coffee outside Le Bloc. The clientele, men two, three times my age, were gambling, watching a game. Wrappers of sugar cubes flecked the café, bright spots in relief on the dirty linoleum, against their backdrop that would not resolve.

It was just the day after, and already one of the squatters of Le Bloc spoke bashfully about the attempt on Opéra. "For a moment there we did believe in it," he said to me, "a little bit."

Police evicted Opéra on a Saturday. In the days after, on Sunday or Monday, the Russians informed me that Valentin would need his room. I left a bottle of vodka, which Oleg drank. I wrote my thank-you note across a baby's face, an ad I'd torn out of a Métro newspaper, hoping Anastasia would appreciate the joke on me.

Guy forbade me to sleep in the office where he practiced—unsafe, too close to the doors.

On someone's recommendation, I forget whose, I asked the *tonton* Marco La Mouche to put me up. I approached him after the weekly meeting Monday night. He was drifting in a wheelchair he did not need, an affectation.

I moved into a spare room on his floor, the sixth, which was calm and quiet.

¶ *The Night Watch*

I thought I might wait for Le Bloc to fall silent.

"Go back, go back to where you live on the outside," said Jesus, pointing at the sidewalk where the trash would go.

Papers lay on the desk at Reception—sheets of prayers from which small strips were torn to serve as filters, a calendar. Ashes, scribbles, plastic cups. In a vestibule for use by guardsmen there rested a mirror, broken, a three-legged chair, a fire extinguisher, traffic cone. A cat made of Styrofoam cloaked in gold sequins, missing its head.

The inner doors had cracked dramatically by then. Jean-Luc used both hands to pull them open, dragged out seven dumpsters.

Settling in, he spoke of training in the army. He found it had prepared him for this work by night. A poster fluttered. Jean-Luc said in explanation that below, a door hung open.

Whether another finding was significant I can't, however, say—if it was typical of Le Bloc, or of Paris, November, first frost in the late-stage metropolis that at three a guy my age or younger came through those doors having no other place to sleep. Named Mohammed, he lived in a suburb to the north, his parents from Congo, Sudan; fatigue cut short his introduction. Action, who lived on the ground floor, fixed a dish of stew, and with it Mohammed sat in that half-room for guardsmen, nodding off.

Jean-Luc and Action discussed the inadequacy of the young man's outfit, the threat of that night's cold.

Over my T-shirt I was wearing sweaters of two hefts, a heavy coat, a scarf—my uniform in the common spaces of Le Bloc.

Cold could make a homeless person drink, Action remarked. Sleep was a threat.

When at four I descended to the –2 a man lay curled on a couch. Another decorating walls with dollar signs was spraying paint, loops lazy as a fly's. A small woman in a sweatshirt was dancing, bobbing, another man photographing the hands of a DJ.

Up at the desk I found Dominique the younger. He'd been the one to buttonhole the lawyer at their hearing. He had white, tired skin each time I saw him. On Le Bloc he was eager to share his opinions, this time in the officious guise of percentages. Ninety percent of the squatters were good, while 35 percent of buildings in Paris were empty, enough to house the city's homeless. The empty hallway perhaps caused his voice to echo. He spoke with aristocratic diction, inverting *paraît-il* as no one did, exaggerating vowels in *heure* and *cœur*. Dominique's politics were that he identified as "royalist." He made and left unexplained a reference to Louis IX, a thirteenth-century king of France in the Capetian dynasty, who would "come in here and say, you nasty ones, out, the others can stay," Dominique the royalist said.

Yellow light from streetlamps was coming through the front doors where it parsed the cut-out letters BLOC.

People came and went, or came and leaned on Reception resting, with no appetite for conversation.

Jean-Luc moved a chair so it gave him a view of the side door; at five, a Frenchman came in, weaving. He sat as if relieved to have pulled that off. He was handsome if you found unusualness handsome, which I tended to, mistaking the sensation of noticing for that of admiration. He had blue eyes, red hair, was very slim. He wore a boat-shaped fur hat, which he removed to set it on another chair while complimenting me. I offered a small bar of chocolate, which he tidily, without eating it, accepted.

"The world today lacks elegance, I find." Unlatching a silver box he drew out a cigarette. "We live in a world of vulgarity," he said in English. "I try to resist. Maybe I'm wrong. But here, I will never, ever try to, I am keen on—do you know what is a dandy?"

"Like Baudelaire?" I asked. The poet forged a permanent association between this term and his version of artful living. "Do you mean you are a dandy like Baudelaire?"

"When you say you are a dandy you are not one. You do not admit it. You live for elegance. You live for a certain sense of beauty. But the world you live in is not made for it," he said, again in English. "You live in a vulgarity world."

A ranking of priorities in which career beat out love seemed to him a generational disposition that he did not share. The world was full of people who wanted success, but to this man it was unclear what success was if not love. He was a singer, loved the Beatles and yet found his accent in English was an inhibition to his singing in my language. Periodically as we spoke he did sing, absently, a few bars in English, always with a helpless, almost embarrassed look, for his accent or as if he couldn't help himself. He let his wiggling fingers tip the cigarette.

I asked his name and he said, with chagrin, Nicholas. The second most common name in the world, he said. "What I always hate," he said, "is vulgarity, and vulgarity, in its first meaning, is that which is common..."

He ate the chocolate square by square and stood.

After Le Bloc opened it didn't lock, Jean-Luc told me. Not every door. Through the night he had patrolled the seven stories. After Ludo came to Le Bloc he did this with Ludo.

As a matter of safety, women were not to keep the watch alone, unsuited as they were to scaring off *petits voyous* who came asking after fake *soirées*.

"And then," Jean-Luc said, "there are times when it's all quiet and we whisper and communicate with just a glance," even as I knew he didn't mean himself and me.

The opera house of Garnier would fill with light, gas powering its proudest installation, the mighty organ. One operator sending air to stir innumerable pipes would command with them the range of expression worthy of modernity.

In 1862, the year after ground was broken for this theater, during rehearsals at the old site for Auber's *La Muette de Portici* as the dancer Emma Livry—a baron's bastard considered by critics ugly, skinny, and yet celebrated for her precocity and seeming weightlessness in leaping—was moving into place for a second act as Fenella, the mute girl, her fate was sealed by a shaking out of skirts. These set in motion air over a nozzle for the gasworks. In the newspaper's account the garment was afire instantly. "She tried to pray," according to another source, and ran over the stage and in the house before a fireman, with blankets ready, caught her.

Fireproofing had been, this danger known, available. Dancers are said to have refused it out of fury that it left fabric stiff. Livry actually is said to have gone without regret, in her suffering deploring still the fireproofing and its rough distortion of the ballerina's raiment. Her wounds turned septic. She succumbed at twenty to a poisoning of the blood. Of course they'd seen only her ghost.

Jean-Luc dozed. A man I recognized, Caravaggio's cousin or a good friend of his, came to the desk.

Another man was shouting at the royalist. "You talk too much, too much, only blah blah blah…"

The friend or cousin, who spoke no French, only Spanish, had seemed to me mild-mannered, a judgment for which, I realized then, I had no evidence other than the silence hanging awkwardly about him. He sat back and yanked a knit hat down. The sky was brightening. He asked what I did at Le Bloc and suggested I'd come to make money. A fluffy German shepherd nosed my feet.

"Would you like it if people wrote about you?" the man asked in Spanish. "Your life, your hopelessnesses. People don't like this, when you write about them."

My Spanish was rusty.

"¿No comprendes?" He was disgusted. "Comprendes lo que quieres."

He asked where I was staying. I explained that Marco La Mouche was hosting me, a revelation taken by the man as clarifying; he offered in follow up, as if at last understanding, that I was involved in "naked photos." I wrote down what I told him, later saw that I'd forgotten a Spanish word for "share," unwittingly replacing it with badly pronounced French. I saw that what I'd said was without meaning. I rose and, at seven in the morning, wished the man a good night, throwing out the chocolate wrappers. My knees were stiff with cold, I found in climbing the six flights.

¶ "It's not a tragedy," the man I didn't know reflected, calling in response to the message I'd composed on Facebook having never met him. "These are things that happen every day, my dear. He listened to people who didn't listen to themselves. So he was available, and it was a vampiricism. He wasn't careful. I don't get why you want to put this in your book. He became an urban legend. It's a catastrophe. In such a way the world is made. It is obligated to kill all the nice people. All around us, people are horrible. There is no need to novelize."

The man, to match his thin, collapsed voice, had a thin, collapsed chest. "If he'd called me at the time"—the name given for "he" was a *tonton*'s—"said *ça va pas* your friend, I would've come, I would've slept in his room, and as I sleep lightly, if he'd have fallen, I would have woken up. Unfortunately... he fell onto the wrong side. And I don't know what kind of drugs he'd taken. Listen, I really don't know. Because with the autopsy, when he was buried, we didn't know... So, he died in his vomit.

"After that, when the family came, they came and saw me, because they knew that he was like a brother to me. We'd spent five years together, going from right to left, and *voilà*. And no one helped us.

"But *voilà*. In squats, nobody helps anybody. It is no brotherhood. They're not brothers. They're destitute. When you're a squatter, you're not doing it for the fun of it. I don't think so.

"Ludo had a connection with animals. All the dogs wanted to play with him. He'd throw himself on the floor to play with dogs. It was something impressive, you know. He had this thing that no one has.

"Ludo was a nice guy, adorable, and nice people always get seen as weak. And in a squat there's no room for the weak, eh.

"The squat swallowed him, raw.

"The city lights"—the man whistled softly—"they sucked him up. Squats killed him. It's a shame.

"One might call this an interview with a vampire.

"I met him in Nantes. He came into my tattoo parlor pushing his daughter in a stroller. I never saw his lady. He goes, 'I'm Ludo, *tac tac*. I'd like to learn tattooing.' No more, no less... After that he comes back on his own, stays the day, and as I like to be around people—not, like, people that do nothing—right away I say, 'Listen. Go get some cigarettes.' I trusted him more and more. I gave him twenty euros, a hundred euros, and I saw he was an honest guy... I sent him out shopping, to test him. Turned out he really was a super honest guy. One day he says, 'I draw a little.' He brought me some of his drawings. I told him, 'Listen. It's not bad, but you have to put in some work.' After that I trusted him, and I said, 'I'll take you on as an apprentice.' I gave him three hundred, or four hundred, euros a month, that's not so bad. He got to be my apprentice. I bought his machine for him, my gift to him out of friendship, because *voilà*, he deserved it.

"Later on I says to him, 'I have a plan for the squats of Paris, come with me.' He was happy. He didn't know Paris.

"So we got to Paris. To Le Bloc. People there took their time, eh. They thought both of us were gypsies. You saw the photos. My little brother, you'd say. And they really respected him. Me, as an artist, and him, as a person. And then it happened, *voilà*, like I told you. He chose the city lights.

"I go, 'We got it, I found the apartment. We're good, I found the spot. The premises. For tattooing. We're ready, Ludo, come back to me.' And then I see something's up. And then he comes to see me, he says *voilà*, it's like a second family for me here.

"I was like, 'Ludo, stop it with that. This is not your family. If you want to get a little more custody of your girl, follow me, get out of here, climb up a little socially speaking. We'll get you there.' It was a little bit selfish on my part, because I relied on him to climb up, too. I'd had to close up shop because I was sick, and there we were.

"But that's not how he saw it. His experience of this was that it was the most beautiful time of his life, the time of necessity and of the need to share. See? When he got to Paris, my beauty. *Pfft*. I don't know. It was Le Bloc. It was them. Everything he'd dreamed of out in the sticks, it was there at Le Bloc. All the graffiti artists, the artists, the whatever. Stardust in his eyes. To my mind it was stardust in his eyes. I had trusted him not to go and leave me. He gave me his word. But a word that's given can be taken back too because *voilà*, it's his choice. And so he decided to stay there. And with the fact that he stayed there"— here, the man named another *tonton*—"quickly realized that this was a super guy. I'm giving you names, but don't put people's names in there.

"To get to the point: that's what he chose. And me, I says every time 'Ludo, come over.' I always had him over to eat, for dinner. By the end he wasn't eating anymore, not Ludo. He drank all the time, or he smoked, a lot. *Pfft*. He fell into the trap of the storm, where everybody says he's super, that he's cool.

"For me, all those people, they killed Ludo. They have nothing to say to him... See? No." (He did not believe that I had seen.) "He held onto them and held on, held on so much that look, bravo. Another side of things, you'll hear a thousand. See if I care. And *voilà* and *voilà*. And one day I get a call, I'm out in the suburbs, I hear, 'Come back. I have bad news. Ludo is dead.' I go, 'Dead of what, dead of nothing, your joke is seriously not funny.' *Et pof*,

I come down from the suburbs. I cut short my job, I get there, and: in effect. They had brought Ludo I don't know where... Then the family came. And when the family came it was funny. There was nobody. Just me and them. In tears, I am not even telling you. The little sister crying all over me, it shattered me. And the day of his funeral. We came from Le Bloc and out of all those decent people there were twenty of us.

"A bunch of...

"Better finish it, your piece of shit of a book," he said, almost spitting it out. A pause.

"For me, all those people: they killed him. They're no friends of mine, not anymore, and there is no one I still talk to out of all those people who were pretending to be Ludo's friend. He was never their friend. Because he was nice and so naïve, he never saw anything coming.

"You know, at Le Bloc we said that no squat was so strong. It can swallow you and it can kill you. And *voilà*, Ludo was the proof of that. I could have wished for somebody else to have been led there, me being selfish. Unfortunately, this fell to him. For me, all those people"— the word that followed then was in a language unfamiliar to me; the man had Roma family, he'd come by way of Spain, and after that word picked up briefly in Spanish and, again, in French—"*basura*, rot, trash. They don't want you to climb up. They want you to stay with them, in their shit. And you get used. That's what happened with Ludo. But he didn't see anything, he didn't see anything coming, and he understood nothing. He was so obsessed with that door. Shit I say, wait. The doors to Le Bloc are not your career. Effectively, he kept an eye out for the entrances and exits."

I cut in. "They told me he was, somewhat, the night watchman."

"The what watchman? The what watchman?" In English, he said: "*Fuck off*." Continuing in French, he said: "Two hundred people can't keep their own night watch? It was he who thought that, who gave himself an importance that he never should have had. But he had such a need, maybe to feel loved, that I don't know, but love he had plenty of, with me, and with our friends in Nantes. See? That's what a shame it was. But that gets us into the complexity of the human animal where at a given moment you give him some importance. What is he going to do with that importance? For me, all I know is that for my part, I did my work to the letter. I had found the apartment. I had found the studio. We were supposed to return to Nantes and live out our buddy story to the letter. And unfortunately *voilà*. Life takes away, life takes away. *Alors pfft. Shhhhh.* They're not the only ones guilty. Him too. He didn't take care of himself. How many times did I take him to the dentist to redo his teeth. We don't know what he died from really, understand? What I mean to say is that he had a dental situation that was a catastrophe. And you know very well that, with teeth, there's a lot that goes with. If you don't eat. If you drink only *archi* strong alcohols. If all you do is smoke your *bong* somewhere it's disgusting, that's rotting, all black, and outside of that, what we got were good qualities. This was a fantastic guy. Nice. Seductive. I never saw him at a loss for ladies or for love, see. But I don't know what happened in this squat. I don't know. And I will never know. Understand that?

"All I know is that this squat stole from me my best friend. *Alors pfft.* So my apologies if I hold it against him or hold it against them. I don't know which is the more pathetic of the story. I got everything ready for him. I go, here it is, we've got the dough, here we are, the spot." In English he added: "*Come on let's go.*

"But he didn't go along with the thing," he continued in French. "What do you want me to tell you, my sweet.

"*Bah voilà*. This was really a good person. Obviously everyone loved him. Are you kidding. You couldn't hate him. This was a good guy, an honest guy. Clear. When he asked people to pick up their trash because it was getting disgusting, *euh*, he didn't do that to be in charge. It was just a matter of walking the hallways.

"*Bah voilà*, my beauty. What else do you want to know? That life is shit? That people are assholes?

"He could be somebody very comforting, as I can be at times. That's the reason we got to be friends. Because we were very much alike, in a number of things. Understand? *Mais, euh*. No no no, there are a lot of people who will add their own things, because at that time, I wouldn't say he was a star, maybe a star in the making, but—the book you'll write, it'll be me, when I'm dead. You'll see to what extent I had friends and to what extent as I speak with you today I don't have them. Nobody. Just people carrying on in a relationship with me for their own personal gain. Really personal. You want a thing? Write your thing. I'm here. It's not for nothing. Everywhere I go, it's not for nothing. My solitude is wild. But it's mine. Since then I got to be a strong man. Used to living with his solitude.

"You realize, it's like if somebody stole away your sister. Under the same circumstances. Would it make you happy to see these people, *ah nah nah ni, nah nah nah*. They wrote it all across their face and then you tell yourself, a band of assholes. That's not how it's written, not like that. You don't go, '*Rest in peace*,'" he said, saying those last three words in English. "Fucking sharks. I apologize for addressing you like this. I said, no no no. Pay for it with your soul. You're talking, and he's dead. Shut up. Live it. Don't take that path. Are we good?

"Very young. I don't know, baby. I think he must have been thirty-five, or thirty-six.

"We did for the sake of doing, smiling... I looked at Ludo, and he smiled back, you know. He's happy, I'm happy. That's how it is. See. It's nothing explicable. That's why I told you that this guy, for me, he was like my little brother. *Mais voilà bon...* It's no big deal, you know. Sometimes there are things that you're never going to be able to write. That me, I couldn't even paint them. You don't have time, and I get it, but downstairs there's my painting workshop, and I don't really feel like showing it to you, because time is short, you have things to do... *Enfin bon.* I knew he would've followed me, we could have gone *mais bon écoute.* You can never expect anything from anybody.

"It's like if somebody came to you and said, 'I love you.' Wow. You think those are the magic words? No. There's no word for it. You can never put a word to what's going on. And that's what went on between Ludo and me. We never said to each other, 'I love you.' But I look at you, you're dying laughing, day after day... and we walked the streets laughing all to ourselves. What do you want me to tell you. Sometimes it's not possible. You can't write it. Can't be written. All the most beautiful things that were our experience together. They get to be ridiculous, too easy. *Bon.* That going to work for you, you have enough?

"Don't thank me anymore. I'm going to have closed out your story with a beautiful love story."

The man, to tell me the story, had invited me to meet him in a suburb thirteen miles outside Paris. The house where we spoke belonged to another man, prominent in the Hell's Angels as my interview subject explained; my source was living in the unfinished basement. He encouraged me to "honor" the lady of the house, in whose home I was a guest, by making time to speak with her; she, however, lounging on a sectional with four freshly bathed children, another, older woman, and two dogs of two mean breeds, didn't reciprocate interest in either of us. I interviewed the man who wanted to be left anonymous in the quiet of a bedroom belonging to one of the children. It had wood floors and, nailed to a wall, skateboards served as shelving.

We sat at the desk, with its globe. Five and a half years had passed since Ludo's death. His friend flung open a window to smoke.

¶ *The Sixth Floor*

The room I then obtained was to the left of Marco's, which, directly below a governing *tonton*'s, had the same luxury of space. My room was about six feet by ten. It had been, before I moved in, vacant. Marco's custom was to leave a buffer against the noise that neighbors, being neighbors, made. A window showed the driveway at the side of the building. Over the summer a couple of the residents had headed out there carrying the fixings for a cookout: to a *leftover strip of city never intended to bring joy*, as I would write. Besides my notebooks and recorder I had brought carrot salad and a tub of hummus. There was a desk and, on it, a basket. I put my food in the basket. Occasionally I stopped by my house on the Rue de Crimée, getting my teaching things, and right away I would scramble eggs, craving hot food, and take a shower. When I left the little room I locked it with a chain, as I was told to do. The filmmakers would use it, too, by day to secure their equipment. Marco had left a futon as well as a padlock and a space heater. Casting about in the room that held so little I found a tube of sturdy cardboard and, in imitation of Jaouad's system, wedged it into the doorframe, where it fit.

I interviewed Marco La Mouche in his large room featuring a prize possession, the collection of linoleum tiles that he enticed the artists of Le Bloc to sign to him. He had returned many to their places after this improvement but had not returned all; he had left holes overhead.

Marco explained his importance at the squat by claiming that, while he would participate in making the decision to evict another squatter, he could never be himself evicted. He was a locksmith. Engendering debts, he did everyone's door (Marco said; around the squat, I saw mostly padlocks). He had a tag of his own, a stylized treble clef, which he sprayed on floors, never walls due to his hatred of disorder. Freedom began, in his opinion, with the throwing of a bolt. It was the power to lock oneself in. "I'm for equality," he said, asked about any politics he might have had. "I'm for justice. But life is unequal and the world is unjust."

I asked about the management of the squat, about conflict resolution, questions Marco construed as dealing with violence, the containment of violence. He answered at length, giving examples. A hypothetical situation he favored in formulating these examples was that of my own rape. He kept bringing it up. Such an eventuality was, in one example, as likely outside a squat as inside, human nature being what it was.

He had obtained a police report about Le Bloc. He asked me to guess what his son—on principle Marco did not bring him to Le Bloc—wanted to be when he grew up. Marco insisted that I guess. "The unimaginable."

I played along. "Not raves... Not locksmith... Not artist," I added, sucking up. "Baker? I don't know."

"He wants to be a cop."

I reacted with amazement, according to the tape I made, and that reaction may have been genuine; I don't remember.

"For the reason of a sweet utopia," Marco said. "In his opinion, police are there to serve and protect you."

"That's funny," I said in answer. "Because you can be a utopian for really any side."

When a squat couple fought, he would call her *bourgeoise*; the accusation flowed in that direction and most couples, at Le Bloc, were heterosexual in character. I did not think of this as interesting, a source of information. A white girl from a nice family, I had, at the squat and after, more of a concern about representation, that my work not advance in the reading any chauvinism of classism or racism. Still, despite these hazards of identity, the occupation as a form of political action was, I came to believe, powerful, elegant precisely for its simplicities and intensities of method (*I am here, with others and with our lives*) and demand (*I, and others here, deserve with our bodies to live*). A squat was achieved by placing one's body within it and staying, done by trading on the body, the body in its difference.

Marco came to my door in a towel. A drunk man had in the night breached my setup, easily shifting the cardboard tube. "Hey look," the drunk man had said, "there's a girl here." It had inconvenienced Marco to shoo him away, I had slept through this, Marco made a show of his exasperation. He went to find something I could use, from his room—a knife.

It was a butter knife.

Marco, the locksmith, rolled his eyes and, in demonstration, jammed the handle of the door.

It is a commonplace to say of intentional communities that within them the society from which they have supposedly withdrawn, the society with its problems, is reproduced in miniature. "It's the legislative elections of Le Bloc," Anastasia said. Marky, the Guianese man living on the fourth floor, had an *association* incorporated on the theme of furthering Guianese identity with which he intended to take over the squat's management. It seemed he thought the *tontons* had not done enough to forestall the eviction that was coming. What he planned to do, besides stay, was unclear, and among the squatters accustomed to going along with the *tontons* it was an item of gossip divulged in high-minded disapproval that Marky sowed false hope among Le Bloc's most vulnerable. Privately I passed judgment on the filmmakers for their prurience as they shot him going door-to-door, soliciting signatures—whether for a petition or to establish the organization's membership is, from the footage, uncertain. Marky, anyway, played to the cameras, casting glances that had something sheepish in them.

It was thought that the bombast of the Opéra opening would deter police from evicting Le Bloc outright. That might require closing major roads—Rue de Belleville, the Place des Fêtes—and dispatching hundreds of men. More likely, *tontons* thought, the electric company would receive instruction to cut off power to the squat. The police would have Le Bloc plunged into darkness. They would make it as cold as the street.

In other business, they still owed the lawyer some money.

"La Miroiterie has stayed as we are a long time," Vincent had said, heading up another meeting, meaning with a verdict to evict.

"They'll leave and I'll stay," Marky said now—wearing a blazer, carrying a folder.

He was shouted down; Vincent brought up fines payable by those named in the suit, as Marky was not.

"A little reminder," Marco La Mouche piped up, lounging in the wheelchair, "if you stop them from cutting it off inside, they cut it off outside, and if you stop them on the outside, they cut it off a little farther."

The Guianese theme of this *association* was no accident; when I interviewed him, Marky brought up colonialism naturally—"Everybody squatted Africa"—and just as he cast squatting rhetorically, in the service of his postcolonial critique, others at Le Bloc made the same turn in the service of a critique of inequality, or an ecological critique. "The earth was naked when we got here," Roberto, the Médecins du Monde activist, said to the cameras, an image evocative in French, with its feminine noun. "We all squatted it." The analogy suggested that even on the brink of eviction, squatting, to these men doing it, felt like power, arbitrary power.

A white guy living at Le Bloc was involved in La Petite Rockette, the collective of ex-squatters a couple of whom I'd interviewed about a *convention d'occupation précaire* they had obtained. They were moving up in the world, as the Bloc resident said around Le Bloc in those days. After having operated in the otherwise unused space the city had made available they were paying, now, a real rent. "To go from a squat to a precarious lease to renting a space, it's quite a beautiful experience," the squatter remarked. "For a lot of people I think it's seen as a model."

Getting to sleep I heard bangs, crashes. Cabinets were falling from their moorings on that hallway and, by the light of morning, stood quietly.

"Violence is always cowardly," Guy, in his office, remarked.

The filmmakers asked some of these squatters to reenact for their cameras quarrels that, naturally enough, arose. "I feel like I'm in prison," Caravaggio joked—under surveillance.

"You live on the side," said Jesus.

I interviewed the *tonton* Vincent, president of the *association* Le Bloc, over five hours during which he used a terrible machine atop a rolling cart to tattoo his own right thigh; he was right-handed.

In his official capacity he confirmed that *tontons* had looked into appealing the eviction before a European court, the grounds those of a French violation of the right to housing. They would have needed tens of thousands of signatures as well as the support of a nineteenth arrondissement official, or so they had concluded.

He preferred to place any hope he had in boys from the Place des Fêtes neighborhood, adolescents who in frequenting Le Bloc drew lessons from it, a "school." He confidently anticipated that people like these would, thanks to their experience of Le Bloc, open further squats, housing the needy.

Doudou, who was receiving instruction in giving tattoos, waxed nostalgic in recalling Le Bloc's early days. "I fell in love every five minutes," she said. "Each of us came here after a rupture of some kind": in employment, in a relationship.

Living and working in squats—Vincent painted, too— had altered his personal feel for time, which seemed, increasingly, ephemeral. He had seen some eight squats perish in five years. He sprayed his leg with disinfectant, wrapped it in cellophane, and left us.

Between floors two and three a man taking those stairs, going up, asked me where the exit was.

At Saint-Antoine Hospital there was a legal clinic. "Papers don't make you happy," Jaouad said, in the Métro. "Money doesn't make you happy," and yet we went, I with him.

Where we changed trains, at République, a man playing guitar was singing along apparently in Arabic; passersby had gathered in the tunnel. Jaouad stopped for us to stand a moment at the fringe they made of bodies and sang quietly, he smiled broadly, it was obvious he knew the song. Every few blocks he would ask someone else for directions, somebody new. Delighted to be out in the city, flattering me, requiring explanations as to why, again, I wouldn't marry him.

In the office with its eye chart he showed thick, frayed folders filled with documents in French and Arabic. He had come to France the previous year, as he told the lawyer, marrying a Frenchwoman for whose sake he had left behind his Moroccan family (seven brothers and sisters; he liked remembering nights out with friends lasting until daybreak, wedding parties). But they had divorced under messy circumstances, which Jaouad attributed to a racism indulged in by his in-laws, who were white.

The lawyer didn't like what she saw; Jaouad was missing the first page of one document, the last of another.

It took a long apprenticeship to develop expertise such as Jaouad had in Gnawa music; he made his instruments, explained songs with their corresponding stories, and from his music drew a feeling of security: he would always be able to earn a living. In those days he played in the Métro, played at a Moroccan restaurant. He worked occasionally at a shoe factory, unloading boxes. He showed the lawyer a binder of photos, some of his performances for he had been accepted at Le Bloc on the strength of his musicianship.

Marriage would not work in his favor, she said (leaving his artistry entirely to the side). Clearly he didn't live with the spouse, as one had to. In learning about his circumstances she was alarmed to hear that immigrants of such irregular status were living in a squat on the precipice of eviction. They had to get out of there. To Jaouad, she added: "Stop playing in the Métro. Don't get yourself arrested."

We exited into a night of neon bars, a woman holding an orange umbrella that read, in English, "Paris Bar Crawl." Another woman slumped in a doorframe, asking repeatedly for fifty cents. Ahead of us was the green Bastille pillar and its angel of metal.

In the Métro, Jaouad got a text: *Expulsion du Bloc le 6 decembre les gars.*

Eviction, December 6, a mass text. It was November 28.

Le Général told me in a hallway he'd gotten a commissariat on the phone and heard that date.

In another hallway Morgane, studying one of her grand formats, was clutching a bottle of Absolut vodka.

A mostly black painting, she was calculating as if whimsically the outside chance of finding any place to put it.

Puddles, lakes were forming in the hallways of the −1 with such an air of mystery I guessed the water of the −3, the −4 might perhaps have been rising through the basements, forming condensation.

In the third-floor room, a child: Valentin's son. "Don't ask direct questions," said Valentin, "he is a philosopher."

On the fourth a man unseen by me was singing, the stairwell accommodating his song so beautifully that I was stopped.

Le Général approved of my move to the sixth. "The closer you get to the sky, the better it is," he said.

Outside that room where I was staying a man prematurely gray was dismantling cabinets cheerfully. I recognized him, a friend of Marco's. He said the good French wood would be useful.

As I was filling an electric kettle in the third-floor bathroom a neighbor on that floor, a man I'd met just recently, came in to ask if I would bring him cups of tea or coffee. He had a guest. He followed me back down the hall to Valentin's, where the kettle went. He took a seat and spun.
  I gave him teabags, cups of plastic.
  He asked if I would also bring the water, when it was ready, and I said I would not be available. He could wait with me, if he liked, for the water to boil.
  "Everyone around here is mad today," he said. "It's the tension. Do you have anywhere to go after this closes?"
  I wondered if he did.
  "I'm still looking," he said, spinning. I asked if he had any friend to stay with. It was time to pour his tea and wrap plastic bags, all I had, around the crackling, buckling plastic cups so that he wouldn't burn his hands. Three times he asked if there was any sugar. At last he left.

"Those who have left cannot return," Marky told me. "I will not let them back in."

Marco La Mouche, on my return to the sixth, offered whisky, which I accepted only after ducking into my room to grab—I was *starving*—rice cakes and hummus. Those, however, Marco did not care for.

Marky, during meetings, began to stand up front, alongside the historic *tontons*. "This is a public building," he announced. "We are neither squatters nor robbers."

The filmmakers had three cameras going.

"Hygiene, hygiene, hygiene," Dominique the elder said, rising. "Don't let trash pile up. Don't use too much water."

The resident named Fred wanted to know if any provision was made for the cats that belonged to no one.

The leader of the housing-rights *association* Droit Au Logement, Jean-Baptiste Eyraud, nicknamed Babar, there for support, made a speech to the effect that while eviction in the middle of winter had come to seem normal, it was not. He shouted, taking off his glasses. He spoke of fatalism, the degradation of the building.

"But to close without resisting it is stupid," Anastasia, standing, said.

Fred had been an engineer. If power were cut, he said, any attempt to hook it up again would be life-threatening.

Valentin got to his feet and, before the crowd, proposed they all, at his count, throw open every window to send paper airplanes sailing out. Accompanied by blaring trumpets: an image for any interested media.

To this meeting Marky had invited a guest speaker: clergy of Charisma, a megachurch, as subsequent research would suggest, in the Parisian suburb Blanc-Mesnil, Seine-Saint-Denis, where it served many immigrants from parts of Africa and the Antilles. Congregants came with. Marky introduced the Black pastor, who stood. "It's not up to Hollande," he told the room. "It's not up to the state. Your faith can make the choice, this time, about eviction."

Dominique the elder was on his feet, taking the relay. "Think of this place you live in," he said, almost angrily, "the walls—the people who made them were fighting for something... You have this on your shoulders... There's not only your little *guitars* and *paintings*, which will end up, *we all hope*, in a museum." People got to their feet, cheering. "In Paris," Dominique went on, "there are homes open still. La Miroiterie!" he shouted. "La Miroiterie!"

Anastasia and Vincent each called out in turn they'd host sign-painting parties in their workshops.

"We must be in Technicolor," cried Dominique, waving his arms.

Churchmen formed a circle. Residents were lingering, some joining in as these believers began singing. "Be glorified," they sang, a command that in French ends on a vowel amenable to lifting. And the man preached in the dim light. To twenty of them, who were holding hands. Rapidly he spoke, speech punctuated by the fast refrain "Eternal Father." "Eternal father this place belongs to no government this place belongs to your children... This building will believe what you want it to Eternal Father ... If you don't take care of them Eternal Father they will be in the street for capitalism is the world today... Life has only just begun there are no old people here Eternal Father for the life is with you Papa... Here there is only love Eternal Father... This place is a miraculous place Eternal Father... Take it back for your children... There are no impure thoughts here Papa... Your children here deserve forgiveness... The Assemblée judges them Papa but you don't judge them."

Calls of *amen* sounded, claps.

Jaouad approached, spoke through a bad mood. "When I open my heart to someone, I don't do it lightly."

I sat against the wall, pulling in my knees.

A young girl, the charge of one of the Charisma

congregants, with no one to play with ran over the stage, losing her breath. The hollow structure amplified her step.

I went up so we were the same height. She had used to have glasses like mine. They had broken. "What do you talk like?" she asked.

"A foreigner," I said.

Light had become unreliable in Anastasia's workshop. But the cables being stripped were phone and internet, a *tonton* would assure her. "I can only protect my territory," she said, the smell of incense deepening as she put on music, gathered trash, and swept. She swept the floors. She had whitewashed those walls, closing windows, painting over.

Her music, that voice was Alexei Khvostenko's. He had quit Moscow in the seventies, a dissident, for the squats of Paris. "Anarchist, alcoholic, artist, bard, painter, surrealist, director," Khvostenko was another of the dead. In life he had belonged, for Anastasia, to "a kind of phantom underground."

In that day's work she was emphasizing packing tape. She had clipped papers to a clothesline (a black-and-white drawing of a babushka, a QR code) and could take them all in case of sudden flight.

Entropy—a theme of hers.

Say you have a bookcase, she went on. With old stuff, your administrative papers, cigarette butts, bad books for which you have no use. Clean it out, it gets that way again.

Like the squat, I said, a little obviously.

There were people she didn't know, bums, camping out on the -1, leaving their beer cans. "I don't know anyone anymore," she said.

She brought up her childhood, a foreigner's childhood.

She spoke Russian with an accent. Speaking it she was a girl, and yet there was a part of her she could not share in French.

Overnight the Soviet girl would find she had no country of her own and in the wake of this, her "first eviction," would make herself over, into a "French foreigner." "Then punks, squats, art..." Her first training was in applied art. Anastasia learned restoration, able to update the frescos of churches understood she was no artisan, went back to school. She liked what she was learning there, "a kind of applied psychoanalysis."

While a student, living in a squat at the age of twenty-two, the age I had just been, on the same day that one of her grandmothers died, Anastasia became pregnant. What she wanted was to be a bum and not live in a house.

Anastasia's mother moved back to Russia.

"Mademoiselle," Anastasia said the French doctor said, "there is a heart that is beating." She understood that something had gone wrong.

Her sister, younger, was enrolled at an elite Parisian university, she would become a journalist, a commentator. Anastasia delivered a son. She considered her feelings, her positioning, to be in contrast to her sister's; she felt right within exclusion, in the "cabinet" of her Bloc workshop, in the larger world feeling that she lacked the tools to communicate her thoughts, politics. This thinking was, even it, "on the order of intuition."

"I find I don't give much," she added as I took that down. "I'd like to have the strength to give more."

During an event at her son's school she'd seen the mayor of the nineteenth arrondissement in person and felt limits of her own: she didn't know what to say, exactly, on whose behalf to make Le Bloc's case. "I'm a novice in the squats," she said.

So was I—I rushed to assure her.

"I'm not a politicized squatter," she said.

Candles had melted down this time to shells, took turns to gutter out. She lifted, tilted one it to give a light. She spoke of middleware, a concept from computer programming picked up thanks to an interest of the child's. A layer separated any two worlds. The French underground was a catch-all. "Between dream and waking, between joy and sadness, beginning and ending, that's where you go."

She was using incense to spread the thriving fire, helping its transfer from candle to candle. She brought over and plugged in a huge square spotlight. I had so much light to write by.

Someday her baby sister would be dealt a reckoning by the system she loved, which ate her up, and on that day, Anastasia reasoned, Anastasia might be of use to her.

In her workshop that evening she spoke, eventually, about her epilepsy. These episodes, aftereffects of a car hitting her in adolescence, a strike that at the time had occasioned stitches in her forehead, came over her with no special frequency after drinking, after taking drugs; they happened, instead, on clear mornings, most recently that of the squat's hearing. Five minutes, that time. A feeling came over her in the way of an orgasm, so intense it was painful, a full-body sneeze. She thought dying might feel that way. So she came to: eyes black, teeth plastic, son at home, unremembering. *La pauvre*, her parents always said, take medicine. For many years she tried. This was a cliché, but she required the experience of sorrow, as she called it, to feel joy.

"*Voilà*," she said. "I've drunk Bordeaux and told you everything."

She rose, turning up a Russian poem Xeroxed onto filler paper. She gave me this, the copy of a poem that I could not read. "Still, it's funny, this departure without head or tail. We're here, *voilà*, and we know we should get lost."

Nails stuck out of a black felt hat; Anastasia set it on a tube of plastic wrap and held up the assemblage to the light. "To be or not to be!"

All around were bottles of acetone, a wooden barrel blackened, collapsed with age. A box with thumb-sized paint tubes. A pillbox filled with nails. On a wall, cross-section diagrams, a human arm. Images as if of thumbprints. Terracotta mask, pursed lips. On an end table, a chess set in its box: "I could keep everything or leave everything," she said.

Singing along to Khvostenko she took three poles and propped them together, using a clamp, tulle. Khvostenko couldn't take care of his children. For his art he had, by night, to stay up until five, as she said without judgment: their mothers did it. She brought up the wife of a squatter we both knew, the squatter American, his woman who'd taken a vow to spend the year of Le Bloc speaking in gestures. Compromise had happened to Anastasia, though she loved her son.

She went to bed at midnight, ate well. In using glue to harden clothes she modeled a hallucination she'd experienced while sick in bed at three years old. She joined me to pour out M&Ms, positioning among them tampons and a rubber band, at the table opened wine I'd brought, not the Bordeaux.

"You must dare to do it," she said. "These are the last days, but you have all the maturity that you can bear. In my work it's in this phase I am most aligned with my environment. All the past is there already, things have their stories."

She mentioned a person, Camille, who had lived at Le

Bloc and filmed its beginnings.

Someone else told me a *tonton* obtained by threatening Camille that Camille's filming cease.

"You need time to feed the thing," Anastasia was telling me, "and that goes the same for everyone."

A dusty cat came to us, raising its tail.

"Oh," she cooed to it, "the cats, the cats, they know that it's the end, what will become of them, the cats, they are exhausted."

That night I caught a glimpse of Anastasia in the third-floor room of Valentin's, taking a shot of holy water from the screw-top bottle on the shrine.

¶ The Police Report

"'Prefecture of Police. Commissariat Report,'" Marco La Mouche read. "*Nah nah nah*. 'The persistence of serious, recurring disturbances of public tranquility and risks for the safety of people in and around the squat...'"

He skipped ahead. "'The building initially had been settled by artists, for them to use it as workshops and as exhibition space for their creative work.'" He interrupted himself. "So far," he said, "it's niiiiiice.

"'The number of occupants was, then, limited. And the squat was not intended for habitation, not at the outset. The squat thus can be regarded with a certain benevolence. However, with the onset of winter, the first squatters soon allowed entry to a steady trickle of occupants with more diverse profiles, come in search of a place to live.'

"So that means it's cold and we give people a place to live. Well, that's not... *pft*." Marco looked back at the document before us, which looked authentic enough, and continued to read it aloud as I taped him.

"'According to our information, the squat in this way took in homeless, marginal people, and notably individuals identifying with the "Rasta" trend, who progressively settled the other parts of the vast building.

"'Often under the influence of alcohol and other intoxicants, these new occupants made a huge racket until very late at night, yelling, listening to music, and playing the tam-tams'"—a term colonizers had used and still, apparently, favored in referring to the West African djembe.

"Oh my god," I said in English.

"I play percussion," Marco said, "and I've never played tam-tams in this building. In the basements, yes. Well.

"'Frequent violent brawls took place as well, as the

neighbors can attest. Police quite obviously were not called by those concerned.

"'Young women, introduced by a spokesman of the squatters as very free-spirited American tourists, also took up residence at the squat, putting into circulation a rumor of prostitution.'"

At that I stopped taking dictation. A friend of his came in, and Marco snatched away the document. No commissariat would speak to its contents. The police would not, put technically, respond to a request for comment. As a means of authentication I was left with my own apprehension of this text's similarity, in its themes, to the landlord's themes, after the removal of the very most outright racism (the Rastas and their tam-tams) and misogyny (the whorish American girls) to the case of the state. The document's fixation on, repeatedly evoked, large numbers of drunks is taken up by the judge, in the order for Le Bloc's eviction.

¶ *58–62 Rue de Mouzaïa, the Nineteenth Arrondissement of Paris, France, December 3–6, 2013*

I found Valentin and Anastasia in her workshop in those days when the first thing asked by anyone, throughout the squat, was if you had a place to go. To a pile of blocks that was an eviction totem, topped by a placard that read "NO," Anastasia had added a cutout from a magazine—"Jacqueline," it read—slicking it on with glue. A chalky high note rose from the cassette deck as Valentin, using the mute, played along, and Anastasia excused herself from conversation by speaking of an impulse to create. The protest banner would not let her interest wane. Out of wood, she cut a house, excising a rectangle to make a door, and draped it with a chain and padlock. She gave me a table patchy with paint, fruit of her excavation. "It weighs nothing," she said.

She sat on Valentin's lap. He played quick runs, stock ominous, used the wrong end of the mouthpiece to uncork a bottle of wine as she shook out a sack of oranges to free the netting. She pinned that up decoratively. To me, the Russian they used with each other sounded sardonic, almost snarling, I thought for the reason of a contrast between it and French.

Dominique, the older one, joined us full of hope. He was holding a press release put out by Droit Au Logement in a show of solidarity with Le Bloc's cause.

"An end-of-the-world scenario," said Anastasia. "We've seen everything."

The lapsed philosopher in joining us saw Anastasia's house and lost it. "We should get all the lovers who hang their locks on the Pont des Arts to secure Le Bloc instead."

Sprawled as if disassembled in a hallway, in an armchair, lay a clochard—alcoholism in his face, wild gray hair—sleeping. I thought I'd seen him before, outside at the Place des Fêtes. Some squatter had draped a fleece blanket around his body.

On waking I looked out: satellite dishes, a radio-relay tower, and, far off, a forest. In the hallway stalled a shopping cart of empty liquor bottles. In the stairwell I opened a door that came off its hinge and hung stupidly.

Downstairs Luís, the Spanish vagabond, stopped me to deliver a piece of news. The eviction was canceled.

I found Guy in his office. Dominique was there, too, like Guy brimming with good cheer. He gave me a hug. "I was so sick of losing, losing, losing all the time." He was opening his mouth to smile, beaming, shaking his gray head softly. "I didn't sleep." He coughed, laughing. "I didn't sleep all night, I packed my bags, I was all ready. I got myself used to it."

Guy, laughing too, was texting his writing workshop regulars to share the news: Droit Au Logement and Médecins du Monde had prevailed in a heated negotiation on Le Bloc's behalf, which had gone on through the night, looping in the minister of housing. "That means we're credible. *N'importe quoi*. It's too good, really it's too good. Oh we have our work cut out for us, we really have our work."

In that hallway music rose, competing strains. The flautist was wandering.

"For once, we can say it's as if victory has gone to the righteous," Guy said as if in wonder. "For once, victory to the righteous, a thing we've never seen."

"Good news or bad, I'm not sure," a squatter at Reception

said, cutting points out of the ends of silver ribbons.

I WANT TO KEEP MY FRIENDS INSIDE WHERE IT'S WARM read one placard. Valentin wore a sprig of pine in a buttonhole and transferred it gallantly to my left lapel.

Droit Au Logement came with cowbells, a banner. "We *Bloc* evictions," their leader said, riffing into a megaphone, "that's pretty good." Sympathizers came alone or in groups—Communist Party members, a city politician—stamping feet and lighting cigarettes against the cold. A TV crew. A Jeudi Noir activist who had criticized Caravaggio—sharply; I had him on the record—told me when asked of his stance against the eviction of any building if work wasn't planned and another, against eviction in winter.

The route was my walk home, along the park. Our crowd of a few dozen soon unspooled to reveal dancers, a ragged drumline, flutes. A wordless song, call and response. Jaouad played krakebs, heavy iron castanets, and sang; Guy, solemn, drummed on an empty water keg. A man wearing a clown nose was juggling adroitly with one hand.

Morgane held an especially large sign: *WITH LE BLOC LAST TIME WE TRIED OPÉRA WHERE WILL WE BE NEXT?*

Singing, the group spilled onto a square before the arrondissement mayor's office. Out of the building came a wedding party, and the newlyweds paused before the protesters, who with much joy improvised a concert in their honor.

"You know, you have the right to protest," Anastasia told her son. "It is a citizen's right." He gave the locked house a heave, finding the beat.

To me he conceded, shyly, that the day was beautiful,

and that he did feel like stopping at a nearby McDonald's.
WINTER TRUCE FOR ALL, a banner read.

Audience was granted; only five protesters could go. There was, among the assembly, disagreement as to who did: a *tonton* and a Christian squatter, Médecins du Monde, the Droit Au Logement leader, Dominique the elder; yells from our crowd had it this selection, white men exclusively, was racist. The point was made that it didn't represent the artists.

One of the filmmakers climbed to the top of a bus shelter, getting a shot.

"We were into the idea of letting it die," one of the squatters told me privately.

Music went on: the drums, a tuba, the trumpet, Valentin red in the face. Buses pulled up, nosed away. In the facing strip of Buttes-Chaumont Park, a digger was working, scooping dirt.

Tontons, emergent, said the arrondissement mayor, needing to read up on the issue, had asked them to come back the next day, December 5.

"We're not going anywhere!" Dominique the elder cried.

Babar, the Droit Au Logement leader, said the mayor was actually personally unsure whether an eviction would be happening on the sixth. "It's a psychological war," he said then, to applause.

By the time we returned to the squat the optimism of that morning had spent itself. The rumor was dead. There was, on the ground floor, conflict: a slamming of palms on walls, stand of metal toppling.

I heard yells, and: *There's no art here. Only parasites. Who are the people who come and sleep on the ground floor, on the –1, these were meant to be common spaces.*

Those people come to steal, I heard. *They don't come to meetings.*

A bailiff arrived eventually, delivering an eviction memo for every defendant. Two days remained to Le Bloc. Anastasia accepted Valentin's on his behalf, calling herself his woman or his wife.

Night fell, and a Christian squatter, one of the believers, swept me with him into Marky's room. We were going to pray. The Charisma churchman, having returned with a half-dozen congregants, young men, led them in their song, forming a ring of bodies that the squatter and I, it became clear, were to complete.

"So," the pastor said, silencing his men, addressing the Christian squatter: "You have received a letter that says you will be evicted tomorrow, you, her, all of you."

"All of this, and all this work, will be over," the squatter said heavily.

Things happening did so, alas, as the result of God's will, the pastor said; for instance, his own mother-in-law, or perhaps his godmother, had died a few weeks previously. "You will be evicted if God wills it."

For me, he had a question. He asked if I believed in heaven or hell.

I was not very religious.

I, too, would die one day.

Another song broke out, and for an instant, on hearing the lyric "We are all fishermen," *pêcheurs*, I was delighted by the earthy metaphor, and then I realized the word of course was *pécheur*, sinner.

The air trapped within Marky's homemade recording studio, which filled half the room, grew warm as the pastor conveyed Charisma's will to undertake an evangelical mission at Le Bloc.

The squatter said amiably that it wasn't just up to him, but as far as he was concerned that would be fine.

They prayed for the squatter's ex-girlfriend. Fervent, they prayed for my soul.

At my side, the squatter ventured a question. "Don't you want to do a prayer for the building?"

"We don't need to pray. If God wills it, you'll leave tomorrow, and if not, if God wants you to stay, we'll come back."

I was so tired; I'd slept nine hours without meaning to. The trees in view of the little window were yellow, no leaf fallen. The day, sunny. Fine, stretched clouds suggested in their dispersion the vastness of the sky and, with it, possibility. A shed roof rippled with water.

In the stairwell, lights were out. Treads of the stairs had worn off.

In the windows of the −1 a man I didn't recognize was harvesting bamboo, still tall and verdant in the atrium. It was full, thick with leaves despite the season. Stepping around the disco ball he sawed down plants, below his boots trampled fallen stalks of them, the sounds he made like mastication.

I sat, taking notes at Reception as the squatters came downstairs carrying suitcases, space heaters. Courtney, a Jamaican man I'd met on the fourth floor, joined me. We spoke English together, naturally. A lot of guys on the fourth floor were in his position: undocumented, with no place to go. He had a theory of his own about the impending eviction. It was in retribution for the noise of the protest the day before: for that dissent it was punishment.

Luís, similarly, pointed out we had only the *tontons*' word that eviction approached. He suspected it to be an inside job, a plot to shake off all but their closest followers. He clasped my hands in his, said he found me honest. He hoped to reach me from a call shop, but in call shops he was often followed. "Life is hard," he said in parting. "Don't let them manipulate you."

In that day's *Le Parisien* a half-page spread devoted to Le Bloc and its eviction showed in full color the building's façade and, bright with graffiti, some hallway.

At Reception, a Senegalese squatter was hanging a poster advertising a party in that country's tradition to take place at Le Bloc that very night. To Le Général and me he said all were welcome, and that the Senegalese ambassador would be there.

The light of day intensified, the city's trees casting shifting shadows on the building. A big painting came downstairs, hitting each stair.

I wondered what had happened with the arrondissement mayor. I found Big Vincent in his room on the fifth floor, which he didn't plan to pack. Everything there would stay, he said grandly.

Sounds wafted our way, a fight. He opened his window to hear and rushed downstairs, leaving me with the chairs that had been his, the table, couch, beer cans, instant coffee, cups, laundry detergent, a scattering of eggshells. The lamp with a wrinkled shade.

Out in the hallway a man I recognized was doing something weird to a terrarium of mice. Lavender paint ringed their container in fat loops, still wet; more paint on the floor spelled out BLOC. That squatter and another who was helping him lifted the mice by their tails one at a time, transferred them to a metal vat, and set them, trailing straw, onto the circle of floor. Each mouse, apparently unsure what to do with its freedom, at last breached the barrier, getting paint on its back, dragging paint, becoming a comet. "This building is still occupied!" cried the man whose mice they'd been. "They can multiply as much as they wish and in that way they will remain."

McFly was spraying tags everywhere, hearts, his own name, *QUE DU BONHEUR, MERCI AU BLOC.*
NOTHING BUT BLISS, THANK YOU BLOC.

On the fourth floor, where admittedly I hadn't spent much time (not having, either, lavished time on the first, second, or seventh floors), I interviewed a man named Bobo quickly, amidst packed bags. Dreadlocked, he did identify as Rastafarian; sharing a link to an online shop, he spoke of his work to peddle posters, other artifacts of that movement. Having previously lived in the Netherlands, he thought he might return there. "I thought the Winter Truce existed, but it doesn't exist," he said.

Another man, Soula, had worked at Le Bloc for two months; a music producer, he used a room there as a studio, from time to time spending the night.

Rarely had I gone door-to-door and done a survey. That week, however, knowing everything would end, I'd prepared a list of clear, basic questions, and I thought I might try and talk to everybody. Quiet loomed in the hallway, decorated to my eye like an American frat house with its weight bench, with a curtain of wooden beads.

An artist, Ousmane, who'd lived at Le Bloc since March, was busy taking out the trash. "I don't know where to go," he said. "If they put us outside, we'll be outside." Those of them whose visa status was irregular kept to themselves, he offered, and most, by then, had left.

At 4:30 p.m. a bailiff served a fresh set of papers, one letter for every defendant, all stating police would arrive the next morning at 7. Le Général accepted the letters on behalf of those absent, making remarks about them. Valentin's name was called, and Le Général offered a character sketch for the evident pleasure of sketching: "On the other hand, he drinks vodka." He found an opening to introduce me. "My journalist," he said.

Reception teemed with people talking, laughing. "You need a megaphone," the bailiff said in irritation.

McFly, in the throes of a directionless aggression, was raising a revolt, smashing something. I looked over and saw the first doors shattered. "I am *protecting*," he screamed, "my *concept*."

The others worked to calm him.

I helped Valentin carry down a table and some chairs from the third floor. He was making trips using a shopping cart to Anastasia's apartment.

Cardboard boxes piled, marked in black and yellow for disposing biohazards, found onsite and being used in the big move.

A photographer wandered, snapping. Squatters swapped numbers. Living in one building, they'd had no need to call.

I had been meaning to interview a man living on the second floor whom I anticipated being unable, after eviction, to reach. A neighbor of his had referred me. What intrigued the neighbor were distressing vocalizations, salvos of a nightmare or waking nightmare about—the neighbor's example—US American helicopters.

San Wrtel, the strange name he guided me in spelling,

came from a rich Parisian family that, in his telling like the "system," never helped. For two and a half years he slept by the Seine, pitching a tent. He made music and sculpture. "As long as one has no apartment, no home of one's own, one cannot create," he said, and in his room there was no sculpture or other creation, instrument or sign of music.

In fact the room was bare, apart from a thin mattress. Dim, red lamps lit it like an incubator. San's face twitched expressively. He lived off the RSA. Asked what he did with his days he spent them in wait, even then, for the system to fall. At his side were a duffel bag and backpack, packed.

Jean-Luc, in a hallway, implored me to show in my book how the state had acted, wrongly, leaving behind its own records of children, the agency's archives, to rot. He recalled repainting walls; France had left the building in poor shape. "It was a beautiful flower, and then it reached maturity, and the leaves fell off," he said. "We should have taken photos when we got here."

Word spread that Ludo would have wanted all of them to take their leave of the building, given its condition.

Outside the rooms where Anastasia worked, she kissed my cheeks goodbye. "Farewell, Jacqueline." The artist, elegant in hiking boots, had slung stuffed bags across her back. From one hand dangled a totem, her creation. In the other was a pole, a walking stick. "I will not be back. Farewell, Le Bloc."

In her absence the workshop's doors within their bank of cabinets looked like all the others, blank.

The Italian boys had vanished. Where had they gone?
"Be careful here tonight," Guy told me. "People will come in, run through, try to take the last things, and be very drunk."

Anastasia's workshop—I looked back—was dark. So was Valentin's room on the third floor. Someone, Valentin maybe, had taken the padlock, unscrewing to remove and take even the metal it latched onto.

Bangs sounded like cabinets having taken flight. Past me ran McFly, sweatshirt coming open to show winding lines, a tattooed chest.

On the sixth floor, doors had broken out. A property of the frosted glass was its profusion of fault lines. Smashed, these doors shattered into fragments like jagged sugar cubes, the green translucent. They lay in piles, in floes.

A strong memory of childhood in Connecticut overtook me, a happy memory. Walking over broken glass in boots felt like crunching road salt on a snow day.

On the ground floor, I ducked back into Guy's office. Wine and sandwiches were being shared among the artists in attendance. "They burn it behind them," he said.

"The squat is a laboratory of wickednesses," Guy said, and yet, as they fell to playing again, vocalized I thought sympathetically with Le Bloc, rapping on the water keg. "Eviction," he riffed, voice reedy, whiny. "Everyone outside... eviction tonight."

Another of them playing plastic pail.

Guy closed his eyes softly, shaking his head. With percussion, he said, no need to do anything quick, complicated. Better a simple rhythm, one that breathes.

Another squatter sang along in Spanish, her language.

On the −1, in the concert room, a ceremony was taking place. It was a Baye Fall ritual, of the Senegalese Muslim sect. The men of the community, their shoes off, circle single file, counterclockwise, letting their echoing voices meld, join. They bring up their hands like a DJ trying to hear. The chant was repetitive, lulling. Gray paper covered the floor. Off to the side, women draped in shawls minded plastic plates of madeleines.

A real marabout, their leader, was on the scene. I would hear he was very well regarded. I got his number so that I might describe the sight with, after some follow-up, cultural sensitivity, and left it.

At 10:30 p.m. Le Général, in his office, told me with satisfaction that a journalist had been there, *Libération* had sent her, spending an hour. Rubber bands piled on the desk. He shot one at the wall. "I used to do that all the time as a kid," he said. To passersby he introduced me, his biographer. He played a radio segment from that morning, a report on Le Bloc, and shared out a tray of cheap sushi. Guy was interviewed. We heard him say musicians at Le Bloc were relegated to the −2.

Le Général didn't really have a "political culture," he mused. He was not, for example, an anarchist. His was "a world apart."

A clock I couldn't see was ticking, packed. My tape began.

Briefly he spoke of logistics: his prison term earlier that year, monthly handout, identity card (of his he had only a photocopy, for some reason, showing me), a bank statement (a few hundred, happy to have). He described a mechanism for an international transfer of money subject to no customs duties.

"You're interested in the sharing economy," I said politely.

"No," he said, "it's the real economy. It's a parallel economy, because it's not declared. You live between the two. You live only in little interstices into which you can slide. I don't know how I can explain this to you any better...

"I got out of prison April 13. Normally we should have been just doing parties. The artists wanted to do artistic stuff. They wanted to make an association. So why didn't they do it? It's up to artists to do the association, it's not up to me who's just out of prison... So, we'll all have reference people. For art, music, et cetera. But afterwards, people forgot they had lives. They have artists' lives. If you play music you have to practice. Waiting around like this in an office is complicated if you're an artist, a musician, a painter..."

"It's complicated for everybody."

"No. For me, it's not. It's simple. You see what I mean? So because they found somebody who could be there, they could do their thing. Little by little they erased themselves... As for me, I don't feel like shutting myself up in an office, even if I like it well enough. For three months no one's visited this office. No one comes to talk, to squat the office... I'm not a specialist in cultural projects," he said finally. "Art doesn't speak to me at all. Music, still less...

"*Voilà.* We've stopped with the monthly fee. So the lawyer won't get anything. Not until the state gives her the legal aid. Seven times eight, she'll get five hundred euros. On top of the fifteen hundred she's got already. See? All good. A small job, it didn't make her sick. We're not thieves. Nor are we killers. We're nice people all the same, don't you think, Jacqueline? You know, sometimes I feel like, sometimes you have, because people can give you funny looks. I'd like to run a simulation for them, *Hostel*, you know. It's an American film, I think. It takes place in Bulgaria or Romania, I forget where. Two American students, they decide to go off and have fun with some pretty Eastern girls... Except there's one, he wakes up the next morning... And they kidnap people, rich people, *bah* they kill Americans. That's the story. But afterwards, there's the plot of the film. One gets away and so on. People have fantasies about places like this. Squats are druggies, people shooting up, people drunk as others lie around on the floor. It's not that, as you've noticed. Drunks, there are a few. From time to time they yell... Truth is, today, it's a mess. But you see, today is an exception. We're out of here tomorrow morning at seven. But this isn't one of those squats you see in American movies."

I got a call. Another woman who slept at Le Bloc had to tell me that a third woman, like me a foreigner, was suffering for fear of what the night might bring. The woman on the phone wanted to know if I would go and talk to the other foreign woman; possibly the Frenchwoman was leaving under some constraint of time, catching a ride. Multifaceted, prismatic negotiations like this were typical, even constitutive, of Le Bloc, routine; though I rarely took note of any, I explained this one to Le Général for the tape to capture. I said I'd be back.

"I'm here until seven," he said, "and there will be no one else to come and see me."

At Reception there was some commotion. The fluorescents were ablaze, lobby strewn with bulging backpacks, the odd acoustic guitar. In this gathering a rumor had been traveling that cop cars were pulling up already.

"I don't feel like fighting battles from which I know the soldiers will flee." Jean-Luc was leaning on an umbrella. "I see their plan of attack." He pointed here and there.

Another squatter read on a cellphone that Nelson Mandela had died. The death, of a lung infection at the age of ninety-five, nevertheless offered, in the opinion of at least two of the squatters, a crazy as if fated correspondence with Le Bloc's eviction.

At Reception or elsewhere, I did reassure the other foreign woman that I, too, would stay the night, as I remember; most often I neglected to keep records of such gestures of my own.

On the third, the water wouldn't come on. Sinks had shattered in one of the bathrooms. On the floor lay their ceramic shards. In another, the bowl of a toilet was filled with spinach leaves.

Across walls ran more tags of McFly's. *QUE DES BONNES RENCONTRES*, a nicety so fatuous that it is hard to translate. *ONLY PLEASANT ENCOUNTERS, NICE RUN-INS ONLY.*

I asked Marco if I could leave my writing on a ceiling tile for him, and he gave me one, half-covered in white paint. I sat with it, unsure what to write, fibers of the tile clinging to my jeans.

Practicing in my notebook, I copied from memory a few sentences of work-in-progress that I thought I could shrink to size: *Those who live in Paris are famously ambivalent about their city. Some monuments make them cringe. The joke goes: the best view is the one from Montparnasse Tower, because it is the view without Montparnasse Tower. Those who hate the Eiffel Tower say the same thing about it.*

But I worried Marco might take this the wrong way.

On the third floor his friend was carrying off cabinet

doors.

Also on that floor Valentin had left behind a length of lace, a box of matches, phone books dating to the sixties, Russian paperbacks, a shell, a leek, and, among these other items, a clipping from a magazine showing an onion dome below a bright blue sky. On the table: a pencil sketch, convincing, of a friend of Valentin's I recognized. On a wall: drawings, winged red figures.

In hallway after hallway lights were out. Ceiling tiles missing, films of lights all peeling, laying bare the bulbs.

They held up X-rays to the light in Marco's room, appreciating their look. Marco bragged he'd gotten them from the hospital by explaining that he was a locksmith.

As for my tile, I had, with relief, reached a decision: to write something about my writer's block. But, casting about, I saw the only marker available was white, like the tile.

Around me they were asking to hear again their favorite parts of Le Bloc.

On the ground floor, the people who'd thrown the party for Senegal were loading wooden planks with paper plates heaped high. Spiced meat and potatoes, salad, bread: they offered the food around freely, to all. Pairs of men were carrying, joyfully, each of the planks, which were surely, I reflected an hour or two later, cabinet doors.

At 2:45 a.m. I found Caravaggio with Le Général in his office, rubber bands littering the hallway just outside. Le Général was zipping up garment bags as, for Caravaggio, Opéra came to mind. "Imagine the parties we could've done in the safes." Le Général unfolded a blueprint of Le Bloc's −3, lines fine as a spiderweb's.

I asked Caravaggio where we'd put the car batteries, which was something of an inside joke. He replied, laughing, they'd put any American out front.

Le Général pointed out a shopping bag: he had a lock in there, ready for the next squat.

They talked over empty buildings. Oan and Oan's mother were "on vacation," Le Général said.

In Caravaggio's own view he'd made a difference in Parisian history. He was going into business for himself, sick of "social work" he told me. He would miss the people, he would come back and help them, but between prison and the squat he confessed he'd done "a lot" of living "in community."

In the hallway now darkened by writing, by tags, keyboards lay on a table. Beyond it was a heap of green glass, a broken door, on which a fire extinguisher lay *almost legibly*, I wrote. It was 3:30 a.m.

I found myself again in Le Général's office, where there were black feathers on the floor. Caravaggio was gone. For the two of us, Le Général reconstituted Nescafé.

I loved it. "The last coffee before the end of the world!"

"The end of the world, the end of the world..." Le Général rolled his eyes. "And if it really were the end of the world—can you imagine?

"I am going to industrialize the process," he added. "I am going to train people with the single goal of opening and animating a place."

He mentioned deaths he'd witnessed as a boy. He got up and, in the hallway, used the fire extinguisher to squirt some passersby.

I started the tape.

"I don't know what I told you," Le Général said.

"You just told me that you had an early acquaintance with death."

"The earlier you get to know death, the earlier your mind takes into account a certain reality of life. That's my opinion."

"What was your experience of death? We've already spoken about it. You were eleven or something."

He sighed. "What can I have said? *Bah* there was my neighbor who was shot at... my other neighbor who killed himself, threw himself out a window. My next-door neighbor got a mail bomb."

A man came to the open door. "Hi, I'm looking for a room? Are there any rooms left?"

Le Général told him, evidently a friend, to piss off.

The interview went on.

"Ludo had another life. With us he had a new beginning. It's often like that."

Muffled on my tape, a crash of metal.

"Always a nice word to say, always of service," Le Général continued. "He was a little insomniac, so it worked out for him to keep the night watch."

A whistle.

"It was really a few weeks after Oan was born," I said a little stupidly, feeling myself to have been ambulance-chasing, "and so it's like that, life, death, everything changes..."

"*Bah oui*, life's like that. It's not sad. Suddenly it is sad, it's funny. You have someone who's there, who plays a part in your everyday and suddenly he's not there. See, that's how I see things. But we've had so many friends around us disappear from one day to the next that it can be a little normal, sometimes—

"But don't take it! It's missing one, a little end—"

A man in the hallway was saying something about

staying another year. I got up, too, leaving the tape on.

His friends had been upending tables, doors, a bookcase to make out of the hallway an arena in which they could be pelted, each, with scraps of wood, rubber bands, paint cans. Laughing, they ducked behind the furniture and coughed. The extinguisher was again engaged, drippings tracing the walls busy with tags.

Le Général fired off a round of rubber bands, aiming for the nearest ears and pelvises. "Sleep and you're dead," he called out. He tossed a dart that stuck thwack in a baseboard; he upended a wooden statue of a woman and a box of DVDs, their cases cracking, whispering. He ducked into the office, panting. "This is the moment of calm," he said, "around four-thirty in the morning," tore a candy wrapper for a filter, again rushed from the room.

The flautist, pausing in his wanders, asked what had gone on. "All the DVDs, it's bizarre."

"Oh but it's perhaps some video boxes that have committed suicide," Le Général said. "They've given up the ghost... We were here, and we heard nothing. The baby? We sold it."

Another squatter dropped in: "Did you piss in the electric box?"

The filmmakers joined us in his office as Le Général, gesturing at the skylight, evoked his vivid dream of building a spiral stair of iron, culminating in a terrace, a hut of pallets. This would have been an easy thing.

He rifled through parts, washers, said he'd set traps for the cops in their cars. He rose and threw the box of parts into the hallway.

A man I didn't recognize came in to hand a crowbar off to him.

In the hallway: planetary bangs. Metal bookcases were being thrown and dragged over broken glass and the foamy, wax-smelling effluent of the fire extinguisher.

Le Général plugged in a bulb that bathed him in a light like chicken broth. It was after 5 a.m.; using his iPad to browse the internet, he shared news of two deaths. In Aix-en-Provence, people like us had died. The organization Morts de la Rue tracks mortalities among the country's unhoused and contributes, as it can, to funeral expenses. In that year, 2013, it counted 454 deaths at an average age of 50 as compared to 82, the average life expectancy in France.

A man showed in the doorway—holding a can of Heineken, clutching a stuffed tiger, saying his goodbyes.

I opened a door to the −4 and heard, in the darkness, water gushing as if from an open spigot. Papers carpeted the floor as far as the stairwell light could reach.

On a landing a bottle of red wine, shattered, was attracting mosquitoes.

The −3 was dark.

The −2 was also dark, and deep in the dark a whir was sounding, feedback of something electronic. In the stairwell, a bookcase had come to rest akimbo, apparently thrown downstairs and sprinkled with cigarette butts, beer cans. A hairbrush. Lights were out.

On the −1, where puddles widened, I smelled sewage; trash bags piled. The floor was shingled in hazard-yellow pamphlets that offered information about—I looked closely—vaccination.

In a side room I had somehow never been to there was, there still remained a workshop. In ruin, it had been a carpentry workshop. I ran a hand over the surfaces soft with sawdust; the smell of it was thick. On sawhorses lay scraps of foam and wood, smooth perfect stones.

Crashes sounded. *Try a door*, I wrote unclearly,

recording, I think, what I was hearing. *It's stuck shut. Try another.*

On the sixth, a wall had peeled off and lay in triangles on the floor. Always Marco La Mouche had, keeping to principle, sprayed the treble clef that was his tag on floors. Here a single treble clef, red, was on the ceiling.

A mattress, piles of glass, bamboo mat, traffic cone, fragments of cabinet. Orange, blue, and lavender paint had spilled to streak the seventh floor. Wet footprints led away. Cabinets hung open, clothes spilled out.

On the fifth-floor landing gleamed lost keys, a couple dozen. Since the escape of the mice, the paint had dried.

Handles of doors that separated the fourth-floor landing and its hallways had gone missing. In Marky's room, I found him. "Look how they broke everything, up above. They are the savages, we are the civilized ones... The fourth," he said, "is the only floor without breakage.

"The police won't come today," he added, out of his politics of opposition to the *tontons*.

A light on the third floor blinked wildly. A long lake was new. Somewhere, a filmstrip had come unspooled, and it trailed the length of a hallway.

On the second, a squatter I was meeting only then was wrangling a hot drink for a group that gathered in its huddle on a mattress. He served in plastic cups. He was carrying, under one arm, a box of white wine. "I'm sorry," he said, "but I have never seen a building given up in such a state. It's hallucinatory. Now Le Bloc will get a reputation as destroyers of buildings."

People, tired, leaned into one another. On the first, where I hadn't spent much time, doors were tilting similarly, unhinged.

From a corner of the ceiling a cord dangled like an invitation.

By 6:30 a.m. a man working at Reception was taping up a cymbal, music from the party spiraling to meet him.

Activists from Médecins du Monde and Droit Au Logement came in support; a ban on eviction by night lifted at six, and so the hour after was reputationally the tensest. In the unbroken dark they were placing a couch, chairs, a small table along the sidewalk. There were a dozen squatters drinking coffee, tea, their hoods up.

Valentin returned again to fill a shopping cart with drums, asked me what to do with them.

More film was trailing in the hallway that had given onto Anastasia's workshop. It threaded the dirty footprints of cats.

There were Christians cleaning up the ground floor, wearing rubber gloves.

To his shopping cart Valentin now added a toy guitar, for his son, a paint can, speakers. He came across a cigar box and attempted, on the first passerby, to pawn it off.

At seven exactly, Le Général handed me a cup of coffee. We ventured outside, still dark. A taxi displayed a green light.

People were moving easels into a truck.

Valentin wheeled off the shopping cart, again to Anastasia's.

I craned my neck to take in the façade. It had been, in the night, improved, some person's reach extended with tools to block out capitals that were, however, hard to read: some tag. Out a window was lolling a slim tongue of silver, a banner.

The sky, brightening, looked as if dusty. The journalist from *Libération* wandered, getting shots. I was sitting on the couch's arm with the young philosopher of art.

Dominique the elder sang softly. 7:30. I couldn't feel my feet. A woman walking a dog let slip a curse that had the lightness of an exhalation.

Small talk was of their shared appreciation for a ray of sun, of the injustice they felt in waiting at an hour when their countrymen were warm in bed. "Who wants a trolley?" Valentin asked. The shopping cart was empty. "One euro." Happy with his joke, he asked again.

Convening a meeting for 8:30 Vincent announced that some defendants, for fear of fines, would go to the commissariat right away and sign something saying they were vacating. Shame spread at that night's trashing of the place, which I found, given the urgency of their concerns, surprising; yet an exhortation sounded in the assembly that they all help with the mess.

The Charisma pastor, having joined us, said as if reproachful that there were, at Le Bloc, people whose lives had been risked in getting to France, the "country of resistance."

"It's a thousand euros a day," came the answer, from a French squatter, "that resistance."

At Reception, in a stagnant quiet, a slight Black man I had not seen before and who might have been younger than I was asked haltingly in English where everybody was and if we had to go. Abubakar, who went by Shaker, had come to France from Ghana, as I learned. Explaining about the eviction I brought him to the sidewalk, where the activists from Médecins du Monde were working. "Tell him to ask around his networks," one of them told me. Shaker had stayed at Mairie de Lilas but could not return there, he said with emphasis from which I concluded, right or wrong, that he had been in danger. He led me to an upstairs room where he was living. In the door there was a rough-edged hole through which a cord was looped, its lock. In the way of personal effects there was one thing, a New York Yankees cap with a flat brim, which hung high on a wall. Shaker took it down and held it out. It was for me, just then preoccupied by efforts to refuse the gift with grace. He clasped my arms in both his hands and moved in for a kiss. I stepped away, handing back the cap, and led Shaker downstairs to Guy's office, where a heater had been running. Guy and Dominique suggested he join them in warming up. I asked Guy for a word planning to tell him, out in the hall, that this person was in real trouble, that we had to help. As I was leaving the room, Shaker rose to follow me, and Guy blocked the door so he would not. With Guy in the hallway, preparing to speak, I, to my astonishment, burst into tears. Guy gave me a hug and sent me home to rest. I did. I called the university and said I was too sick to teach any of my afternoon classes.

My phone rang. I had a favorite filmmaker; I might not have picked up otherwise. He asked if I'd been sleeping.

I was sleeping.

The eviction was happening.

Le Général was shooting the breeze with plainclothes police, telling them of his ideals.

Marky and a few others were thinking over, at Reception, the prefecture's request that they compile a list of those in need of emergency shelter services—an occasion for suspicion and confusion.

White vans blocked off traffic. The squatter who had made me pray took my hands in his and said a prayer.

Guy appeared on the opposite sidewalk, wearing a backpack.

Le Général was eating gratin dauphinois out of a baking pan.

Médecins du Monde said to police that eighty squatters were rehoused already, some in other squats.

Across the doors that read *LE BLOC* another message had been added in paint, *ICI NOUS*, "our place." The doorway filled with a man holding a Christmas tree.

Blue vans pulled up, gendarmes. The dancer stood in the street, brandishing a sign, *NE PLUS MOURIR DE FROID, DON'T DIE OF COLD EVER AGAIN.* The filmmakers captured her, as if stretched to stillness. There were 150 gendarmes, I heard a policeman say into a walkie-talkie. Armored, they led their charge into the building, visors fastened, as the dancer moved to stand and hold her sign before the door. Within the building there was singing as a few came out, squatters with their suitcases and trash bags. Duffels lay in clumps, with kitchen equipment, with a canvas showing a lone figure below a tree.

In one of the ground-floor rooms that had been a gallery I found the pastor from Charisma with the squatters who were Christian holding hands. The prayer they chanted fled the building through high windows. *Chasse les sécu et tous ceux animés par un esprit destructeur, un esprit satanique...*

Nous chassons tout esprit de Satan de ce lieu...

I climbed the stairs. Doors, one by one and with a sound like rain, were giving way of course to clubs.

"Anyone up there?" The officer was shouting, skylight brightening his face.

Gendarmes were marching. On the seventh floor, they held the clubs *at 45° angles*, I wrote. The filmmakers were prevented from taking any more images. "Go farther," a man said.

But I was escorted out. At the doors I found the pastor, singing. *Sois glorifié, sois glorifié, Seigneur...*

Cans of paint had been poured out of three windows so the building appeared to be crying: orange, red, blue.

A cold wind rose. It got through clothing. A Christian squatter came out of the building holding up a poster for the cameras, LE BLOC LABORATOIRE D'UN FUTUR POSSIBLE.

Another of them, the dreadlocked Frenchwoman, addressed the pastor furiously. "You sleep inside where it's warm," she said to him. "That's why you're singing."

Dominique the younger, royalist, was drifting with the officials handling emergency housing. In a white van, one of two, a half-dozen squatters took seats, Le Général first of all.

From outside the building we could hear the gendarmes working: thuds, whistles, a shatter of glass. The Charisma pastor switched to "La Marseillaise," the national anthem—the lyrics are criticized for their racial definition of France as Gallic.

I had packed a bag of peanuts and shared it around, the others partaking by eating or flicking them into each other's mouths.

The flautist came out, carrying a saxophone, percussion. So did a man I didn't recognize who allowed his knees to buckle. "God help me," he said. Speaking at, toward, a gendarme, he reached skyward in jerking motions—"Help us, help you"—and, turning, approached the exit as if to return by it, though another of the gendarmes was standing by. The flautist reached to lay an arm carefully along his body, guiding him away. "We are driven out in the middle of winter," the staggering man declared.

Gendarmes came out, four crowbars slung across the back of one, another just sheathing a club.

The last squatter was a man I didn't recognize. He

came out laughing, carrying a microwave.

"This is really the end," Dominique the elder said.

At 4:30 p.m. that December 6 gendarmes were, at last, securing their perimeter, stretching tape between the building and a tree. At intervals they formed a blockade, the corps scaly with armor. They moved out.

Jaouad dashed back in to get some things he'd left, a bailiff accompanying him. It was his thirtieth birthday that night.

A Christian looked up at the building, yelled his thanks.

Gendarmes advanced. The dancer approached their line as if in mockery, swigging from a can of beer and singing, keening, swaying. The squatters of Le Bloc caught and held her.

The moon was out, a slim bow slung over Place des Fêtes. They sang again in English, everything was gonna be all right.

Guy had put on his glasses and was watching from across the street, apart from, topographically higher than the others. I joined him there. "Nothing to be afraid of," he said. "I know this kind of procedure, this is not the first time."

We watched them as the light grew low and gray. The flautist played. The others danced or formed a knot against the cold.

Guy laughed quietly. "There's nothing to say," he said. "What can they mean by that, the dance? They want them to put them back in Le Bloc?"

¶ In my room above the bakery I went through my notes. I knew the names of many people who'd been squatters at Le Bloc, including names I hadn't known even a few weeks earlier. Provisionally, I had substituted private nicknames. Now, with ink of another color, I corrected them.

Dozens of unfamiliar names would stay that way, however. Much later my favorite filmmaker, making reference to a squatter, cued up a clip to show me who he meant.

It was a scene of singing; after the eviction, the man who'd prayed had hosted a few of those left homeless at his apartment, a nice place in some district like the second arrondissement. A balcony gave onto a courtyard, which was visible in the background, hive of lights. The music of a tuned guitar, night air.

"It's a beautiful shot," I said.

"This is dumb," the filmmaker said. "We can't see anything. It's all dark."

¶ Of course he had not been the only cameraman to haunt Le Bloc on its last night. A half-hour video would go up on YouTube, "LE BLOC dernières images," "last images." Shot by Camille Robert for DOC du réel, a self-described activist YouTube channel, it is in tone very dire, partly the effect of a cello backing it.

> Regulars at Le Bloc had never seen the building in such a state.
> On the last day, certain residents of Le Bloc ransacked the place themselves. For hours, others cleaned up the traces of these desperate acts...
> This documentary of thirty minutes was filmed the night before police arrived, the night before the eviction.
> Without commentary, it presents the remains, the artworks that would be destroyed, the occupation of a place deemed illicit.

True to these promises the video, after the cello, after other instrumentals, includes no commentary. There is the rarest murmur, overheard words. The camera pans over murals, messy tables, dim blue scenes, all of which in combination with a headlamp's white beam leaves an impression of underwater ruins. The bearer of the camera breathes loudly, unless that breath is an effect of the music.

Images of figures flitting at far ends of hallways are as if by accident loyal in a representation they make of Le Bloc, which had an optics of secrecy. More characteristic of this video is its avoidance of any human subject—its insistence, resilient, on framing walls and objects. It is like a nature documentary in reverse, waiting for the people, its quarry, to go into hiding. It is a premonition, showing the building not as it is but as it will be, empty of life.

¶ Except that light was shining in the building that had been Le Bloc—a light left on. In a ground-floor window a dog was shivering, curled on a wrinkled sheet. It belonged to a guard, it had found its way to shelter via instinct and the whorl of that parking garage.

The man who tended bar across the street greeted me warmly. I asked if he had noticed anything, unsure myself what I expected him to say. A guard kept watch or else the signs were random, like the firing of a dying brain.

¶ Along with making up those classes for which I'd called in sick I had a pile of exams to grade. One evening as I was leaving the university, a colleague of mine who was avoided and of reputation fallen buttonholed me in the parking lot. A Frenchman of late middle age, he had been caught by our boss teaching more courses than the rules of the public institution stipulated. That night he chose me as his confessor for additional sins, apparently for the reason of my nationality; the yearning of his off hours was, it came out, capitalistic. Pink dusk bloomed above the trees authorities lobotomized each fall. "These civil servants, they are just *lazy*," my colleague said. "Fifteen hours a week, I mean *really*... and *that* is where hypocrisy lies." He had a fine, British English and took clear pleasure in it. "In America, would this ever happen? Would a teacher who wanted to work longer hours be prevented?"

He didn't know about my habit of taking notes, and I didn't share any of the aperçus with which I had begun, lately, to sprinkle my notes as if afraid I'd be called on to justify my activity—this sprinkling a kind of writer's block—epigrams about the illogic of understanding various things and, namely, housing as a market. The man, I sensed, was out of money. I said I didn't know.

"No. The answer, I think, is no. Well, goodbye, Jacqueline."

¶ I caught up with Le Général a week after Le Bloc's eviction at a squat opened by *tontons* three years previously, as he informed me casually. He was eating cabbage out of a trough-like bowl and sawing at a lock, which gave off sparks. The occupied building in a suburb to the east was low and vibrant with graffiti. Stained glass patched the walls below its eaves, drooping shapes like a child's drawing of lakes.

I followed him out into a cold night. He waved at vines and said that in that house, squatters had stayed ten years; the proprietor had left for Algeria.

We paused at an overpass as I was overcome by the open feeling not achievable within the city. In the cellar of his boyhood he had found fermented cherries. He had been, coming out from underground, stricken by love, love for the sky.

He had fallen with a car into the Seine, he should have drowned. We looked down on the traffic. "They're all running," he said. "Running, running, running…"

He had been assigned a berth in Villeneuve-Saint-Georges, a commune to the south of Paris. A service the French state offers is to provide, to members of its homeless population, emergency shelter in low-cost hotels; entire hotels in the Paris region are given over to this purpose. Jaouad was placed in a different hotel from the sixteen or so Bloc squatters who stayed, as I heard, where Le Général did. Possibly Shaker had received a room. After the eviction I had received from him a text that I thought meant he'd taken a place in one of the prefecture's vans. Possibly he had gone through something worse. Many times a day he had tried calling, texting pleading propositions.

In a deserted lobby of locked doors I recognized a

former squatter of Le Bloc's second floor. Le Général's room, which Le Général shared with Hassan, was twice a double bed in size and very warm. Above the double was a twin, the frames made of curving white plastic. Attached to this was the allotment of four coat hangers, also of white plastic and continuous with the bedframe. No occupant would steal them. The walls were roughly spackled; the hallway bathrooms, shared, were of plastic like an airplane's, continously cast. There were sixty-nine rooms, the prices thirty-six to thirty-nine euros a night.

I found Le Général there on Christmas Day, finding him by walking from the Villeneuve-Saint-Georges station below which a main street flecked with litter was lit by joined storefronts of sushi, kebab, and Chinese restaurants all open on that day. Saint-Georges was a church of brown stone, softly glowing from big lamps. I passed an old-age home whose largest window, that of its cafeteria, revealed attendants wearing Santa hats, old people eating early, silently to me. Following an empty road I could hear airplanes on their way to Orly pushing at the barrier of sound. The dark deepened, one house appearing as a dotted line of Christmas lights. "Roads nobody uses," Le Général said, dragging a finger across his tablet to manipulate the map of them. "We're at the end of the world, Jacqueline. Look, the real *banlieue*."

He had asked me to bring food, and I had picked up madeleines, chocolate, baguette, a bakery loaf studded with chocolate chips. Le Général explained, tucking in, that breakfast cost four euros. Oan and Oan's mother were staying at her mother's in a suburb to the east so that Le Général had to travel, taking the suburb train and Métro, at last a bus. Oan was receiving treatment for fluid in his lungs, and still a calm temperament had taken root in Le Général's son. "He looks at you like he's going to kill you," Le Général said. For himself he wanted to open another squat as soon as he could. "They throw you in here, but you're supposed to go on with your normal life. It's complicated." He did a lot of relaxing, was reading *The Peter Principle*, a 1969 satire about "the incompetence of hierarchy." In French translation, a paperback: "I found it at Le Bloc," he said. "I saved it out of the wreckage."

It was obvious to at least one of the Bloc squatters that I had no family in France, and at his invitation I had spent the prior evening, Christmas Eve, with a group of them, in a western suburb. The apartment, which they had discovered furnished in Suresnes, the western suburb, belonged in their understanding to a family whose ailing son, the occupant, had been committed to an institution. The family, which in my understanding the china, the houseplants belonged to, had not sued. Those who'd left Le Bloc, getting together, asked each other where they were staying; the answers varied.

The next day, in the gloom of a winter day that would not fully break, the squatter Fred, the engineer, walked me to the tram. We passed apartment blocks and houses in one of which a chandelier of silky glass was shining, long rays casting into goblets. In another was a family below an artificial bough, one man just sitting down. "Oh, people who are eating," Fred said absently. The sidewalk steepened, giving way to a set of stairs, and we followed along, touching the handrails lightly. It seemed to Fred that Belvédère, the stop's name, derived from *belle vue*, "beautiful view." (The origin stories for Belleville's name are similar. From its heights, the Parisian looked homeward besotted to cry, "Beautiful city.") La Défense loomed to our left, the top floor of Montparnasse Tower shone blue, and Sacré-Coeur showed slightly. The Eiffel Tower leaned away from us, gathering its skirts. Within Paris, the city's hills, Belleville, Place des Fêtes, were expressive, inflecting the experience, but at that remove Paris looked flat, uniform and low.

On the opposite platform boys closed in on a soccer ball. At their backs, across from us, in an enormous picture window a tree was all ablaze, electric blue. "I wouldn't be able to sleep with that thing on," Fred said.

I agreed quickly. "It looks like a visiting UFO."

We stood in silence and the tram pulled up.

In my company Le Général would visit social workers at the Place des Fêtes, not by appointment as I realized when I turned up, but as a walk-in. Though Le Général had been the one to name the time, it took nearly two hours after I called for him to appear. Eventually it was obvious he had forgotten. I found a newsletter, *À Paris*, put out by the city, and perused it closely. In a spell of bitter cold, I learned, taking notes, emergency housing had been contrived to fill gymnasiums, arrondissement offices.

Le Général, when he got there, couldn't resist letting the staffers know about the labor by which he had personally ensured Le Bloc stay open—social work, as he explained it, offering up a sampling of his homilies.

They had to get something. Le Général delivered himself of an aside. "It gives them an opportunity to reflect on their work," he told me.

"Something good will come of it," Anastasia said that winter. "It's like Valentin with his trumpet; you can't tell him otherwise."

I was moved. "It's a little bit in pieces right now," I said, "but that's the sense of the narrative, now."

¶ The cold was bitter, night falling early. Strings of Christmas lights in side streets led always away, like lures. *This winter, during extreme cold, the City of Paris has opened 920 places in 12 gymnases. Last yr, btwn Nov. & Apr., more than 650 ppl benefitted from this help.*
"À Paris," p. 11
Hiver 2013–2014
Le Général and Caravaggio, when they went out scouting vacancies, took the filmmakers and not me. Their cameras were off, and, as Le Général offered, I was a girl. I could not, then, corroborate the filmmakers' reports: of a door that swung open, dark windows, a medical building on Paris's fringes; of guards spotted or their traces, radio running, hum of a fridge, the fur of a dog so easily taken for dust.

I met up with my Russians, with Le Bloc's. Coming in out of a drizzle we saw mimes playing a theater having made the journey from St. Petersburg. Valentin knew them for some reason such that we stayed. We drank vodka with the mimes, their faces red and scrubbed.

Or Anastasia treated the rest of us to a dinner costing one euro, dumplings big as two fists and filled with ground pork. The cashier heated up the dumplings; at a table, a girl bawled, twisting in our direction as if appealing, mouth howling, steadying herself in the gale of her own tears by clutching rungs like bars. We laughed at her, saw ourselves laughing in the mirror behind her, peeled plastic from the dumplings, went out into the wet road.

They knew of poets, also Russian, who'd be reading in a white brick *cave*, a café basement.

We sat with one in the upstairs restaurant as another of them, a woman with childlike features and long gray hair, was holding forth also in Russian, the first poet liking this so much that he leapt up, knelt at her chair, burrowed underneath the chair until it tipped and caught her just to hold on as she nestled in, with and against her will. He stroked her hair. Her poetry was rhythmic French, wonderfully accented—*Je t'aimais plus que Paris la ville des rêves des artistes et des ambitions*—while the same man, playing guitar in the background, writhed so forcefully he broke a string. A different one went to buy wine, bread, cheese, chips as we helped ourselves to the bar's stemware and spread out on the sidewalk glossy with rain. I complimented the woman poet, who had put on a beret, and she replied I was the future. Her English, too, was lyrically broken. Her own generation was lost, geopolitics bogging it down impossibly. "The KGB, et cetera," she said wearily. "Vietnam..."

Another Russian turned to Anastasia and used his French to ask about me: "Friend?"

"No! She is... she is an American spy. She is a novelist... She has been following us for almost three years. She comes to all the trashiest spots in Paris. She is always up for improvisation. When she first came, she spoke no French, she only took notes... I have told her a lot of my problems, but she never tells me any of hers... She is neither friend nor enemy..."

Conversation shifted to the neighborhood, Belleville, a new crowd there. That café was sending the projection of a village scene onto a wall across the street.

Je ne suis pas riche... The Russian man was singing, warbling, Piaf, between breaths asking for a cigarette. *J'habite à Paris... ça me suffit...*

He had a sweet voice and, when he sang, lost the Russian accent that tinged his spoken French. I declined a swallow of his wine.

"Be modern, Mademoiselle! There is Edith Piaf just

beside us! Let your future go!"

"The present!" Anastasia cried. They raised a toast. "The present!" Anastasia fed Valentin his sandwich with her fingers as Valentin explained some jokes the others seemed to trade in Russian. "This is Cossack humor, of a fine subtlety."

"This is the chance to make a wish if you want to," Anastasia said. "As for me, I have nothing to wish for."

The man had on a long brown beard, a Santa hat.

"He said so," she went on. Taking my hand he covered it in kisses.

Globes at his back were set afloat above the Rue de Belleville, lights for the Chinese New Year.

Valentin and I arrived at the theater where mimes had played to find it dark. He suggested I join him watching the cars go by, and we rested on one of the benches subtending the *grands boulevards*. He had on him half a roast chicken, friends had given it to him. We ate using our fingers as he spoke tiredly of a dry problem, return to Russia.

Separating from Anastasia he fell to practicing that winter at a squat in Bagnolet, a bad one. There too he made his practice room in a low parking garage, its walls of cinderblock. In whatever state of disrepair the room's piano was supporting shards of mirror. A man to whom Valentin must have introduced me brought a tape roll to his mouth, used teeth to cut, readjusted the position of a snare drum. Valentin switched on his metronome and left. From a large room ours gave onto he sent forth notes that burst. Returning, ducking under hanging painted canvas, he paused. "Yes," he said coquettishly, "my problem is alcohol. I prefer knocking one back to hanging out with idiots."

In that room tarp was patching convex plastic in the

ceiling, a skylight. From there, I learned, a man had fallen to his death. I had it confirmed later. The hole was gaping. We looked at the area of floor where the man had died as dutifully I noted down this tragedy.

At Valenciennes I recognized a painting for its style: pastel colors, melting lady. Babar, the Droit Au Logement leader, confirmed that three Italian boys had been to stay. I recognized their way of painting from Le Bloc, and I had lost them. From there, too, they had gone away.

Finding Valentin at the bad squat New Year's Day I learned that he had made no resolution. "What is there to hope for? The love of a girl? I'm kidding." He kissed my ear and stood. Dancing was a man whose lip was split and chapped. Another, who introduced himself, a sculptor, showed me to a door of broken glass, a man who had pink jeans on backward there to tell about its state.
"Again?"
Cracks cobwebbed it. A vending machine's glass was fingernail-sized fragments, none fallen in or out, on a platform for the Montreuil-Sèvres line at République.

On a ledge a cube of glass enclosed a diorama. Anastasia had made, at last, a real place for him—her tiny dummy she had dressed in a felt shirt, trousers, little boots. It sat on a tiny bed with threadbare pillows sized to it, a burlap scrap. Around this figure were arranged a tiny book, tiny suitcases and loaves of hard doll's bread, small plastic bag, green bottles, cardboard sign and beggar's upturned hat, and, in the doll's lap, a tiny, gleaming trumpet. A gallery in the eleventh where her work was that February exhibited had listed it at six hundred euros, *SDF mon amour*, "Homeless bum, my love." Hands and head were thickly bandaged in pure white.

The eviction of Le Bloc had led Anastasia to work in miniature, she told me, fitting art and its materials into her home.

¶ Typing up these notes one summer, I left off for the day. A birthday would be celebrated, my friend Juliette's, on the Île Saint-Louis. I put on makeup, pulled on jeans one of my roommates could approve. I wasn't buying many clothes but they were new to me, a man's old jeans. Emerging after workdays in the summer I was like a dog with its head out the car window.

A madman was, I saw, walking in my direction, crossing the stone bridge that led him to the Right Bank. In speaking he was addressing a cloud of gnats as he followed the bridge, turning its corner.

This was San, as I saw, San who had lived on Le Bloc's second floor. His hair had grown out, mantling half his back. I sensed, wrong or right, that he wouldn't recognize me. Certainly he was preoccupied. He paused at locked trapezoidal boxes, the riverside booksellers'.

I couldn't make out what he was saying. But I recognized an intensity in his gestures and expressions. He no longer suffered from the tics that had been his characteristic at Le Bloc, however. It was as if, having hovered between conditions, spinning, he had finally shifted, clicked into gear. This lent him an appearance of wellness relative to how I'd seen him.

He walked off. I took note of a riverboat's music, the thrum of cars, lichen below my notebook. The spires of Notre Dame that, in their way, split the dusk.

¶ One night that February, at 3:14 a.m., Jean-Luc called—I did not answer—and then texted: *Mon amie on a ouver 1 endroi vien. Apel moi.* "My friend we've opened 1 playse com. Cal me."

I rolled over, the buzz loud. I had been, already, edgy. A call that I would miss from another Parisian number had woken me up in just that way, back in December. I had redialed until four in vain, sure I would learn of a newly opening squat.

Having turned up the radiator before going to bed, I was sweating. I had gone slack or sane, apparently: I nodded off again.

3:19: *Apel moi!*

Jean-Luc was drunk, his voice broad, happy. I heard a woman and got him to put her on. The woman who had run *récupération* at Le Bloc was dating Jean-Luc; she suggested delicately that perhaps they were bothering me.

"Not at all," I said. "I would be delighted to come if it's possible."

I was not invited. She would call.

¶ *Knowledge*

The first images from those days and nights show pedestrians traveling on a sidewalk not quite together; that they have split up and at times go single file gives a sense of the length of the journey, which takes them through two suburbs in the dead of night. Out ahead walks the American, her hood up. Le Général, after the filmmakers and I spent the depths of that winter clamoring to be taken along, set to the task of opening a building in February of 2014. He would name this occupation in which documentarians would be involved from the start La Connaissance, "Knowledge"—as if to make fun of us, though he let the joke go unexplained.

We stood in wait under a bus shelter. A *tonton* dropped a cigarette to grind it underfoot, lifted a garage door of metal to beckon us under. The target. "*Venez.*" Le Général, panting, led the rest of us upstairs.

Fluorescents switched on automatically. Linoleum reflected them, smaller in the reflection. The halls were long, white, and windowless like the halls of a clinic, and without life the building had a clinical, sanitized feel.

Doors to every room but one were locked. Le Général took out a drill with a lamp on its snout, and we heard the chime of metal landing on the floor beyond. He knelt, swearing, and wedged in a crowbar. Jean-Luc folded his arms. The filmmakers set up their tripod. I rested my head against the cold wall and closed my eyes. I tried to remember how old Le Général was.

"It's not possible," he said quietly, and wandered away, the lock's setting torn. The other *tonton* managed it.

The room was huge, sealed air still colder than the hall. It had a faint, not-quite-neutral stale smell, like packaged bread. Le Général returned to peer into my face and, though careful to stay quiet, laughed at me.

Jean-Luc was to stay and watch over the building as, downstairs, the locks remained unchanged. I would stay, too, take notes. Behind Le Général, *tonton*, and filmmakers, at 4 a.m., the grille fell. Jean-Luc bent to test the handle.

We spoke in whispers though the room where we would sleep was at the rear of the building, selected by Le Général for discretion. Periodically we remembered we didn't have to speak so softly even as, anew, the impulse dawned. Light from streetlamps or the moon found a column at the room's middle. I spread my coat over my lap. There was silence. The scratching of my pen could fill it. Jean-Luc's whisper filled it capably. He asked how I was managing, writing in the dark. The light those windows parsed as squares lingered, shifted. In the hall a light flicked off, which startled me.

We slept past noon to stay motionless, each of us heaped under covers like that couple of Beckett's in trashcans. I wanted to blame the cold, which was deep, for the heaviness in my limbs. The room was so long, it looked low from where I lay although the ceiling was, I mused, of normal height.

I remembered the date and wished Jean-Luc a happy Valentine's Day. At last he rose, capitulating to curiosity, leaned over a wall that was mottled with brown mold in small spots like fingerprints, took a shingle of the wall between his fingers, tugged it off. This, in his estimation, proved the building was abandoned. It legitimized our occupation.

To warm up I paced the halls where other doors, still locked, shuddered in the breeze I made as they returned, like lungs, to rest.

The footage takes light as its first subject (before whispers, ours, heaped sleeping bags, building materials caught in the void of a hall). Sparks rush from locks under assault. A moon swells. Gusts hurry clouds by, and behind them the moon is dry ice left to steam. My favorite of the filmmakers lay on his belly to get that shot; just as I got down the detail and, pushing up my glasses, made a record of the gesture, so did he film a kettle boiling.

The American is a frustrating character, very passive. When her nose turns pink in the cold Le Général takes the liberty of tweaking it. But she is not uninteresting in writing, with one intelligently angled shot showing how she writes. A camera at her left captures her way of holding a pen so it rests on the third finger, not the second. She writes by the light of a headlamp affixed to a spiral binding. They were like humans in the Martian zoo...
Periodically the filmmakers took stills, and in one the young woman is faintly smiling, hair tumbling over an eye—a smile of pleasure, though what makeup she has on is smeared and she's wearing something disgusting, the sweater gray, "colorless" maybe and found in a squat (Le Stendhal, chilly night at summer's end); where she looks a spill of water slicks the floor—for, despite the absurdity of her embedding in surroundings so plainly sordid, she is delighted by, again, the notebook in her lap, which she works to fill.
For me this image is a bit misleading, and I'll now take advantage of the force of my own medium to correct it for the record. I have found what I believe are the corresponding pages, which include a mini portrait of the filmmakers and filmmaker, my favorite—crouching at the edge of sight, pushing up his sleeves—as well as a note it's for his benefit that I've set my lips in what I imagine to be

an attractive cast. *I don't know what I could possibly be doing in the movie*, I add—dishonestly, because it was clear my writing was of interest to the filmmakers, and I remember writing rapidly to let them get a good shot.

Le Général's origin story resumes at his eighteenth birthday, still in the Rouen *cité*. His stepfather, to get across the message that this young man will have to pack his bags, serves a rectangular cake complete with a handle formed out of cream. Le Général coolly shares the cake around the neighborhood that he then leaves. He opens a discothèque, which rises to national prominence, and buys a house.

The point in any case is that he becomes self-reliant at eighteen: another time he told me that at eighteen, having funded his specialized training by stealing, he went into business as a locksmith with another, older man from his *cité*. That man did shoe repair, Le Général charmed customers, and soon they ran, together, half a dozen stores throughout Rouen. So the years passed, until in '95 or '96 Le Général came face-to-face with a version of himself. He could place this event in its sequence after the birth of his daughter Marie, an aid to memory.

With Marie's mother he goes to Sunday dinner at her aunt's. The village, equipped with a river and castle, is, as far as country villages go, "one hundred percent typical." For the aunt, Le Général's whole look is something to remark upon. In that village there is one of him already, she explains, a man identical to him and named, like Le Général, Antonio Xavier. This Xavier lives just across the street. Le Général goes and rings the bell.

The man who answers has Le Général's compact build, round face, wide dark eyes. Recognizing Le Général immediately, within twenty minutes he makes out a check. "This is for all the birthdays," he says. Le Général's dad's house is prefab, concrete. He lives there with children, his other children, and works in construction. His disposition is like Le Général's—"always good, never bad"—but it will not accommodate the revelation that Le Général has been to jail. Thus his father "takes his distance." The next year, 1997, Le Général, zooming by motorcycle among the franchises he manages, collides with a car. He flies through the car. He will never again remember a dream.

He spends six months in a coma. Five months and twenty days, he spends. The slow days quicken as he engages in a reckoning with questions that bounce around his head, experiencing them, uniquely, as a "crisis of self-interrogation." He recovers just to learn his business partner has sold the shop and vanished, robbing Le Général of "a hundred fifty thousand euros in today's terms." Le Général asks around their *cité* and after some time finds the guy.

Some stories he repeated often. By Sunday dinner in the country village he had collected many Xaviers. Into this submarine for Knowledge he had brought a comic book, a 1987 edition of Marvel's *Special Strange*, which he kept with him, he said, always. The boy, hiding in his cellar, had known already that he shared a last name with the character named X, short for Xavier. "When you see Professor X, Charles Xavier, who has a school of X-men, and you are all alone in the *cité*, all the other kids speak a language you don't know and they don't have the same types of interests, they like sports or music, nobody will go to the library with you... That said," he added, "you have a lot of friends, a lot a lot a lot of friends." He had once built a website for Jesuits, staying six weeks at a monastery. As a thank you they traced his lineage, making a genealogical tree. "The first time I stole, no one told me, 'Go steal.' I trained myself. I was the one who trained the others. I guess I've always had good luck. A lucky star. I'm not religious. I've never believed in God... But in this way I learned my ancestor was St. Francis Xavier," a sixteenth-century missionary born in Navarre. Searching online reveals he died on an island in the South China Sea—waiting for, of course, a ship.

"There is a certain genetic memory," Le Général said, "a memory of the body." By night he was wearing a headset, blue light flashing at his right ear. The room was dark. Taking a handful of candy he lunged and made a ghostly sound. "I'm going to listen to the house," he said.

Upstairs a staircase of treaded metal made a steady, binary sound like tennis. At the top were doors. A terrace wrapped around. We made our way over to a corner, stepping around a depression where water had collected, and stood as if at a ship's prow. Orbs, streetlamps, were seeded between buildings, cranes mid-project arced as if in prayer. We looked in the direction of Paris without seeing it. To one side was a skyscraper, green glass. Le Général had pointed it out. He could see himself in there, he had told me, shooting a film of his own.

A floor at the top was lit from within. Workers, he said. Taking it apart. It was empty, the tallest thing in sight. We wiped our feet, Le Général locking up, and moved between the empty rooms. "Millions of euros in rent," he said absently. "Make believe you are walking on eggs."

By day I slipped away to interview one of the Médecins du Monde workers, something I'd planned to do. Robert Bianco-Levrin was beloved in the squats of Paris, known to all as Roberto. Ahead of our talk he'd asked me to read up on countrymen of mine, the Diggers, a San Franciscan group that, late in the sixties, performed street theater and operated free shops in the Haight. I was taken, during our interview, by Roberto's holistic understanding of health. To marshal figures, he brought up life expectancy. For those below the poverty line, far below, sleeping rough, this was about forty-five, as compared with that figure of eighty; even just that many spent outside the welcome of society could be arduous. In occupying a building, by contrast, one exercised the prerogative of the living to be originators of action. "Is there life after death?" he said, to remind me of the old question. "The joke goes: is there life before death?"

Unlike Le Bloc, La Connaissance did not occupy a government building. This privately held building didn't show any major sign that it had been left to ruin, mold notwithstanding. It wasn't clear who would move in or why they needed the place so badly. Jean-Luc and his girlfriend were planning to live there, two drifters. Le Général could have stayed at the hotel. In our newly opened squat I'd dream of usurpation. At 9 p.m., unable any longer to read by headlamp, I fell into a deep sleep lasting until 9 the next morning, during which I dreamed, more precisely, of having my photograph taken before I was ready, standing on a bridge; of being accepted to medical school, where I didn't want to go; two women I knew in my dream to be girlfriends of the filmmakers' threatened me as in my confusion I sat on a bed. Conforming to a characterization of Frenchwomen that Gertrude Stein favors, giving it in *Paris France* and elsewhere, both had sturdy legs. I had been unsure of what Stein meant when I first read that, but in my dream it became clear.

    The men slept late. On rising I changed my clothes and washed my face.

By morning Le Général complained to me as if enjoyably that he'd gotten only half the circuits working. A small, black bruise was forming at a corner of his right eye. He had fallen down as he explained. The building's lawful owner, the *de juris* proprietor, seemed to him, meanwhile, unworthy, even fraudulent. Le Général judged the construction job slipshod, done in a hurry to take a photo and show it to investors. A boyhood dream came to mind, that of a "crime school." "But *organized* crime," he said, interrupting himself. "We'd have barges and jet skis, go by way of the Seine, the Rhine, the Rhône. We'd exist outside society, in parallel, reentering only sometimes."

He got to his feet. I heard it too, a banging on the door below. We took the stairs.

"Open up!"

"I'm calling the police," Le Général shouted back.

"The police!"

"They were here," Le Général bluffed, "yesterday," and dialed the number for emergencies. We heard hold music.

"*I'm* calling the police!"

"Madam," said Le Général, "there's someone trying to get into our house. There's my wife, my children, my friends who are living here." He gave the address and yelled, switching to the rude *tu*, "Stop drilling the door," as the screamer, a man, indeed seemed to be doing. "That's a home break-in, what you're doing!"

"Open up!"

"We're waiting for the police," Le Général said.

"Yeah me too I'm waiting for police!"

"You've made an emergency call. Please wait."

"Don't be violent," Le Général called out, over the hold music. "He's trying to drill it," he said, "because, well, he doesn't have the key. And he seems violent. There are forty of us."

I could hear the responder. "What does he look like, this man?"

"I don't know," said Le Général gravely. "I haven't seen him."

"But how—is he making noise?"

Le Général pounded on the door. "Sir, are you still there?"

"Yeah, I'm waiting! I'm waiting for the police too!"

"But who is this man?"

"But who are you, sir?"

"When the police get here, they'll tell you."

"Sir"—Le Général took a stern, patient tone—"Who are you?"

"I have nothing to say to you."

"Did you hear that? He's violent." Le Général hung up. "Stop it. I'll open the door when the police get here. Are you the owner?"

"That's none of your business!"

He ran for something to barricade with. The screamer held his peace. I stood in a murky light at the door and heard rain. Tires sliced it, sirens following.

Oan's mother had been settled in already, baby in tow, several days since. Sticks of furniture had been arranged under fabric strung up into canopies like wings. In that room the officer made out his report, the mother asking, even then, "All right, my heart?" of the baby she was pushing in a stroller all around the vast room, suitable for cubicles, to kiss his forehead.

Médecins du Monde arrived, saying a precarious lease might be arranged. "You're a journalist," a property manager said. Le Général, being tackled by his man, had cried out, "Jacqueline, record!" "What's going on?" The manager, sweating in a black puffy jacket, had a drawn face, red hair wet with rain or sweat. In the end he took a lot of pictures. I gathered that he was the owner's son; the owner, as another of his agents would inform us, had immigrated to France from Algeria by necessity after the Second World War, a Jewish man. By working as a hairdresser he had built up a patrimony of which this property was the lion's share.

That night, after the departure of the proprietor's people, fear set in. As no official had come by to document the occupation, with no lawsuit filed, this owner might do as he liked—it was thought—send thugs. Gathering in one of the big, empty rooms we drank pastis, the reinforcements, and a man I recognized, a sculptor working at the squat where Valentin was staying, made mention of Le Carrosse. I had been introduced to him, "Pascal."

I stared. I had assumed of Pascal Hollemaert, old boss of Le Carrosse, that in making such an entrance into legend he had been lost to history, but this was he. Having been warned against him in hyperbolically strong terms I might have been expecting a person eight feet tall, not six-foot-four. I looked again, for—undoubtedly—a sign, at the sinewy, scarecrow arms, his open face, the bulbous eyes unblinking behind glasses that seemed from his expressions to cloud and not to clarify his view. "I've been looking for you," I said, surprising myself. I tried to explain and, again to my surprise, quickly succeeded. Pascal was glad and unsurprised himself to be the object of a search. "Do your thesis on him," the "policeman" said. "He's the oldest opener. He's the doyen of the squats."

He rolled a sleeve to show me a tattoo—winding lines, a lady angel, the woman that had saved him, he explained.

At Le Carrosse he'd made a fortune selling sculptures just to spend it on two overdoses after which she'd seen to it that he relocated to the countryside. "I was the prince of Le Carrosse," he said. "I am Le Carrosse. Le Carrosse is my best friend."

¶ *Correspondences*

So I looked for Pascal until I found him, but in other ways my project had evolved. I had arrived in Paris two years ago as part of a cohort of fellows; the others had gone home. But I was kept company, still, by a vision of the city that in Year One another of the fellows had presented to the rest of us. A visual artist, Zoe Schade painted cubes and other shapes from nature. She made it so they fit together and allowed the patterns to compound. When in this complicated process an error was occasioned she kept it, allowing it to direct the production of subsequent layers so that mistakes compounded too. Schade was explaining she aimed for maximal density. The Eiffel Tower was visible in the windows. The building, a center for American art, was old, it had floors of sun-bleached parquet, but not grand, and all throughout the atmosphere—pretty, faintly apologetic—was of a piece with an attitude I seemed to sense among United States Americans in Paris. Personally I was in the habit of asserting I was not a Francophile, and "expats" freaked me out—what were they running from?—but finally I came to appreciate in these Americans how they could recognize the humor in their situation, that of being a guest, resigned to a love that afflicted them for something that didn't need them. About the series, *Error Cube/ Infinity Box*, and its relationship to the city, Schade has written to evoke "traces of great tides of people" and of the importance of a "physical layering of these archeological remains," for her "key" to an "experience of historical time" and "an analog to the structure of [her] paintings."

In the city's literature there exist many instances of figures running into one other, making cameos in stories underway. The example relayed by John Merriman, US historian of the Paris Commune, is full of slapstick humor. It is in fleeing policemen that, in Merriman's account, Raoul Rigault—irascible radical and follower of Blanqui, the great imprisoned anarchist—jumps onto the roof of a train. He climbs down in Fontainebleau forest, south of the city, and there spends two days wandering. Dirty, starving, he trips over Auguste Renoir, who naturally enough is out painting. The Impressionist, ready to beat him away with a cane, becomes sympathetic when Rigault explains his situation, making him a gift of paints and smock so that, like the humble watercolorist, Rigault can go unnoticed. Madman as revolutionary, revolutionary as fraudulent artist, writer as king: in one case of mistaken identity, the mistake is Guillaume Apollinaire's. He lay dying of Spanish flu as the First World War was ending and a chant wafted in, *À bas Guillaume*, "Down with Wilhelm," the enemy head of state. Delirious, the poet trembled, thinking the mob was coming for him. Rigault would end up serving the autonomous municipality of the Commune as its chief of police.

Were there any bohemians left? Whose inheritance was bohemian Paris? Anastasia and I compared ourselves in salvaging to squatters of the squats. So too did "bohemians" of the nineteenth century see themselves, Benjamin writes, in the figure of the ragpicker, whose work the scholar Antoine Compagnon sums up by naming two substances: gold, and the mud from which it was in strokes of luck extracted. "Bohemian" was first applied to Roma people thought to have come from Bohemia, an etymology on which the *Larousse* dictionary does not dwell. Instead, having picked a fight with the *Académie française* (for the lexicographers once believed strongly *bohème* should be spelled with an *ê*), it presents contradictory assertions as to whether bohemians by definition have any talent. Balzac, in a novel, says they do.

Benjamin, in a posthumously published essay, is similarly generous in stretching the definition. In Baudelaire's day, many Parisians could be classified as "bohemians," including "professional conspirators," a label that Benjamin borrows from Karl Marx, who by professionals means conspirators—activists—without day jobs. Benjamin likens Napoleon III to such a professional for his "surprising proclamations, little two-bit machinations, sneak attacks, and impenetrable irony," all of which could be found, Benjamin continues, in the theoretical writing of Baudelaire, little emperor. The worst bohemians of all traveled in the actual imperial entourage: compared with the hangers on of one count's memoirs, "a Mimi or a Schaunard seem honest enough and plenty petit bourgeois," Benjamin writes, naming two characters in Henri Murger's *Scènes de la vie de bohème*, a novel appearing in feuilleton in the 1840s, attracting imitators and adaptations, including the one surpassing it greatly, Puccini's opera.

But the ragpicker was not a bohemian, Benjamin writes, analyzing a poem of Baudelaire's in which a ragpicker is compared to a revolutionary and a poet. The comparison with the revolutionary is magical, it being an apparent metamorphosis that the ragpicker's moustache, as Baudelaire looks on, droops like "old flags." And much like a professional conspirator, the ragpicker is a schemer, which for Benjamin implies he would rather have been fighting on some barricade like the barricades of 1848, an uprising with which Baudelaire in life sustained an ambivalent relationship. (The briefest of revolutionary hopes seems to have dawned on him along with the notion it might have provided an occasion for the assassination of his stepfather, a general.) The comparison with a poet is more oddly located.

> A lot of the time by a lantern's red light
> Of which wind bats at the flame, teases the glass,
>
> In the heart of an old faubourg, muddy maze,
> Where all humanity teems, a turbulent ferment,
>
> You'll see a ragpicker come along, head nodding,
> Throwing punches, and running into walls like
> a poet...

If I feared, as I was working to describe real people, that the product would suffer for ignorance of what they hid, if a barrier did block off the other culture at its core so that in getting close to city and people I ultimately would hit a wall, I could take comfort in knowing that for Baudelaire, a certain Baudelaire, such collisions were characteristic of poetry practitioners. They couldn't help themselves. Compagnon, lecturing on Baudelaire's ragpicker at the Collège de France, culls from Parisian history evidence of every writer's dependence, meanwhile, on the frenzy of the ragpicker, whose gleanings were used to make paper.

Le Général, after I moved away from Paris, landed interviews with other journalists. He would complain, warning me to proceed with caution, that they never really understood him. But it is in reading an article at an online journal of pop culture that I feel a pleasure like cracking the spine of an offering by a familiar author. "I live in the margin of the margin of the margin," Le Général tells the reporter, as he had told me many times. "The normality of my life is," he continues,

> for the majority of the broader population, extraordinary. I belong to the elite of the margin. Picture a wheel. I decided to live between tire tread and pavement. Except that now, at forty-nine years old, my tire's a hundred inches across, and I'm in the eighth lane of the highway. When I come to a stop on the shoulder, I open the doors, I get out, and I realize everybody's been lobotomized, more or less. Every other human being is in a big rush, which intrigues me to no end. They're stuck in traffic. All they do is pass, they run after time. But time is more than just money, time is life. When you're out of life, you're dead, and that's for good.

Repeatedly he situated himself on the outside of a field of text. What do you call a poet of few metaphors? The journalist asserts that Le Général is a little crazy (*un peu siphonné du bocal*). Sure, fine—and yet I can't forget how compelled I was, and am, by a remark made by this Général before the cameras at Le Bloc. In participating with the anti-austerity protesters who had camped out at La Défense in 2011, he had observed of many of the most devoted activists, those who stayed the night, that they were homeless as he was: they were already there.

The labor of the ragpicker was "a kind of homework undertaken in the street," wrote Benjamin, who carried notebooks everywhere. Hannah Arendt, a friend of his, notes that he felt at home in Paris right away. Entering his perspective, she describes the city as an "interior"; the façades flush with each other are like inside walls. A distinction between home and street was in this way muddied, and reportedly Baudelaire, too, was insouciant about the boundaries of houses, known to wander the Île Saint-Louis, where he lived, in slippers, an attitude like that of San from Le Bloc when, months after the eviction, I could glimpse him, its survivor, in that place; it seeded wonder in Laurent Penisson, a music journalist who lived at Le Carrosse beginning in 2002, that the squat "was never like an underground center" but rather "like a private mansion open to the outside." All Paris was material, and about Paris there was always more to read, as Benjamin writes: "Many of the main thoroughfares have their own special literature, and we possess written accounts of thousands of the most inconspicuous houses."

The publication history of "La Bohème"—the last of three parts of a Baudelaire study to appear in print, none before Benjamin's death—was ill-starred and in this typical, unfortunately, of Benjamin. On completing another, "The Flâneur," the author in a letter to Theodor Adorno, his editor by then based in the US, compared the experience of drafting with a "race against the war"; it was October 4, 1938. Adorno savaged the essay in his return correspondence of November 10, the day after Kristallnacht. The French translator of these essays and the *Arcades Project*, Jean Lacoste, levels against Adorno that he "perhaps did not completely appreciate Benjamin's distress, nor to what point Benjamin would feel obligated by his project on the arcades to remain in France," and Benjamin did leave too late, or at the wrong time anyway. Having packed morphine, he killed himself after getting over the Spanish border and learning that, because of a technicality having to do with an exit visa, a matter of bad timing, he could go no farther. Lisa Fittko, the resistance fighter who had acted as his guide, much later committed to writing her memory of a heavy "briefcase" Benjamin lugged with him despite a weakened heart. This contained, he told her, his "new manuscript." It was, however, lost.

In reading "La Bohème" one is struck by how neatly it ties up a lot of the threads of Benjamin's thinking on Baudelaire in his *Arcades Project*, which in fleeing the city he had had to leave unfinished. He died in transit having written, in his theses on history, of proletarian gunmen firing into the faces of Parisian clocktowers all at once as if by prearrangement to "stop the day" (in the words of an "eyewitness" Benjamin does not name). That was during the uprising of 1830. To understand time, Benjamin renders it in various ways as space, and these theses are characterized by a casting about for standstills, for the present, which by its nature slips away. One thesis is well known; it deals with an angel in a painting of Klee's, which—the interpretation is Benjamin's—stays in place, experiencing the present, only instantaneously, by a very great effort. It flaps its wings furiously against a wind pushing it into the future as meanwhile it looks back at history, which piles up like trash, and thinks it can salvage something.

Murger's *Scènes de la vie de bohème*, though folk art rather than philosophy, is also concerned with the present—with stalling and deferral. Murger claims to admire in bohemians that for them, daily life is a matter of "art" (what we might today call "lifestyle"). The end of bohemianism—theorizes Murger, no Benjamin—coincides with the end of youth. Murger's arrested adolescence differs from Benjamin's present in that, therein, future and past are kept at bay without effort. There is no treading of air, no cost. This period ends for exemplary bohemians in the sale of their work, in which eventuality all is well. Selling out, in that it ends the story, is like getting married in a novel, bohemianism having been, like life, a tryout after which you go to heaven or hell as you deserve, to use another set of metaphors. The view, either way, looks conservative. In teaching it's better to sell out than die, Murger claims stakes that are suspicious: was he forced to publish his book on pain of death? His characters don't struggle against the incoming present, as Benjamin's angel does, so much as they grumble about it. As the book opens, a rooster wakes Schaunard. In his garret, he lets out a curse. "*Sacrebleu*," he yells. "It's not possible that it's today already."

Very early in the morning of November 1, 1999, artists slipped into one of the grand Haussmannian buildings on the Rue de Rivoli: Number 59. It had been an office of the bank Crédit Lyonnais, and, though this is a district like a mall, it had stood empty fifteen years. One of the artists, who using the name Gaspard Delanoë periodically mounted stunt campaigns for mayor, told me in a 2012 interview that the long vacancy lent them legitimacy. In ways that mattered, they were inoffensive. Their irreverence relieved the commercial tedium at Châtelet. The press they got was positive, the Socialist mayor won unexpectedly, and the rest is, as they say, history: Paris cut them a deal and, after the renovation, some artists stayed. Another of my early interviewees, Dan Steinfeld, who worked at the city's housing bureau, said that the precarious leases "protect us from other forms of squatters" in addition to effectuating "artistic relationships"—and the imprecision in that "artistic" struck me as suspect. Gaspard, meanwhile, told me the goals of 59 Rivoli were to "democratize" and "desacralize" art. When I visited the "after-squat" around that time I took note of its inventory: reasonably priced skylines, on-the-spot tourist portraits. One artist offered dildos modeled on the Eiffel Tower. I was very young and wondered why everything was ugly, cynical and like a Christmas market.

Later, in March 2013, I went to a relevant panel at Le 6b, an "after-squat" in Saint-Denis. A municipal official who handled precarious leases (and had for that reason acquired the nickname "Monsieur Squat") said that the case of 59 Rivoli had been a turning point in city policy. Gaspard then spoke, and his speech was heated as he asserted that artists who signed such leases were no less "radical" than those who didn't. "Not only do we not participate in gentrification, we participate in degentrification," he claimed. I was more interested to hear from a younger artist, Vincent Prieur. He was of the new school of squatting, and he was very frank. "We've always worked by negotiation," he said. "When we set ourselves up in a building, we've always tried first of all to meet the landlord, explain our project, and tell him we're ready to pay rent."

The case of Le Carrosse, evicted in the spring of 2012, was unusual. Rather than award a contract to the artists who were living there already, the city, which by that point owned the building, gave it to a different collective after the eviction. The organization was called Curry Vavart, and it was Prieur's group. I interviewed him late in that year. He had of course known about Le Carrosse. He had gone to a concert at the old squat. Among the members of his collective they had said to themselves that if they didn't take the place someone else would, he told me miserably, and they'd been threatened by eviction where they were before. The city fixed up the old garage, where it would be ever after strictly forbidden to sleep. "A piece of the roof fell off into the street over the summer," Vincent told me.

Infrequently, I kept up with the Carrosse squatters. In particular I kept up with a man who went by the name

Yabon Paname, by birth Franck Hiltenbrand, and his companion, Catherine Poulain, both of them artists. They had been generous in taking me in and each was, fair enough, eager for me to publish already. Catherine occasionally expressed this eagerness in connection with a worry about Yabon and his wellbeing.

"Paname," a name he had adopted, is slang for a gritty people's Paris, like calling New York City "Gotham," and there were people who saw him, as he wanted, as its symbol. The name had played its needful role in all the newspapers around the turn of the millennium—*Libération*, *Le Monde*, *Le Figaro*, *Le Parisien*—and for a time in certain circles the interest seemed to hold. As late as 2009, *Technikart*, an arts magazine, profiled Yabon, giving him a raffish, Robin-Hood glow. Though that coverage too was in the past by the time that I knew him, it lingered on in his thoughts, perhaps as a constant companion for Yabon tried out on me a line I recognized. He would wander Paris haunted by a longing of empty buildings, which called his name, he said—as he had said before. One of the journalists who had reported about Le Carrosse in its day, David Langlois-Mallet, who had done this reporting for *Politis*, told me, "He's one of those people who are a little bit the soul of Paris, in my opinion. His grandmother lived in the fourth arrondissement, like my family, near Notre Dame, and was evicted by Chirac, by the construction projects." Inspired by this, I asked Yabon if he really had lived in that district, which street, and his response was approximate; the street, whatever it was called, was right by the arrondissement mayor's office.

By the time I met Yabon at Le Carrosse, late in 2011, he would emerge from the room where he slept just to brush his teeth in the kitchen, the building's sink. He encouraged me to email a city official about my project and name my American university, remarking to Catherine that this might give a *piste*, a way in—he was hoping the city might recognize Le Carrosse as artistic and grant it relief from eviction. He had accepted the baton of the squat's leadership, he'd been the one, and when eviction came that spring, Yabon resisted it with dignity. The barricade he raised was made of "Scotch tape" as Anastasia, there to see it, said; yet she admired his commitment to the gesture. He moved in with Catherine, her suburb an hour's train away. Infection developed in his lungs. Doctors who examined him attributed it to "professional stress," he said. All that summer he worked with Catherine to make a tapestry out of flypaper and, when he left her, threw it out, as Catherine said. She was keeping, for him or herself, an archive of clippings about Yabon. In a blue dusk I followed her home from the station. She reached to switch on the light of a fish tank. "I'm the one who feeds the fish," she said. "I'm the one who feeds the rabbit."

In the early days of Le Carrosse there was almost a "rule," Penisson said, that "artistic quality was not to be evaluated or discussed." To me Yabon spoke rapturously about an effect that was atmospheric rather than specific. "You stayed ten days in paradise, Jacqueline. It was paradise, that place." In paradise he'd made irreverent installations: delicate webs of trash, a neighborhood noise machine, a campaign of his own for mayor. He rigged up rubber gloves filled with water to gently slap the squat's guests into awareness. Over the years he expressed, in alternation with his eagerness for me to publish, a suspicion that anything I ultimately published would betray him, and at times he made obscure excuses for his art. It was craftsmanship, Yabon only an artisan.

He had wanted to make people happy, his work suitable for children as well as adults. When I asked in 2014 if he identified with any lineage of Parisian artists, with any group of artists in Paris, he answered he wasn't Picasso, he wasn't Modigliani but resembled them in that he, too, suffered. We had come from a meeting at an arts center, a legal one, in a former industrial building on the Rue de Charenton. Yabon would have it that I go along to watch as he failed to sell the administrators on himself. He had put on weight in the suburbs, his beard whitened and grown messy, and that day he held a wad of tissue paper to a thumb, a cut. "I was like the *bête curieuse*," he told me afterward; I watched the blood bloom. And yet the very décor of the space, a loft, was lifted from the art squats to which Yabon had devoted himself, he continued. Forty-nine, he feared he was old for opening squats. In gestures, subordinate clauses, he made apologies so small I wanted to assure him they weren't necessary but couldn't bear to wound him by my show of having noticed. He deplored the precarious lease and the artists at 59 Rivoli who'd signed and yet, occasionally, gave me to understand he had deserved an equally nice deal.

After the eviction of Le Carrosse the journalist Langlois-Mallet wrote in the online journal Rue89 to polemicize against what he saw as the city's cultural politics and decry the treatment to which it had subjected, even by "blackmailing" them, the local cultivar of "artists"—or so it seems to me; this article, saved to my hard drive, has since disappeared from the Web. What I find instead, linking back, is a response by Julien Bargeton, "cultural adjunct" at the offices of the twentieth arrondissement, where Le Carrosse of course was located. That March 28 he too wrote for Rue89, first to valorize the local culture and second to instruct Langlois-Mallet that Langlois-Mallet was laboring under "dangerous illusions." When the city preempted the building of Le Carrosse in 2005, it had "proposed" to rehouse those living there in greatest need and bring the building up to code then to assign it, by a *convention précaire*, to the Le Carrosse squatters. In return, Bargeton went on, the squatters were meant to keep promises of their own: to refrain from hosting events or in any way turning a profit; to accept, meanwhile, no new residents. They fulfilled none of those, he wrote. Catherine told me there had been, during the time of her residence at Le Carrosse, no talks. Yabon would claim he had turned down their offer. They stopped the mayor in the street, said Catherine. I'd asked Bargeton, recording him, about the squat's eviction. He'd closed a folder, rapped it on the desk. "It's not enough to call yourself an artists' squat," he said. "They're liars." He meant that they had not been artists. It was for this reason that Yabon had been left homeless.

What kind of bohemian was Yabon? Murger, introducing his novel, presents a typology. There's the *Bohème ignorée*, made up of artists doomed to obscurity, unable to publicize their efforts. "Innocents," disciples of "art for art's sake," by Murger's definition they die young, once in a while leaving behind something worth laying eyes on. There are, too, "amateurs," drawn to bohemianism out of rebellion against their families, and they have "nothing in common with art." In the end they will just "marry their little cousin" and live out their days as "notaries." At last there's "official" Bohemia, per Murger composed of artists and writers destined indelibly for visibility, notoriety, for—this word does not appear—*success*.

A Type One bohemian, then—or not. An important error I find in Murger's typology, occurring in that first definition, is in his use of the phrase "art for art's sake." Murger gives this a contingent sense, art which does not catch on, but *l'art pour l'art* had taken on in the nineteenth century a meaning of its own, intrinsic also to the work, aesthetic. Flaubert, one of the few contemporaries of Baudelaire's that Baudelaire liked, is famous for wanting to write "a book about nothing"; he is considered a proponent. Movement like this has been characterized as a response to events of the 1848 insurrection, events of ambiguity and failure after which artists and writers found it difficult to throw themselves into supposed socially beneficial work, for which there had been a vogue in the 1840s. Baudelaire changed sides. "He proclaims around 1850 that art must not be separated from utility; a few years later, he defends art for art's sake," Benjamin writes in "La Bohème." Characteristically, Benjamin presents this shift without judgment (and, just there, without context), but because he is similarly studious in transmitting the notion of a useful art, there is, still, the sense of some purpose from which Baudelaire can be understood in one direction only to have fallen. Unlike Type One bohemians, he wanted badly to sell his work, stuffing letters to his mother with assurances like the one he'd write a saleable novel or two that very month if only she sent money. "La Bohème" ends, its closing line, on this Baudelaire who "looks already for a buyer."

After Le Bloc's eviction, after the opening of La Connaissance, spring 2014 became summer, and though I had been all year very busy in the squats, I at that point took up with a boyfriend. He was forty-nine to my twenty-three, an artist, and the language with which we carried on in our relationship wasn't native to either; he had emigrated from Syria to attend the Beaux-Arts; notes to himself left strewn about his apartment in the fourteenth arrondissement were to me objects of curiosity and mystery. In Arabic, I couldn't read them. Similarly, because I wrote in English, he couldn't read my work without great effort. He would have introduced himself as an *artiste-peintre*, "artist-painter"; the expression may appear redundant but is standard in French, conveying an important, honorable distinction, like "medical doctor." Daily the evidence was mounting that he was a real artist. Presented with any piece of fruit, he knew just how to cut it up beautifully; from apples, he removed the skins in peelings that were not only continuous but of even width. And he was very sensitive. Returning to his apartment after a walk—because I lived at the other end of the city and was dramatically underemployed, I would stay for a couple of days—I, just once, took out a scarf, picked up at a *vide-grenier*, Parisian pop-up flea market. I thought I'd give it to my mom. He looked at me in wounded horror. He was extremely allergic to dust, any textile that came in from outside was suspect. He gave me a plastic bag to put the scarf in and we never spoke of it again. Very influenced by ideas of his about art, labor, and time as well as impressed by the artist's sensitivity, I tried asking his opinion on whether squats were a good subject. "Of course," he said, sounding nonplussed, "anything you've been working on for so long will be good." This strikes me, in some moods, as simple, as the nicest thing that one adult can tell another: to keep going.

In my heart I didn't know what I wanted. Just as I was getting together with that boyfriend I ran into another guy I'd met briefly, at a party at one of the Brians'. He hadn't seemed so talkative but had followed up the next day with a long email about Venice, where I was thinking of going, a city he knew well. Italian, he was nearer my age, a photographer, and I came across him in Buttes-Chaumont Park, near where he lived too. It was a sunny, beautiful day. He looked a little dazed. He said he had something for me. He had, he pulled it out of his bag, a paperback, a French translation of the novel by Italo Calvino whose title is rendered in English as *Invisible Cities*. He had been carrying it around, he said, waiting to give it to me. Later I would see he had written, as a dedication within it, the book's own last lines, signing his name to them, which struck me as so like a photographer. But my name wasn't there and later still I would think it possible that, while surely he had intended to give the book away to somebody, he hadn't planned in advance that I would be the recipient. From the park we walked together to the Russian Orthodox church Saint-Serge, near my house on the Rue de Crimée, which he had been planning to photograph. We walked around it, a rose-colored building set back from the street on bright green land, a quiet place that was familiar and where I liked to go. He took a lot of pictures. A row of bells, a vegetable garden. I pointed out tall wires standing together, antennae I guessed, and mentioned that they looked to me like the rigging of a ship; later again, after he didn't text back, I would wonder if that had been why, if it was that weird thing I had said about a ship.

    For want of a photographer, then, for want of that photographer, I had my painter, and spent a lot of time at his apartment reading the book this other man had given me. I was frustrated as I read because I felt I had an enormous, incalculable amount of work to do on my project about squats, and reading the book was taking so long; it was full of involved terms from architecture and urbanism I had to look up, and it wasn't even a French book; surely there existed English translations just as good, but there I was, killing myself. I read on a hard bench my boyfriend dressed with a nearly flat mattress to use it as both couch and bed; to my right was the hot plate of a kitchen, the shelf crammed with books. (There was one book in English, Hemingway's *The Old Man and the Sea*. Pencil marks, translations, filled the margins of the first two pages.) To my left was a window giving onto a quiet courtyard on the other side of which a neighbor, quite visible, let prayer flags fly. As I read my boyfriend worked in the apartment's other room at something for which he didn't need a studio, stencils perhaps, or something on the computer, or he would prepare food. I didn't like to offer my help because he was old and set in his ways and the only job he would trust me with was the washing of herbs "one leaf at a time" (*feuille par feuille*), a phrase at which I still recoil. I looked out at the late light and wondered what would become of me. Automatically I'd received the opportunity to renew my contract with the university for another year and I had done this very naturally, not having any other job, and so I was going to stay on in Paris one more year at least. I had filled dozens of notebooks and got mad at the suggestion that I pile them with spiral bindings alternating so that the stack would level out. I had a lot of quotes; as a student doing the reporting I had waited impatiently for a squatter to say anything of metaphorical resonance. José-Xavier of Le Stendhal, among others, had obliged. "We'll never win it," he'd said, about an eviction suit. "We can only delay."

About the book I was reading I had developed an idea that it was an important one among books about cities, I would have to read it for my project. In the end the argument for getting through was that it had been given me, it was what I had. As Calvino writes: "You take delight, not in a city's seven or seventy wonders, but in the answer it gives to a question of yours." The paradox of Paris Syndrome—a psychic ailment that tourists from Japan, paradigmatically, came down with when the European city failed to live up to some dream—was that while sufferers may have had Paris in common, Paris didn't suffice to explain it. In that summer I began to think of writing as a compromise by which a thing could last, as a precarious lease on life.

¶ While I was shadowing Le Général in his work to establish La Connaissance, Guy sent me a text; it read something like: "Hello, Jacqueline, are we mad at each other or what?"

How strange, I thought. I wrote back, apologizing that I hadn't been in touch. I explained, as periodically I found myself doing in that stage of my project, that I was helping to open a squat. I looked forward to seeing Guy afterward.

He picked the café Ménil on the Rue de Ménilmontant, just uphill of La Miroiterie—a nothing, run-down bar, the décor pessimistic, premonitory of its own decay. Wall panels at angles, misshapen tiles worked to camouflage cracks in their development, anticipating them. My recorder picked up sounds of traffic, laughter. I can be heard asking Guy to speak more loudly. His low voice had changed, I thought, fading, softening, and from the difficulty of hearing him over the street noise I thought he hadn't noticed. He had not made accommodation for the change.

The experience he told me of had begun as a "malaise" and developed into "crisis." At its origin was a feeling of spectatorship that had, at Le Bloc, overwhelmed Guy. After the eviction, he was beset by the worry that police might stop him and ask him to inform on Bloc squatters. Simultaneous with this feeling developed a suspicion that Le Bloc had been "power games." He felt trapped in his spectator's role, unable to act though action might have been required of him as he came too late, he felt, to understand.

The feelings intensified, and he checked himself in. He recovered and left. He then experienced a second crisis. In the end, he was hospitalized for two three-week periods, as he told me at the café. He woke up to a swollen face, gaining weight. These changes in his body scared him, the condition of the other patients scared him, and Guy was able to fulfill the resolution he set firmly, to get well.

I had thought of Guy as my teacher in the squats and deferentially I let him know, imagining he would take this as a compliment.

"If you don't pay attention," he said, "you'll be inside it and not realize what has happened."

Years out and in a different mood he would impress on me the need clearly to state that people on the margins were that way because they had refused, out of refusal. At the café what obsessed him was another revelation, late enough, that the exploitation as well as the violence of the society from which he had sought, in squats, refuge—to which he had sought out an alternative—were present there, were even magnified. "They're worse than the capitalists," he told me. The American girls, Guy added, had been treated poorly. "They want bigger and bigger squats," he said, "it's like the real-estate market." He felt that "bandits" had manipulated "artists," holding them "hostage" in exchange for Le Bloc's respectability. But this predicament did not an artist make; few of the artists at Le Bloc had struck Guy as true artists. "It was as if being an artist was only a role," he said, "as if there was no content." Just the same as bandits, they made money on false pretenses.

A French word for madness, *délire*, is capacious. With the possessive pronoun it can be used to speak of a personal interest, a hobby or pursuit, self-deprecatingly. I knew it as Guy's term for the creative gift. At times it seemed to him that some madness of his had allowed him to see the situation at Le Bloc clearly. Telling me how he would render the squats in his book, hinting didactically at how they might take shape in mine, he said he made amalgams to disguise them. "This allows me to enter my madness as I wish."

At times it seemed to Guy that the connections forged with others at Le Bloc came at a cost, or did to others. He had seen these others pay. A madness of the margins, it had momentum of its own, a tug. "The symptoms become stronger as you find yourself with more and more marginal people," Guy said. "If you choose to be marginal, that's death. It is a system that works automatically."

Le Général had invited him to join in working at La Connaissance and wondered why Guy refused. Guy would not return to any squat. "It wasn't a squat as they used to be," he said, "the squats like Le Carrosse. That had a human scale."

Guy had met with students, not the only ones who customarily would show up much as I did with their projects at Le Bloc, this group students of philosophy. After the eviction they had asked him to sit for an interview about the human experience under extreme circumstances. He invited them to Le Ménil, anatomized Le Bloc's decline, eventually reporting back to me that they scored well, found success, news he was happy to share.

¶ I also kept up with Jaouad, the musician from Morocco who had been my neighbor on Le Bloc's third floor. I would meet him in Clichy, the northern suburb where he slept in a hotel room. The hotel, in an act suggestive of the surrealism that characterizes the *banlieue*, was named the Hotel Seoul. It was a narrow, dour building, posted rates running between forty-three and sixty-nine euros. Small windows at the back framed a leafless tree to which a single pomegranate clung. Jaouad got me past the front desk with difficulty, difficulty that brought on a bad mood. He sweet-talked the man at the desk, saying something in Arabic—I didn't know what he had said—the posted rule being that guests were not allowed. Smoking wasn't, either; on another visit I watched him light up just to be interrupted by a knock, a visit from a clerk who made him put it out. Jaouad did so, on the windowsill.

That window gave onto the street. Through its thin pane the noise of trucks reached us. Within the room's constraints he had cultivated habits, returning at the end of every day to wash out socks. He missed his family. He warned me not to work too hard; he was making money here and there, playing his instrument. He was slowly moving through the steps to immigrate. These subjects exhausted, I would receive, on occasion, a serenade, songs on the spot showing the mark of the training he had received in hospitality in Morocco—showmanship that made me uncomfortable for its tailoring, its pandering to tourists I might have looked like. I was embarrassed by this evidence of a failure to have set myself apart. He made me watch the song accelerate as if getting out ahead, the joke of a ventriloquist whose dummy has gone rogue. Some months after the eviction, in response to the questions I was forever asking, he encouraged me to stop dwelling on Le Bloc; he saw that I was living in the past.

He said the filmmakers had fallen out of touch though they had said something about traveling with him, about a visit to Morocco. At last, after perhaps six months, I also stopped visiting Jaouad.

The picture of Jaouad that comes most readily to mind isn't one I took down in my notes, however. We are walking along the Quai d'Austerlitz where, a year or two after this, during the height of what was termed officially an immigration crisis, a line of men would set up tents. The embankment was cobblestone, the night dark, and Jaouad sang to me, a song everywhere in Paris that year, "Formidable" by the Belgian artist known as Stromae. The speaker is a wandering man who has been cast out from his household, drunk. The form is that of street harassment, a series of interpellations: he calls out, warning bystanders that beauty among other things is fleeting. *Formidable*, Jaouad sang, the refrain, telling me I was formidable, *tu étais formidable*, and swallowing the pun that follows, *j'étais fort minable*, "I was seriously pathetic." My memory is that I was unable to hear the song as Jaouad wanted me to hear it that night. My failure was an inability to isolate the poetry of the lyric from the position of the speaker.

¶ "My buddy has trouble with artists. With artists he's had trouble 'cause with artists, and we call that *bobos*, the *petits bourgeois*, in French we say *s'encanailler*, old French word that means to frequent those who don't have money 'cause it's cool, pop, it's ghetto, see, it's mean, but we don't choose it. They have the choice.

"I come from Spain but I'm not a concierge, my grandma was not a concierge, and I am not the custodian of a building.

"You get there, Barbès. You raze a packet of houses because they are dilapidated, full of illegals, illegals, let's say immigrants, Blacks, *quoi*, or Arabs, it's scary, *fin bref*. Developer arrives. He razes. He builds a new building, all new, we are going to put in *bobos*, the *petits bourgeois*, people who quote-unquote succeed. And then what? Now that it's built and those people are living in there, they have to be protected! The neighborhood is hell! You see? We have to protect them! There are crack dealers! It's *merde, quoi*."

"But with poor people we didn't have to protect them?" I asked, prompting the man to go on.

"We don't care, they kill each other, it's not important."

The man, who wanted to be called by his graffiti tag, Fakom, had participated in Le Bloc's opening team. We were sitting along the Belleville boulevard, a neighborhood he liked because its streets were always peopled. He confessed that he felt lonely except in crowds. He was courteous and forthcoming and emanated a diffuse nervous energy, adjusting his back and hands, leaping up to ask passersby for cigarettes. Tarps framed the terrace; they whipped like sails, combining with the street's noise to make a violent sound behind him on my tape as if that of the city straining in assent that it required, as Fakom was implying, chaos force.

¶ Periodically I stopped by the squat in Clichy where the Femen activists and Branislav still lived. Space upstairs was given over to a Femen headquarters, the walls there busy with murals by a *Charlie Hebdo* illustrator, but the women themselves were often absent, or quarreling. Few rooms of the facility, a former water-treatment plant, were small enough to serve as bedrooms, and the squat had an underpopulated, listless air. One afternoon Branislav granted an interview in an upstairs room he used, where ideas of his took form on a chalkboard. He revisited themes of art, nations—at that time in 2014, he still identified as Yugoslavian; he was avowedly anti-American—and representation. He didn't write to sell, didn't make sculpture to exhibit and so to win glory and, when it followed on, fortune. What challenged him, then, was striking a balance between "spirit" and "body." As he was forced to acknowledge, he had a body to feed.

I offered that showing or publishing a piece of work might be seen as a part of the work. Ahead of making money or glorifying the self as he had said, the aim might be to address an audience or contribute to a conversation.

"Yes, yes, yes," Branislav said, "that's very good, of course, but how can you trust those with whom you're sharing the ideas?"

That was the point, I said—a retort that, on my tape, comes out fast.

That June 5, one of the Ukrainian members of Femen, Yana Zhdanova, ran afoul of French law. What she did was destroy the waxwork of Vladimir Putin in the Grévin Museum, the Parisian wax museum. The occasion was a state visit of Putin's to Paris. On paying a visit in advance Yana had judged the head to be of heavy wax, causing her to rule out beheading the statue and decide, instead, to stab it. On the day, checking that the journalists she had tipped off were in position, she flung open her jacket and sweatshirt to reveal her breasts and, across them, a mirror image of the phrase KILL PUTIN, having been alone in preparing for this happening. Her face contorted as she tore into the waxwork, screaming. It fell to the floor. The head that she had thought so hard broke like an egg, scattered its fragments. She straddled the figurine, slicing deeply into the resin of the body. Drawing back the stake in preparation she had held it for a moment, though, at her arms' highest arc to stare directly into the camera. Surrounding her are a garnet carpet and curtains like the inside of a jewelry box. At a distance of inches were the impassive waxwork faces of Obama, Hollande, and, smiling with uncharacteristic solicitousness, Angela Merkel.

Yana would struggle for years after that day's work to contest the charge of indecent exposure, a sex crime in France. She considered the charges politically motivated. No individual had been convicted in this sense for baring breasts since a 1965 episode that found the perpetrator playing ping-pong on a beach in Cannes, as Yana's lawyer Marie Dosé told me. Even then, the bobbing of the uncovered breasts, rather than the nudity in itself, was judged obscene. Journalists reporting about Yana's protest struck a bemused note, in one case comparing the scene with a slapstick by Jacques Tati as if the action was supposed to be a joke. For Yana it was not a joke. I hadn't known about the protest in advance, but in interviewing Yana I'd begun to understand that her reaction to death threats made on the Femen, to a falling out with the group's French members, and to the shelling of a city in eastern Ukraine, Makiivka, where she had grown up and where her mother lived, was to redouble her commitment to her activism. "You have to have a motivation which is stronger than comfort, your comfort," she told me. "I like risk."

Though the squat would not be evicted for good until October 2016, the case against Yana, Branislav, and their roommates had been settled in the month of Yana's protest, in June of 2014. I visited them there that summer, the hangar full of sunlight. Vines crept in every direction on railings and beams. Courgettes, they were sending out tendrils that closed over air. The kitchen was appealingly dim, floral chiffon draping a window. Dishes lay drying. Cabinetry too small for the space had been propped up on cinderblocks. Thumbtacks lay here and there and books on the shelves were stamped VINCENNES, the loan or plunder of a university. Noise from a construction site was muffled—sounds of metal on metal—and a sliding door that gave onto the courtyard was malfunctioning. It slid open and snapped closed on its own, making a startling sound.

When I met Yana there July 15, our interview avoiding the subject of her attack on the Putin statue, she was working to repair a figurine of a different world leader. A miniature of Tito, at one time the Yugoslavian president for life, it belonged not to Branislav but to a Russian friend of Yana's. It had broken while she was over at the friend's place to watch soccer. She had taken the repair job in charge and, as we spoke, transferred superglue from its tube to the doll's ankles, where the rest of the body had come off the base. The white insides of the figure showed plainly. The Communist wore a commodious jacket, gaze cast downward, hands tucked neatly behind his back.

It was as if, protest over with, she had nothing left to express. The situation of her Ukrainian family was "too complicated" and "not interesting," and she had asked her mother to leave where she lived, which was near a military base. This was the case, I'd been informed, for my Syrian boyfriend's parents, he would say it guaranteed their safety, and I asked Yana if the proximity was any protection to her mother. It was not. Her hair was dripping in her cup. She had to look after her mental health, she said. Apologizing that she was not talkative she took off the rubber gloves she had been using and left for the bank, a personal necessity. She had an exam the day after in a mandatory French class, and she had to go to the doctor.

¶ The *tontons* did, in the end, open further squats. During a vernissage in one such setting in the eleventh arrondissement I encountered, to my surprise, Luís, the Spanish vagabond who, greeting me warmly, appeared happy—I was happy to see him—and healthy. After opening the squat, Fred from Le Bloc told me, another from Le Bloc confirmed, its residents had set out after Luís eventually to find him sleeping in a bookstore, bring him home.

Another of these squats was located, like Jaouad's hotel and like the Femen squat, in Clichy. In retrospect, I might have taken this shift as a signal to leave off reporting. My project about Paris, for which I had moved to Paris, had taken me, was taking me out of Paris; to be precise, it situated me so I lived in Paris and, to continue in the project, regularly traveled that small distance out of Paris, and in Clichy a party was held with many from Le Bloc I recognized. The people living there all lit a bonfire, brewed coffee and pear cider. A neighbor meanwhile had been invited to cook and sell tagine. Girls my age who were jugglers worked one-handed in a hangar like a barn. They took charcoal from a ruminating brazier and used it to leave writing on the floor.

Night fell, and one of the friends from Le Bloc brought out a pair of paper lanterns, big ones, confiding he liked to buy them every time he had a little money. At the mouths briquettes were lit, and these lanterns expanded into golden pope's-hat shapes some four feet tall. It took three guests to hold the both of them as like leashed animals they strained, were whisked out to the street, allowed to rise. The party rushed outside to watch, craning our necks. The lanterns looked like jellyfish. One guest offered that, beyond the right altitude, air currents would flatten them. Another stated they'd reach aliens. What would aliens make of us? Soon the lanterns looked to lack depth. High in their ascent they shrunk to points, small enough to seem celestially far away. They disappeared. We crossed the street and went into the house.

¶ Easily detectable in secondary sources, the architects Claude Parent and André Remondet, working in the "functionalist" tradition, took a kind of care in modulating the façade of the 1974 building that would become Le Bloc to lend it an "organic" character, like "skin": a "readability." Concrete furrows, a form from underground like a rodent's burrow, were to catch light, minimize dirtying, and give the building an approachable appearance harmonious with its neighbors, the houses of "the Mouzaïa," themselves built low in cautious deference to the caverns that underlie this part of Paris. Adjacent to the no-build *Zone*, captured in Atget's photos as "a silent world in which nature is weary and no longer able to afford a welcome to the poor," the neighborhood in question had long been a marginal, minor sector, where the element of chance denied so strenuously by the order of the city center entered in, where business ventures failed, especially the aboveboard. In the latter half of the nineteenth century "ravines" were filled in and, at present-day Place du Danube, a horse market established that "very quickly collapsed."

Among the primary documents, requests to approve plans for construction submitted to city authorities strike an eerie balance of banality and, begging the question of whether something wasn't swept under the rug, portent. Letters sent to the *Inspection générale des carrières* or IGC, a Parisian body charged with monitoring the city's underground, were, just for example, mere formalities, returned with a stamp on the verso: "According to the statistical documents of the Technical Service of Quarries, the terrain of interest in the planned construction is situated to the exterior of the old quarries currently known." But each of the letters eliciting that response had stated formally, "The planned construction is to be built on land located in the zone of the old quarries"—over the years suggesting a feeling strong on someone's part that there was, down below, a void. Many IGC records are not stored at the Paris Archives but are still in use, and the IGC archivist required any inquiry to be approved in a first instance by a mayoral press office, which didn't get back to me. It was therefore in an IGC record dating to July 1, 1886, accessed in the Paris Archives, that I found an attestation to the presence of cavities "along all the length" of the Rue de Mouzaïa. Specifically, these are "subterranean exploitations of a great mass along all its length... presumably backfilled."

To build tall in this place, the state pulled rank. A July 18, 1973 letter to a supervisory authority, the prefecture, from the ministry of health, which had commissioned the 1974 edifice, is coercive and even gangsterly in tone. Parisian authorities, memo after memo, had made known their disposition to the project, "unfavorable" for it made too extensive a use of the parcel. The building was too high-density, especially given its proximity to the densifying renovation underway at the Place des Fêtes. In response to these worries, a man no less than the ministry's *directeur du cabinet*, Pierre Manière, addressed a sugary assurance to the Paris prefect that the establishment of operations of the ministry's in the Mouzaïa building was in the best interest of many, including that of the prefect. (Spillover from certain offices to be accommodated had been taking up space in Manière's building.)

An air of disrepute was old in that place. Postwar, the smaller building then belonging to the ministry of labor was allocated to its subsidiary, one *Association nationale interprofessionnelle pour la formation rationnelle de main-d'œuvre*, National Interprofessional Organization for the Rational Training of the Workforce. The utopianism suggested by this name is of a different flavor from the squatters'. Lost, in many other ways, to history, the group appears at least to have conducted psychological evaluations in this same location in a smaller building designated on blueprints by the abbreviation BÂTIMENT PSYCHO, "psycho building."

By the summer of 1964, the ministry wanted badly to build on the site "two collapsible buildings on the ground floor, for use as offices (orientation and placement center for youth)." The lull of summer had perhaps set in by the time it submitted a request, that July 22, for prefectoral approval. It seems approval was slow in coming. Letters were sent, "very urgent"; the wait was then, from all the evidence, untenable. A handwritten letter dated that September 9 and addressed to the functionaries of the mayor's *architectes voyers* preserves, still today, the words of one concerned person living on the Rue de Mouzaïa for whom there was, already at that early date, something very like a squat:

```
Paris 9 septembre 64

Monsieur l'Architecte

If you would desire to see: How it is possible to
build 2 Buildings of 36 x 9 "Without a Building
permit" come, then, and pay a little visit to 58,
Rue de La Mouzaïa Paris 19th.
```

¶ *The Paris Underground*

A punchline to Paris is that it's full of holes. On July 30, 1880, during a brilliant summer storm and on the odd-numbered side of Saint-Michel Boulevard, a crevasse opened, eighteen meters long and seven wide. The city made sure to fill in, after that, all its foundationally dangerous abscesses—missing at least one. In the night of July 5 and 6, 1979, in the courtyard of 4 Rue Tardieu in Montmartre, another pit appeared, eight meters wide, six deep.

In the seventeenth and eighteenth centuries the caverns had proved troublesome—as in the case of Val-de-Grâce Church, for which the foundation ate up its budget—or lucky, as with the new Observatory. Scientists made use of a cavity deep as the building was tall. For centuries policy had obligated builders to coat houses in the plaster whose gray still characterizes the city, fireproofing it in patches as, out from under where they lived, Parisians took not only gypsum for plaster and calcite-rich limestone but clay for tiles, marl, sand for glass and bricks. Louis XVI, his building projects sagging, established the IGC. In 1777, as he was vesting it with powers of inspection, a house on the Rue d'Enfer, "Hell Street," collapsed into a quarry that lay twenty meters deep.

By the end of that century, neighbors to Paris's cemeteries, which were many and poorly maintained, were complaining of miasma. The soil of Saint-Innocent was thought to strip corpses to bone; its odor was said nearly to have asphyxiated a living person. Bodies spilled through spongy ground into his basement. The city, faced with this problem as well as that of the cavities, began to have exhumed the corpses and use those dead to plug up the holes. By the time the tunnels were ruled off limits an irresistible lore had formed. The doorman of Val-de-Grâce went down in 1793 to be found in 1804, identifiable by a ring of keys. In 2004, police found, in a cavern, a working movie theater.

A year after I had published my article about La Miroiterie's imminent eviction, a year after the *New York Times* had published its ("For Enclave of Rebel Artists, Much in Life Was Free, but Not Real Estate," March 13, 2013), La Miroiterie was still open. I felt happy for the squatters and a little sheepish. I walked by the squat that spring, twice in a week, with a sometime squatter who had helped to get it open in the first place as he said, a juggler known in squats as Snoopy. He shared his real name, Stéphane Bourotte. He had juggled at Le Bloc, and I interviewed him about both squats, one day following a march in protest against the impending eviction of a third squat, also in Belleville, La Cantine. The Jourdain market, disassembling nearby, gave off a smell of fish on melting ice. A tawny dog with spotted paws leapt about and lay down in the road. The façade of La Miroiterie had been re-painted with a version of the *Looney Tunes* last title card in which the rabbit was scarred, smoked, and looked challengingly out, inquiring, "Is that all, folks?"

"The artists I knew have aged," Snoopy told me. "Then, we were all outlaw squatters, and maybe now, those who have been rehoused someplace are happy to have a little place to sleep and not be evicted the next day..." He had spent many years in Belleville, living in a cramped, old-fashioned building with an airshaft for a courtyard, in the nineties taking part in the resistance against a plan for demolition. Headlines called the protests a "second barricade," second to the Paris Commune. Neighbors had met at a squat called La Forge de Belleville, since closed. "Now it's beautiful there," Snoopy said, "because they've let the vines grow."

He smiled knowingly when he heard La Miroiterie was also closing, this time from a comrade, from a person marching with us. Without pretending anyone had been alarmist Snoopy gave the reason why, according to him, that squat would never be evicted. No one could build on the parcel. There were caverns in the ground below. I started. I had thought of the squatters' stories as tall tales, but they had involved a river down there, dark and frothing. Now we saw into the courtyard. The stone wall of the factory, as Snoopy pointed out, was buckling. Men nailing in beams to prop it up saluted us. "They dug out all the stone from underneath Paris and used it to build the city over the holes," Snoopy said. "Smart, right?"

The implication seemed to be that all of Paris would buckle one day, fall, the underground reclaiming it. We walked to Belleville Park and could barely make out the Eiffel Tower. The city's transit system would be free to ride the next day, part of its response to the unusual pollution. A fine white mist gripped the buildings. They faded into the contours of the valley.

On April 20, 2014, during a concert given by a Swedish band called Doberman Cult, a wall of La Miroiterie did cave in. (According to news reports, three people were hurt, none seriously.) To Guy, who had played capoeira with the squat's Brazilian musicians, I mentioned one squatter theory: a tree's roots, growing, had pushed at the wall. Guy laughed. His own theory was that an agent of the neighboring establishment La Bellevilloise, a gentrifiers' bar, had thrown a Molotov cocktail, angling to buy the land.

Police evicted the squat soon after, though Guy believed that the Brazilian men still slept there, climbing in despite concrete that walled off windows. For his part, Guy was on page 240 of his book about the squats. He felt he had hardly begun.

The longtime concert organizer at La Miroiterie, Michel Ktu, whose ancestor was a Communard, lived higher on the Belleville hill. He couldn't reach La Miroiterie in time to witness the eviction. By that morning at six, most of the squatters—though not all—had left, he told me.

¶ Over a span of years I visited Valentin and Anastasia where they worked—the *café de la gare* of a minor suburb with its piano played by Valentin one-handed (the other on his trumpet), a loft in Montreuil honeycombed by studios. Anastasia introduced me to a man who said, "I knew Le Carrosse. I knew all Paris. I even knew Yabon. I've lived in Paris forty-five years and no one knows as many streets as I do. Out of seven thousand I know probably five thousand five hundred. Not even the taxi drivers know as many as I do. I walk all night, and people used to walk all night, but no one walks in Paris anymore." He was slight, sitting on a table. Shyly, a white greyhound approached us.

"What a beautiful animal," Anastasia said.

"Like a doe," I said.

The man asked if I had spoken French already when I got to Paris.

"Very poorly," said Anastasia. She liked to say they'd taught me all I knew.

¶ How many streets did I know, really? In 2019, I moved from Number 25, Rue Alexandre Dumas to Number 11, Rue Alexandre Dumas.

"You have a thing with the Rue Alexandre Dumas," my friend Juliette said.

"No," I said.

"Yes, you do," she said. "You're going to do a writing project about the Rue Alexandre Dumas."

"No," I said. "Too early to talk about," I added.

We were neighbors, and we were meeting where we usually met, at a café on the Place de La Réunion, where the Rue Alexandre Dumas in fact ends. It was a broad and flat circular plaza, all around was housing for families, and in the warmer months children and teenagers would gather to ride bikes, skateboards, scooters, tricycles, and even toy cars so you couldn't sit there in the spring or summer without witnessing, guaranteed, at least one kid fall. Catastrophe would dawn so palpably, but they could handle it.

"I have the impression that something has happened with your French," Juliette said approvingly.

She worked in theater and had visited one in Brussels, a venue she thought I might appreciate hearing about. It was home to a cat, extraordinarily beautiful and of an unusual breed. The owner of the theater, without any dimming of the aura of this animal, owned the cat. Periodically kittens were coaxed from it and sold at a thousand euros apiece. In this way the cat's fecundity supported the theater's art materially, and as Juliette was given a tour she was shown diverse appurtenances—spotlights—all purchases with income from the breeder, which was treated beautifully. Art, far from being independent, incurred debts as surprising as these artists' to a cat.

¶ In March of 2017, Guy told me that his manuscript about Le Carrosse, Le Bloc, and the rest had been stolen. Some thief had taken the computer with the file of the reworked manuscript—then 248 pages, the only copy—as well as the notebooks that constituted Guy's handwritten first draft, complete at some 392 pages. The culprit had broken in without a trace. Guy had titled the book *Le Voisin acoustique*, and it had been a good book.

We were sitting at the café Ménil, our old table. The mirrors had been repaired. I had complimented the barman on the job.

"Who can you tell you've written a manuscript, and someone's stolen it?" Guy was questioning himself. "Who will understand?"

It was as if I wasn't there. It was as if I was the thief.

¶ *The Parisian*

Like his metal sculptures, Pascal Hollemaert was tall and thin. He had mended his glasses with wire or tape in a fresh configuration every time I saw him. Although I'd been warned, long ago, that his scars were disfiguring, he did not seem disfigured, and I wrote in my notebook, "No scars." Just then Pascal removed those glasses, and I noticed obvious lines at his temple, and then near the hairline, over the bridge of the nose. My expectations had been so great I was confused when he proved human. The scars and glasses and long limbs made me imagine Pascal as requiring assembly, patching himself together of a morning to pass among humans who were whole.

To remember names he closed his eyes and chewed his lips, holding the rest of his face still. The effect was tantalizing as if he, too, were hanging on his every word. His lips were fleshy, eyes big, and while regarding me he often did not blink, not out of surprise or excitation but, simply enough, as if he had forgotten, for looking could absorb him, mortal tiredness placed its limits on the span of the attention, one thing at a time. The eyes finished each sentence by widening, remaining open. At this, rather than picking up any cue he had given to speak, I remained just transfixed, of course as if riveted. His sleeves fell loosely on lean, long arms matted with curly hair. The hands were enormous and the forefingers were shorter. The eyebrows were expressive and there was white in the hair and short beard. He swallowed audibly. He was nearly deaf in the right ear; when we walked, I walked to the left. The head lolled like a baby's, heavy for the neck. Outside the room he used at that bad squat, spreading over walls, he had stapled up window blinds, relics of the building, guided by Pascal to curve as seashells. In that room he used in 2014, where I went to meet him, he had collected a quantity of wire, rubber tubing, scrap plastic.

On the first day I spent interviewing him in the room, a former office, Pascal described opening Pôle Pi, a squat in Belleville that had fallen to violence, and mentioned the building's destiny, to become the national architecture school. "We were," he said, "the great Parisian gang of squat openers: Yabon..." He listed others. From a loaf of yellow bread he seized five consecutive slices and ate them together voraciously. One of his front teeth was missing a piece. Pôle Pi had started the trend in Paris for art squats, he went on. The gang of openers had been, however, young, and they had been overwhelmed by the size of the building as well as by others, people who came to it late, "undesirable" elements. Still, the squat was "relatively mythic," and while its first goal had been shelter, Pascal began to sculpt there.

At his window stood half a faceless woman, her metal body ending cleanly.

From deep in the squat a beat reached us. Pascal pulled on boots, tucked a black shirt into black jeans, brushed his hair, and left to bum tobacco—unsuccessfully for, as he explained upon returning, the day after and not that day would be payday for recipients of the RSA.

"Then I opened—all alone—the famous Carrosse. That was my thing, all mine." Summer, 2002, or early fall, the days still warm. Seeing pigeons leaving by a window he judged, correctly, the place was empty. He rattled off square meterage, two thousand. "An immense loft, weirdly arranged but perfect," it was well suited to performances. Pascal looped on a scarf. I saw that he was elegant despite his scarecrow build. He had entered the building by a window, he continued, and as he was an electrician wired it.

Years went by, and the City of Paris bought Le Carrosse. Pascal asked me to imagine the purchase of a building in which there was a fresco by, say, Leonardo da Vinci. The fresco, Pascal went on, belonged to the buyer, and so had Pascal belonged to the city, with its purchase of Le Carrosse. Paris bought Pascal with the building, its fixture, and for that reason could not evict him. In such a way he had lived long years as a fresco, bound to the building in exchange for its dazzling life. "I was a pick-up artist, an exhibitionist. Or maybe I was always just a shy guy... Of course I was always the king there, on a pedestal." "I had a dream for that thing," he said, "and for a time it worked. But then it fell apart, because stupidly, I fell into the drug..."

As his addiction overcame Pascal, he found he could less readily assume the feeling of control over Le Carrosse that he had enjoyed. And so he left, as he had told me, for the countryside—a four-year cure. In that time the squat was drastically diminished. "With me gone, Le Carrosse had little meaning anymore. So they tried to take hold of the reins but they couldn't."

The partner who had saved him was an actor and a playwright, a theatrical director. He could never understand why people like her chose to worry about him. When he considered how close to death an overdose had brought him, he thought, "If I'm still living, it would seem I still have things to do."

One day he said he'd open another squat, "Le Carrosse II." Having opened it, he would hold power over it.

Since making his return to the city of his accomplishments he had lost kilos, dozens. He pulled up his shirt to show me: all skin. Remaining sober at that squat where he was living could defeat him. "I'm always looking over my shoulder," he said. "It's hate, it's fear. And I went too far..."

I asked if he missed Le Carrosse.

"Don't exaggerate. I've grown up, my beauty."

He took off his glasses and leaned back to smoke, ashing frequently, one day giving the name of a documentarian who had made a film about him and his art. *À cœur de faire* was the film. "You can't forget, we're bums, too. I'm SDF. And I am not a victim. I have chosen this." Since returning to Paris ten months ago he'd made no sculpture, though he estimated he had made 240 metal sculptures in his life. Nothing else held his attention in that way. Love, maybe. "I'll never be happy," he said. "All this is too strong, and I am too sensitive..."

Each sculpture would, at some late stage, develop a will independent from his. "It doesn't want to be soldered, to stick."

"That means it's art," I said, "because it begins to have its own internal logic, like a novel."

"Yes," he said, "and sometimes I speak to them."

In the beautiful town near Bordeaux Pascal had seen a neighbor bring home an electric collar, for which the neighbor appeared to have paid a premium. It shocked the dog when the dog barked. "After all that, how do you expect me to be well? I'm ashamed of the human animal when I see such souls... and when you think that man is just a tiny, a tiny representation of the human, there are ones a thousand times more ferocious!... I would have loved to be an astronaut." He spoke of a one-way voyage.

I said that would call for enormous sacrifice. It reminds me of the bargain you struck for Le Carrosse.

"No! It is no sacrifice! I will abandon all of you..."

Pascal gave me a stack of CDs, and as my laptop had no disc drive, I brought them when I commuted. In a room reserved for use by teachers there were two old computers. Between responsibilities I worked to copy every file onto a flash drive, stretching my legs to look out at the Seine, that section of it slow and brown, flecked with dirty swans. I was surprised by the number entitled "Pascal" (as if another person, or a few people, had taken charge of his archives) as well as by the fragmentary nature of images like that of a long-haired woman crouched around a cigarette. Pascal told me another squatter at the place where he was living had stolen hard-copy archives of his. I did like photos of him soldering for a gorgeous play of sparks on stupid film, which could make no distinction between light and solid matter.

Once, meeting Pascal, I mentioned I'd played back the tape of our previous interview earlier that day, I'd listened, expecting this would please him, and he said angrily, "Only today?"

Not until his thirties did Pascal understand his turn to art as aspirational. "To get out of the world in which I was raised." He asked how old I was and compared my age with his, as if we were beginning a relationship. Soon enough, he warned, after I turned twenty-five, my body would stop producing cells. We were seated at a bar across from the mayor's office of Montreuil, a neighborhood bar with crumbling tiles half-open to a hot day.

He was born in the nineteenth arrondissement, not far from where I lived then, with congenital grand mal epilepsy. Born in May 1968, the month of uprisings, he was for a time the only child of a "very violent and crazy alcoholic father." He was twisting, tearing sugar packets and threw them to the floor. His mother had left when he was two, or one and a half, he could not forgive her, having as an adult reopened communication only to close it when she failed to appreciate his sculptures. She should have taken him. His father had painted, Impressionist landscapes. "He locked me in closets," Pascal went on. "He hit me every day for the first ten years of my life."

In his adolescence Pascal had lived, he said, in a home with other boys, in the Pré-Saint-Gervais. His epilepsy worsened, he went to hospitals. At seventeen, helped by one of his grandmothers, he settled down in the Nineteenth and learned his electrician's trade. Quickly he "fell into alcohol, obviously to be just like my father." Most of the scars except for one above the left eye, the work of a knife, resulted from a series of falls during this period, when seizures were frequent. Another scar followed the swoop of his shoulders, still another zigzagged inside a wrist, hidden, a deep one cut his chin in two, and there were more that pocked his face.

When he was twenty that grandmother, his father's mother, died. His dad then stopped eating, electing to drink himself into a coma. Pascal signed him over, away to death. "Up until the end, he fucked me over," Pascal said. He held jobs he considered ordinary until the age of twenty-five or -six, then stopped. "Creation is better in pain," he told me. "It's more interesting."

There were towheaded children in the photos he had loaned me, children in the countryside. He stared away. A grin came over him. "I read the other day," he said, "that the bull—that's my sign, Taurus—is a symbol of power and fertility. And it made me laugh because I still don't have any kids...

"In any case, I'll never be well. I'll always have too many needs, too many desires, I'll always be frustrated... Right now all I need is to get good and drunk to do something really stupid, jump out a window..."

I hardly felt that any experience of mine left me

qualified to reassure him. Of course I would beg him to stop.

Occasionally, he thanked me for the writing I was doing. He called permanence a feeling he could live for. "Not for nothing do I make sculptures out of metal. Otherwise, I'd make them of Scotch tape..."

We returned to his room at the squat, choked with sawdust. He was working to build a counter. He shook sawdust off a heavy album, flyers for his exhibitions. He drank water with the white pills he had taken every day for countless years. To a wall he had nailed torn-out paper on which he listed maladies, his disfigurements—a current project, as he was eligible for disability and had only to apply. He took it down, adding commentary read it aloud:

— Skull trauma
— Hole behind his eye from having fallen,
in a seizure, onto a table
— Dent in his forehead, same reason: they had had
to peel back the skin
— Hearing loss
— Jaw fracture
— Knife wound
— Brace in each shoulder because his shoulders
had so frequently dislocated during seizures
that his arms had to be stopped from falling out
of the sockets
— Another in his left wrist
— Two spindles right here
— Iron plate in his right forearm
— Broken hip

"So, look, I know what pain is..."

"Which pain is the worst?"

"Breaking of the knees, heroin withdrawal, and toothaches," he said quickly. "Those are the worst pains that I have had." In return, he asked, "What are the things that remind you of the past, that it wasn't just a dream?"

"For me it's writing," I said, as fast as I could. "For you?"

"For me, it's my sculpture of course, but also my scars. My scars remind me that the past wasn't just a dream, or a nightmare... Do you think life is a dream?"

"I think we have to define some of these terms first," I said. "What do you think?"

"It's all illusion anyway. I have nothing to do here. I have no business in the universe of men." Music rises from another room behind the voice, a drumbeat like a heart accompanied by murmuring. "As for me, I'm far above all that. If it weren't for colors. Did you know the only colors you see are the ones that don't exist?" He gestured at the day as it entered through a window, shifting curtains.

"Yes," I said carefully. "Something to do with reflection..."

"For example, the red you see, in fact, only your brain sees red, but in fact the light that hits the chair brings out..." His phone rang. "Hello? Yes, fine, impeccable..." The music changes, grows louder, repetitive. "Me? Well, yes, there is room here, but it's not at all easy to live here... Of course you can come work here. But once again, this place may close soon. *Voilà*." A flute takes over the melody. "I've got my friend here who's going to write about me. You know how I love it when people take an interest in me. Kisses. Wonderful. Bye, ciao, thank you..." The music changes again, to Neil Young's "Helpless."

"Oh, yes, so as I was saying, the sun in fact does not

reflect the colors that you see. Your brain, in fact, interprets the red you see there. That means that whatever animal seeing that doesn't see the same color either. Dogs see in black and white—"

"Even among humans, it's possible that we see colors differently."

"Yes, also. All this to say that all this is your brain's interpretation. While in fact, the color there doesn't really exist. As far as you know, that could be not a couch but a dinosaur."

I laugh.

"Yes! You don't know. You don't know anything. Take cats. Maybe they see souls. Haven't you ever noticed a cat sitting in a room, a still, silent room, and yet it's watching some *thing* that moves? We can't ever really know what they see. Maybe they see the littlest moving things and so on. Lost souls. Souls lost in, what's it called, where we're judged?"

"Purgatory?"

"*Le purgatoire, oui*. In between the two, life and death. You! You've been nasty, get down there. You've been nice, go on up!" We laugh. "As for me, I think that after death there's nothing. But I have a little doubt. Doubt! That's what we have left." He picked up a scrap of wood, turned it in his hands, and set it down. "I don't know why I do all this," he added. "I'm really very solitary." In looking at the body charged by tension I could envy him his medium, observing tension in the jaw, the muscles twitching when the face fell still, his focus poised to shift, the hands that did move wildly. Several hours later, at 1:40 a.m., Pascal sent a text: *at Tenon hospital, cannot move whole right side of my body, ribs broken, spine, vertebrae...*

He has jumped, I thought on waking. And I made him think about his childhood. I made him remember Le

Carrosse, as I had been warned against doing. I called. No answer. I called the hospital. He had left, which seemed impossible, given what he'd said about his state. I called Pascal again, no answer. The psychotic break, I thought. The streets. Finally I reached him. He was back at the squat, preparing, he said sweetly, to *faire dodo*, go sleepies. In the days after our call I visited, bringing groceries, and I saw Pascal in pain.

Who had done this to Pascal? Someone at the squat where he was forced to live. I told my boyfriend what Pascal told me, explaining the situation at some length—explaining the exercise of an arbitrary power that this man had over Pascal, injustice that was exercising me in the place of my concern about Pascal's vulnerability. My boyfriend was not amused. "Journalists go to prison every day for writing about dictators," he said. "You want to do this for some *petit voyou*? If I see this guy I'll laugh at him, I'll have a beer with him," something I'd never thought to do.

Why had I not made Le Stendhal my focus? I'd spent enough time there. On a very early visit, in 2011, I had met Croatian backpackers, one untangling a heap of yarn she'd use to knit her friend a hat. She nodded at him. "He is in a motorcycle gang," she said.

"It's not a gang," he said. "It's a *club*."

Pascal, in any case, recovered. One night I'd walked with him in ochre light that gave the alleyway an air of some past century. He picked out cans of beer, which I bought for him; the month, April of 2014, was at its end. He dipped his fist into a barrel of peanuts, as we were stepping outside peeled me a few. "I'll make you a sculpture," he told me.

"That's too kind..."

It was a fair trade, he said. But he would interview me, he would need to learn my demons.

Distracted, wondering how I'd describe the streetlamps, I asked lightly, "Are all your sculptures sculptures of demons?"

He stopped and staggered backward as if I'd shoved him in the chest. "But you have understood nothing." He sat heavily on a doorstep. "You have understood nothing. You have understood nothing. You have understood nothing. You have understood nothing."

So I returned finally, in July 2015, to my country, and in November of that year—two weeks after the passage of legislation, precipitated by terrorism, that gave police in France carte blanche to conduct searches without warrants—I checked my phone to see an email. "Raid in progress," it read. The squatters of Le Stendhal had outfitted a building to host protesters for the United Nations Climate Change Conference. To police who, aiming guns, ordered them to get on their stomachs, they said they were not the black bloc. When, hours later, these police felt able to affirm that they had found nothing suspicious, the damage they had done included, according to testimony, using a knife to slash a theatrical curtain hanging in a "meditation space."

The cognitive dissonance was stronger in no one than in the sympathetic blogger who wrote of the difficulty mothers were having in maneuvering strollers past where police vans blocked the street off, of "a great disorder and contradictory orders," and, similarly peevishly, of the reputation for good citizenship the squatters enjoyed. "The inhabitants had even signed an agreement with the proprietor."

While living away from Paris I returned periodically to visit, and, on a hot day in May 2018, I saw Pascal again for the first time in years. As before he was living in the south of the country, with a woman. Up to Paris he was wearing, despite the heat, a blazer and jeans. I was late, and as he waited at Saint-Jacques Tower, the place I had suggested for our meeting, it dawned on him he might have happened to mishear me, always there was the treachery of his poor hearing, so he ran to Saint-Eustache, a nearby church, only to find I wasn't there, either. His anger dissipated as we settled down to talking on a lawn around the tower. He got rid of his cigarette butt fastidiously, squishing it into a bottle. He was sober, better in every way as he asked me to notice, and when having walked up to Beaubourg we said goodbye, he wished me happiness in love. After all, we'd known each other fifteen years, or ten—we'd met at Le Carrosse.

We hadn't met at Le Carrosse.

He looked at me in astonishment and assured me that we had.

We had not, I persisted, but I didn't tell him fifteen years previously I had been twelve, I hadn't even spoken French, a language that none of my family spoke and which I learned for this project—its open door.

In Memoriam

Masha Guttsait
Ludovic Le Ménélec
Oxana Shachko

Notes

Le Bloc's sale price appears in Julien Duffé, "L'immeuble 'bunker' de la Mouzaïa abritera des étudiants," *Le Parisien*, August 18, 2017. Thomas Aguilera's paper, "Gouverner les illégalismes" (*Gouvernement et action publique*, 2012/2013), combined with research on analogous Spanish cases has formed the basis for a book by the same name, his dissertation, *Gouverner les illégalismes urbains: les politiques publiques face aux squats et aux bidonvilles dans les régions de Paris et de Madrid* (Dalloz, 2017). Beyond the sources already indicated, another paper, "Revendications des squats d'artistes et institutions," by Curry Vavart's own Vincent Prieur (*Marges*, 2015), has since added to the Parisian history that I survey. Médecins du Monde's 2019 report, available at medecinsdumonde.org, gives an overview of the activities, some of which I have depicted, of the ten years' work of its Squat Mission. Information about Droit Au Logement's and Jeudi Noir's achievement in getting "social" housing made out of their squat at 2 Rue de Valenciennes—I have sometimes translated this concept by the American expression "public housing" though the approaches aren't identical—can be referenced in "Paris: l'ancien squat sera transformé en logements sociaux," *Le Parisien*, October 27, 2015. What I write about the Femen repeats my earlier reporting on them published in *The White Review* ("Marianne's Breasts," February 2017).

"[N]ecessitated by the crinoline" is a quotation from Walter Benjamin, *The Arcades Project* (Harvard University Press, 2002, trans. Howard Eiland and Kevin McLaughlin, p. 133: "The widening of the streets, it was said, was necessitated by the crinoline"). The account of attitudes of the Belleville population toward Belleville's annexation, including the information about a poll, is from Christiane Demeulenaere-Douyère, "L'"annexion" vue de l'Est parisien" in *Agrandir Paris (1860-1970)* (La Sorbonne, 2012). The assertion about Rue de Pelleport being Belleville-Ménilmontant's north-south axis is Éric Hazan's in *The Invention of Paris: A History in Footsteps*, also my source for the quotations about Atget and a horse market; they come from David Fernbach's translation (Verso, 2010). The names of taverns have been taken from Jacques Hillairet's unique, magnificent *Dictionnaire historique des rues de Paris*, first published in 1960 by Minuit—the *rue de Belleville* entry—as well as from "Le territoire avant 1860," the article by Bernard Rouleau that I quote at length (in *Le XIXe arrondissement: une cité nouvelle*, Délégation à l'action artistique de la ville de Paris, 1996). Rougerie's claim as to when Belleville came to be revolutionary Paris's center of gravity is from his 1960 article, "Belleville" (*Bibliothèque de la Révolution de 1848*); for more on the Commune of 1871, related to Le Bloc as something like a precedent—in the singularity it has been taken as presenting in the city's history, and for a multiplicity of projects, for a certain dramaturgy—I recommend the oeuvre of Kristin Ross who, attentive to the forms French activism is still today creating, in *Communal Luxury: The Political Imaginary of the Paris Commune* (Verso, 2015) objects strongly to the idea that this was a "perfect tragedy" for its unities of time, action, and place.

Le Général is quoted on the resemblance of his life to a life lived on a spinning wheel in Pierre de Baudouin, "A mort le Street Art, vive le K13," *Gonzai*, July 23, 2017 (accessed at gonzai.com). Arendt's writing about Benjamin and his sense of Parisian space as being an interior appeared in *The New Yorker* ("Walter Benjamin," October 11, 1968). The anecdote about Baudelaire wandering the Île Saint-Louis in slippers, and the quotation, "Many of the main thoroughfares have their own special literature, and we possess written accounts of thousands of the most inconspicuous houses" are from *The Arcades Project*, but the main source for Benjamin's reading of Baudelaire is his *Charles Baudelaire*, Lacoste's translation as indicated, published by Payot (1979). *A New History of French Literature* (Harvard University Press, 2001), edited by Denis Hollier, was also helpful. The account of Le Bloc's first architects' intentions—including the "readability" even they aimed for—according to my notes is from a touristic guide to monuments of modern Paris architecture by Hervé Martin (Alternatives, 1996); I also consulted a monograph on one, Claude Parent (by Michel Ragon, Dunod, 1982); *Paris sous terre* (Yves Manou, Éditions de Nesles, 1980) was my major source for information about the city's catacombs. In 2023 Patrick Rubin, the architect in charge of renovating after Le Bloc's eviction (he had looked up greatly to Parent and the other), in an email while volunteering he had preserved some of the squatters' traces—I could and did see for myself that works of their art, as publicized during the renovation, remained—confirmed to his knowledge the presence of cavities, dug out to mine gypsum, in the ground.

Primary documents were helpful; while those I reviewed from Le Carrosse's case did not, as far as I could tell, substantiate Pascal's story about the Faustian bargain he had struck to keep it open, the thoroughness of their intermixing in files a Parisian friend, Carole Peclers, had kept for him with documents of an ultra-personal nature—an X-ray, a summons, a sheaf of love letters—was its own, deep kind of proof. Florence Diffre, their lawyer then, did not respond to requests made over more than a decade for comment. The lawyer Matteo Bonaglia, experienced with squats, said that what Pascal described was a "great classic" of squat defense; another lawyer said it would have been true "metaphorically." When in 2023 I obtained a PDF of the police report Marco had shown me—from Le Bloc's lawyer Julie Convain, who in 2023 as in 2014 would not respond except by sending documents to a portion of my questions—I saw that Marco had not had to lie. There was, also notably, a reference to a crime ring by which raves were, according to an ongoing investigation, thrown for profit. And while they had been asked to leave before my time—my reporting there having attained its greatest frequency not until the fall of Le Bloc's year—the presence, in that squat, of a group I will not name although it had a name, of graffiti artists of daring and renown who had been invited to Le Bloc for the entire squat's protection, and yet would come to be associated with the worst of violence there, had impressed one of my subjects deeply enough that ten years later, hearing my book would at last be released, her first question, trepidatious, was if I would be mentioning them. This is when you know it was dishonest not to.

But nothing has been invented. Many quotes were double-checked against 6.7 days of tape I made or footage of the filmmakers' they generously made available. My reporting fills, in the end, just about forty notebooks. During the decade I worked on this book I took them with me every time I moved, between apartments of my own and rented rooms (I count twelve moves), never losing one.

I have described my time in the Paris archives, but the archives, in Rouen, of the Seine-Maritime Department were also helpful as, in 2023, I sought to corroborate, without Le Général, the craziest story Le Général ever told me (that, upon locating his business partner after waking up out of a months-long coma following a traffic accident, during which incapacitation this partner had defrauded him, he threw him down the stairs, ten flights, and, with him in the trunk, drove to a sandy forest where he made him dig only to find—at dawn, pulling the trigger—that it was rusty, his gun making "just a click"; the man was spared). A lawyer at Rouen's appellate court informed me there was only one person in the system with Le Général's identifying details and that the offenses Le Général claimed to me he had served time for in connection with this affair—*barbarie, torture, mis en danger de la vie d'autrui*—did not figure on his rap sheet. In France, the person concerned needs to make the request to view their record, something he had put off helping with, and by this time, Le Général was missing. I heard from different people he was in prison in Morocco. Oan's mother, no longer speaking to him, said in 2023 she'd share my information with his children, the last I heard before she blocked me. But in Rouen, rifling newspapers in a building attached to a tall one, the Archives Tower—it dominates Rouen's Left Bank, which in that way resembles a set out of one of Le Général's comic books, but rigged up for an epic battle with the record, with historical truth—I discovered that the accident had happened exactly as Le Général had described it and to him: "Antonio Xavier, un Rouennais de 27 ans." A Scorpio, I knew, he had not turned twenty-eight. It had happened, I read further, on the Quai Jean Moulin, also the location of those archives, where I was just then finishing my reading.

It was still not really this amazing grain of truth that vindicated my inclusion of so much of what Le Général had shared. Documents from trials and police investigations in France are turned over to archives like that one only after decades have gone by, but it was easy enough for the archivists to clue me in on the very real nature of the early part of his career. He stood accused of stealing a car, of stealing objects out of a car, and of armed robbery, and that was just the eighties and nineties. "He was arrested several times between 1982 and 1996 for theft, contempt of public authority, forgery of checks, willful damage to private property," one of the archivists with access to relevant files wrote in an email. More to the point, it was too easy. In reading through three years of *faits divers* I had surfaced many stories, of cars falling into the Seine to be retrieved with people in them, of incidents of color, intrigue, even violence in the woods around the city. This had formed, I thought, my general's imagination. There were, too, stories of homeless individuals who, in contrast to the housed, the paper left unnamed. They made the news when they were assaulted or, in a more representative example, died of exposure. Here was the necessity for the myth, I thought as I read. I felt him, at last generic, fading from the sharp relief of poetry, the lyric and the swagger of his speech, to join the flow of history.

For whenever a source disappeared on me—as "Marie-Laure" of course did, and "Guy," "Odette"—my ability to check out stories they had told me by interviewing secondary sources was impacted (as it was not in Valentin's case: Igor Nasonov, no relation, the trombonist of the band with whom Valentin had fled the Soviet Union as it fell, in 2023 living in Marseille confirmed almost every detail about that flight, about years of their flight; aunts and a cousin of Pascal's, all on his father's side, confirmed what he had said about that father's violence, the violence of his upbringing). I am unable for such sources to make corrections as I am for example by having learned, in 2023, from the "lapsed philosopher" that he holds just a *licence*, in film studies. The Brussels theater's site makes no mention of a cat but is curiously repetitive in invoking a debt of gratitude that is owed to interns. A spokesperson for the national "chamber" of bailiffs did not comment on whether their being paid by the proprietor created a conflict of interest. The DRASSIF, which had occupied the building of Le Bloc before the squatters, furnished a Dada-esque list of all the archives it believed itself to have kept but would not say if it might have left any behind. Primary documents produced in the wake of Ludo Le Ménélec's death, including those of a police investigation, resided, said his sister Virginie Aïnaoui, with their mother, who would be too disturbed by the inquiry for me to ask to take a look. He had died of an aortic aneurism, Aïnaoui said. Funds collected by the squatters at Le Bloc did reach his family. The document about the death that I am able easily to access is suggestive, however, in its own way, piquant. This certificate, which anyone can look up by making inquiries at the nineteenth arrondissement mayor's office or by ordering it online, is marred by hyphens, redaction. It notes that the date, because this death happened in the night, could not established. But, conforming to the French convention of including the occupation of the deceased, listing the place of death it says with simplicity and certainty that Ludo was an "artist," that this was "his home."

In this, a glimmer of humanity appearing through the cracks left as if negligently in official jargon—one ought always to travel in "the little interstices into which you can slide," Le Général, by way of life advice, would tell me often—it was reminiscent of squatters' usage that I have tried to capture in translating what they said. They said they were SDF—"I'm SDF" I have Pascal saying—in an example of this no doubt deliberate reclaiming. I have said that this entire story fought its way to breathing life by exploiting an open door of language. The law's, of course, had helped create the distinctiveness, for squatters, of this period in Parisian history. It was an epoch in full swing August 25, 2009, when the city signed with artists it then reinstalled at Number 59, Rue de Rivoli. At, perhaps, the period's height, anyway in 2014, an NGO wrote to a Jeudi Noir activist begging that group *not* to squat a building. (The email, seeking to appease squatters, makes much of the NGO's affinity for housing rights.) This was a time when storied beauty, the confusion and the pressure of beauty's memory—"I tell myself, we owe them something" Anastasia said, referring by "them" to "Americans" arriving in squats of a city whose cosmopolitanism historically has meant, for artists and for others, refuge; a city where still, thanks to these squats, the Russian and I had been able to meet—sided with political expediency to free up, for the savvy art producer, unique opportunities. These contracts were notable for the vogue I have described in the way that they were used though one I've saved, these long years, five pages with initials in the corners like so many flies or a dropped string, is interesting for a line granting the mayor's office access when it wanted. Maybe all this ever meant for artists was a chance at being singled out for the dubious privilege (sometimes even paying for the privilege) of serving as property guardians...

 The period, anyway, is over. On July 27, 2023, an "Anti-Squat Law"—as it was referred to not only by squatters, making up whatever tiny sliver of France's population, but in blaring, victorious headlines—consigned all this, my story and its possibility, to history. With the steady onward march of progress there had been, already, changes; the period of "two years" after which construction and demolition permits are said, by the 2014 edition of *Le Squat de A à Z*, to expire had by the 2019 edition expanded to three. The mix up in jurisdiction described on p. 108 would not take place in that way now. But the real innovations were this law's. There was, for instance, the tripling of relevant penalties. A one-year sentence was increased to three. A home invasion would be sanctioned by a fine of, no longer fifteen thousand, but forty-five thousand euros, balanced as if elegantly by the reduction of grace, the wait to evict, by one-third, so the three years' allowable delay described on p. 23 was shortened to one. New crimes were created. Squatting itself was a crime, a first in France by one analysis. "Maintaining yourself" in a building, having placed yourself there "fraudulently," was a crime, now, in cases of abandoned warehouses, of refuge taken in a vacant barn or building like Le Bloc's. "Propagandizing" squatting was newly a crime. "There is really a before and an after with the law of 2023," Bonaglia said late that year. And this scapegoating—if, definitionally, *not* the movement's fault—added to its ambiguity in legacy, in the still-forming signifier of its legacy. The vilification of squatters and of whomever they were thought to be harboring, a racist vilification not without its gifts to comedy—*Le Squat de A à Z* had apparently made an appearance, in a context of right-wing outrage, during one legislative session—was being used as the excuse to revise law of a land becoming ever more hospitable to property developers. Meanwhile power's innovations in the realm of temporary leasing, and that of one lease in particular, had nourished an exploding trend for *tiers lieux*, disused train tracks being given over to "businesses" who, though describing themselves as collectives, selling "beer for twelve euros" were ersatz versions of *associations* Bonaglia had worked with...

While Michel Ktu of La Miroiterie did not respond to late requests for help in documenting the revolutionary history he claimed for his own family, I am satisfied that Daniel Pipard, the painter who had lived there, really did exist; in 2013 I reached his daughter, Catherine. "They are there completely illegally," she said of the squatters. "I want nothing to do with those people." It was in a reprint of a 1988 pamphlet acquired during a 2019 exhibit about art squats curated by Prieur (who had also, within the exhibit, taken pains to highlight the importance of Le Carrosse, offering what he described as an homage to Yabon) that I happened upon another story I would never verify, this one telling of a place called Art Cloche, I'd heard the name; no less a personage than the artist Joseph Beuys had, according to this pamphlet, helped found it, on the Rue d'Oran, before abdicating his presidential role due to a quarrel with the artist Jean-Pierre Raynaud over Raynaud's "definitive installation" of one thousand blood-red flower pots all around the squatted building. Now the scene is dead, gone; the lease has reached its term and I discourage everyone, anywhere, from going in search of any of these people. After all a source of bias in my own research was that, as I confessed years later to my journalism professor, regarding blind corners—that I stopped myself from looking into—they had a key feature in common, they "were not able to be checked out safely by me." Caravaggio, echoing the wisdom of this position, told me when questioned in 2023 that he didn't know anything about Le Général's background, had never asked for he was not a cop. Begging to be left alone he would ask me to think of his daughters, a leitmotif of our conversations in follow-up stages and evoked alongside trouble with the law faced already after actions taken at Le Bloc. "Please," he would text via WhatsApp. "I have a family."

What else? Translations have been mine. Names that have been changed, like his, are indicated in the text.

Acknowledgements

Nicole Dirks helped check this book; Alex Milne, Solveig Serre, and Colin Weinstein, just to begin naming people who did, helped with specific research tasks.

I'm grateful to Michael Barron, Isidore Bethel, Andrew Blevins, Joely Day, Max Ehrenfreund, Ava Kofman, Kate Kornberg, Ben Lasman, Cora Lewis, Rebecca Nagel, Caryl Pagel, Hugo Partouche, Alyssa Perry, Hilary Plum, Zoey Poll, Nadja Spiegelman, and Fred Strebeigh for their reads of the text; to my other friends and family of origin, for many other forms of help; and, for their help to cut the facets of the gem, to everyone at Fitzcarraldo Editions. Thanks to the *Paris Review* staff for edits on a passage.

Its deepest debts are for the most part acknowledged within the text of the book. I left off some dozens of names for the sake of shaping a narrative and would like most of all to thank all those who took me in, teaching even inadvertent lessons, taught me French, gave me shelter.

The authorised representative in the EEA is
eucomply OÜ, Pärnu mnt 139b-14, 11317 Tallinn, Estonia.
hello@eucompliancepartner.com
+33757690241

This book is printed with plant-based inks on materials
certified by the Forest Stewardship Council®. The FSC®
promotes an ecologically, socially and economically
responsible management of the world's forests. This book
has been printed without the use of plastic-based coatings.

Fitzcarraldo Editions
8-12 Creekside
London, SE8 3DX
Great Britain

Copyright © Jacqueline Feldman, 2025
Originally published in Great Britain
by Fitzcarraldo Editions in 2025

The right of Jacqueline Feldman to be identified as the
author of this work has been asserted in accordance with
Section 77 of the Copyright, Designs and Patents Act 1988.

ISBN 978-1-80427-140-7

Design by Ray O'Meara
Typeset in Fitzcarraldo
Printed and bound by Pureprint

All rights reserved. No part of this publication may be
reproduced, stored in a retrieval system or transmitted
in any form or by any means, electronic, mechanical,
photocopying, recording or otherwise, without prior
permission in writing from Fitzcarraldo Editions.

fitzcarraldoeditions.com

Fitzcarraldo Editions